# Tax Crusaders

## and the Politics of Direct Democracy

# TAX CRUSADERS

## and the Politics of

## Direct Democracy

Daniel A. Smith

Routledge
New York and London

Published in 1998 by

Routledge
29 West 35th Street
New York, NY 10001

Published in Great Britain by

Routledge
11 New Fetter Lane
London EC4P 4EE

Library of Congress Cataloging-in-Publication Data

Smith, Daniel A.
    Tax crusaders and the politics of direct democracy / Daniel A.
  Smith
      p.   cm.
    Includes bibliographical references.
    ISBN 0-415-91991-6
    1. Tax and expenditure limitations—United States—States
    2. Referendum—United States—States   I. Title.
    HJ4182.S65   1998
    336.2'05'0973—dc21                              97-51490
                                                       CIP

*In loving memory of Catherine "Kit" Graf Fernald,
an inspiring grassroots activist*

# CONTENTS

# ACKNOWLEDGMENTS

In the course of this study I have incurred numerous debts to my family, friends, and colleagues. My editor at Routledge, Melissa Rosati, had faith in my ability to write an academic book that would be of general interest. Her sharp observations and persistent enthusiasm were immense sources of motivation. Thanks also to Janelle Miau, Paul Mooney, Lai Moy, and Eric Nelson for shepherding the book through its many production stages. You all helped to make my job much easier.

My biggest debt is to the many people who shared with me their knowledge about tax limitation ballot measures. I received an invaluable education talking directly with several "tax crusaders," their collaborators, and their opponents. In particular, Barbara Anderson, Douglas Bruce, Chip Faulkner, David Biddulph, Joel Fox, Richard Manley, Greg Walerius, and John Flannigan generously shared their knowledge about the politics and process of direct democracy.

A mini-sabbatical from the Division of Arts, Humanities, and Social Sciences and two grants from the Faculty Research Fund at the University of Denver enabled me to carry out my archival research and personal interviews in California, Colorado, and Massachusetts. The editors of *Great Plains Research* kindly granted permission to reproduce parts of my article on Douglas Bruce. Director Nelson Polsby and the staff at the Institute of Governmental Studies at the University of California, Berkeley were extremely generous with their time and expertise, as were the many research librarians and staff at the California State Archives, the California State Library (where the Howard Jarvis and Paul Gann papers are housed), the California Secretary of State, the Massachusetts State Archives, the Massachusetts Secretary of State, the Colorado Legislative Council, and the

Colorado Secretary of State. I am indebted to Nate Golich, my undergraduate work study for three years, who provided me with outstanding research assistance along the way.

A number of friends and colleagues read or discussed with me various parts of the manuscript. Paula Baker, Richard Braunstein, Robin Calland, Anne Campbell, Tom Cronin, Chuck Epp, Kevin Glynn, Rodney Hero, Robert Herrington, Allen Hertzke, Lora Jost, Dave Magleby, Paul Passavant, Grant Reeher, Caroline Tolbert, and Greg White all provided me with critical feedback. Numerous colleagues at the University of Denver helped me clarify my ideas and made me look beyond my own presumptions. A decade ago, Peter Eisinger, my dissertation advisor at the University of Wisconsin-Madison, introduced me to the rich complexities of state politics and political economy, and has been continually supportive of my research efforts. Thanks to my in-laws, Robert and Leita Chalfin, for their support, and especially to my parents for all their guidance over the years. My mother, Susan Fernald Smith, copy-edited the entire manuscript, and my father, Ronald A. Smith, a historian by training, did his best to keep his snide (but usually apropos) comments concerning political science's "jargon" to a minimum.

Above all, for her critical insights and enduring support, my warmest thanks go to my wife and best friend, Brenda Chalfin.

Denver, CO                                                                          D.A.S.
1998

# PREFACE

## *Direct Democracy and Conventional Wisdom*

Anti-tax ballot initiatives have become an important part of the political landscape in nearly half of the American states. Many scholars, journalists, and of course the tax limitation proponents and their supporters, generally view these ballot measures as products of broad-based, grassroots movements. Backers of these measures, like tax crusader David Biddulph of the Tax Cap Committee in Florida, contend that their citizen initiatives, "will once and for all put the power back in the hands of the people . . . where the power should be."[1] According to Biddulph and other tax crusaders, these ballot initiatives enable "the people" to curb the taxing and spending authority of their state and local governments, thereby returning governmental power to the citizens. Journalists often write about how these tax limitation measures, which are placed on the ballot by citizens via the initiative process, exemplify democracy in action. While remaining dubious of the process, *Washington Post* columnist David Broder calls direct democracy, "a truly amazing form of government."[2] In the abstract, many scholars too find wonderment in the initiative process. They note how tax limitation initiatives tend to spring from the only legitimate fountain of authority – the people. It is the citizens, after all, and not their unresponsive elected officials or the special interests, who place initiatives on state ballots. According to the conventional wisdom, which is an amalgam of these and other perspectives, tax limitation measures are generally understood as being the product of grassroots citizen groups that are able to mobilize fellow citizens in support of their cause.

This book challenges the conventional wisdom. This is not an easy task, as the making and reinforcement of this standard view has gone relatively unchallenged for more than twenty years. With the passage of Proposition

13 in California in 1978, the common perception that tax limitation measures are the result of populist undertakings became permanently ensconced in the American psyche. Subsequent tax revolts, via statewide citizen initiatives, have been widely understood as emanating from the people. The journalistic and scholarly canonization of Howard Jarvis, the legendary father of Proposition 13, has only helped to further this perception. In 1978, Jarvis claimed, and the press and scholars have since concurred, that he was leading "a people's movement,"[3] and that his successful ballot measure, "was a victory against money, the politicians, the government."[4]

Expression of this populist, not to mention popular, viewpoint resounds in the explosive rhetoric of prominent tax crusaders like Jarvis, as well as in the echoes of their zealous and vocal supporters. Equally pervasive, though perhaps somewhat more subdued, this populist perspective informs much of the academic research and journalistic accounts on tax limitation measures. This conventional wisdom – the broadly accepted interpretation of the nature of tax limitation initiatives that a majority of scholars and journalists subscribe to – has gone undisputed because scholars and journalists tend to make two basic assumptions about the initiative process. First, they tend to pit direct democracy and representative democracy against one another as binary opposites. Second, they tend to equate the widespread support at the polls on election day for tax limitation measures with extensive grassroots, citizen participation during the foregoing initiative campaign. These two assumptions, because they have gone relatively unquestioned over the years, have impeded more thorough investigations of tax limitation citizen initiatives. Instead of contesting the conventional wisdom, journalists and scholars have tended to reproduce the portraiture of the anti-tax movement as painted by tax crusaders and their supporters, and in turn, have only reinforced the general public's view of tax limitation initiatives.

A brief word on the two assumptions that continue to influence our collective understanding of direct democracy and tax limitation measures is in order here. With regard to the first assumption, those who promote the populist view of anti-tax initiatives are wont to view representative democracy and direct democracy as incompatible systems of political participation and representation. They often portray representative democracy as being easily and adversely affected by the machinations of special interests and kowtowing elected officials. In stark contrast, they describe the initiative process as a purer, unsullied form of democracy. The initiative process, advocates contend, allows for the unencumbered participation and representation of all citizens, not just the special interests. For example, political journalist James Ring Adams writes, "In voting directly on initiative proposals, the citizen body can directly express its consent to taxation or withdraw it from a level it deems excessive. Unresponsive legislatures have aroused a reaction threatening to repudiate representation altogether."[5] Concurring, political scientist Jack Citrin writes how "direct democracy," in contrast to representative democracy which is bogged down by entrenched professional politicians and special interests, "expresses a positive yearning for voice – for the chance to be heard and to participate."[6]

The second basic assumption, that sweeping electoral support for a measure on election day signifies a broad base of grassroots support for the measure, is equally prevalent. When a measure receives across-the-board support from voters, those writing on the topic frequently assume that the measure was the result of a grassroots endeavor. Eschewing the investigation of organization and financial data of a given tax limitation campaign, some journalists have a tendency to focus exclusively on the personalities of the tax limitation measures. For example, in Florida, Biddulph's Tax Cap Committee was bankrolled by the sugar industry in its successful campaign to pass Amendment 1, its 1996 anti-tax ballot measure. Over a three year period, the Tax Cap Committee raised more than $4.7 million; $3.5 million of the total, roughly seventy-five percent, was contributed by the sugar industry. In 1996 alone, the Tax Cap Committee reported contributions of $549,795. While only thirty-nine out of the 2,842 (1.3%) contributions that year were for amounts greater than $1,000, they accounted for eighty-five percent ($469,033) of the total amount raised by the group. Two companies, U.S. Sugar and Flo-Sun Sugar, along with the Sugar Cane Growers Association, contributed $339,947, or sixty-two percent of the total.[7] Biddulph, blithely acknowledging the beneficence of the sugar industry, stated to one reporter that, "[t]he sugar support has been gratefully received." But the journalist then went on to report, without checking it against the state's campaign finance records, Biddulph's populist-sounding claim that "the average contribution" made to his group was "about $18."[8]

No one questions the fact that an overwhelming majority of voting citizens in Florida supported Amendment 1 at the polls. But success on election day should not keep those interested in the political process of direct democracy from asking the following questions: Is the measure the product of the people? Are ordinary citizens, and not vested special interests, driving the process of direct democracy? Is the initiative process any less corrupted by special interests than the legislative process? Should the passage of a measure be considered a more democratic outcome than a leg-islative vote, simply because citizens voted on the measure directly? Is the initiative process democracy in action?

These are some of the normative questions I try to address in this book. By probing landmark tax limitation measures in California, Massachusetts, and Colorado, I attempt to peel away the thin populist veneer that shields most tax limitation measures so as to call into question the conventional wisdom. The assumptions that largely have shaped the study of tax limita-tion measures need to be challenged if we are to gain a more balanced understanding of tax limitation measures in particular, and the initiative process in general. In order to bring into question these assumptions and move beyond the limited understanding they allow, we first need to criti-cally examine the internal workings of the initiative process and the poli-tics of direct democracy.

Direct democracy, it seems clear, will not be fading away any time soon. There are likely to be over four dozen citizen initiatives on the November 1998 ballots of the states permitting direct democracy. In addition to the anti-tax measures in California, Colorado, Florida, Idaho, and Oregon, citizens across the country will be voting on controversial ballot questions concerning abortion rights, affirmative action, campaign finance reform, environmental protection, judicial reform, and parental rights. Those citi-zens who choose to turn out to vote will be making public policy on elec-tion day.

Beyond these well-entrenched biennial ballot initiatives, the burgeon-ing electronic age portends many exciting possibilities for the expansion, if not the complete transformation, of democratic governance. Citizens voting directly on pieces of legislation, on days other than election day, may in the future become common practice in this country. While inspir-ing, it is also daunting. There are many potential pitfalls in the quest for an unadulterated form of democracy. The three cases in this book provide a cautionary tale against blindly circumventing our representative system of governance in favor of the supposedly more participatory and democ-ratic initiative process.

# ONE

# THE POLITICS OF DIRECT DEMOCRACY

I think we'll be the law of the land. We are talking
about a healthy dose of democracy to put a check on          ⁓
runaway government.
                                        —*David Biddulph* [1]

                                  It's predictable that the politicians of this state, the
                      ⁓           government class, would attempt to use any trick or
                                  maneuver possible to overthrow the will of the people.
                                                        —*Bill Sizemore* [2]

A few months after I arrived in Colorado to assume a new teaching position, reporters from the state's two major newspapers, the *Denver Post* and
the *Rocky Mountain News*, called to ask me to comment on the upcoming
election. With the vote less than a week away, they both wanted me to
assess the chances of Colorado's eight statewide citizen initiatives. The
measures, petitioned to the ballot by citizens, covered a range of subjects –
taxes on tobacco, workers' compensation, election and campaign finance
reform, gambling, obscenity laws, term limits, and cost of medical care.
Being new in town, I intentionally sidestepped the specifics of the measures and talked more generally about the initiative process and the normative implications of direct democracy. I recall responding to each
journalist with a similar rhetorical question: Is direct democracy—and in
particular, the citizen initiative—a good or bad thing?

In responding to my own question, I made specific points on both the
positive and negative aspects of direct democracy. I emphasized how:

1

- Ballot initiatives can increase citizen participation and provide a sense of efficacy by directly involving ordinary people in the policy-making process.
- Concerned citizens can legitimately use the process to bypass an intransigent or inactive legislature by putting tough policy questions directly to the citizenry.
- Citizen initiatives, even when not successful at the polls, can place pressure on legislators to take action on a subject matter.
- The initiative process can generate public debate on serious issues of public concern.

But I also suggested to both reporters how the initiative process is by no means a purer form of democracy than representative democracy. I explained how:

- Moneyed special interests are often involved in the initiative process just as they are in representative government.
- Direct democracy could possibly lead to majority tyranny by allowing the will of a majority (or minority) interest to run roughshod over the views of the community, as founding father James Madison had warned over 200 years ago.
- Citizen initiatives are at times poorly worded, which makes them difficult to implement and coordinate with other statutes or amendments, and can possibly lead to costly litigation.
- Initiative campaigns are often debated through the media, which tends to reduce complex debates over public policy to shallow, sound-bite posturing.

I concluded the interviews by paraphrasing one of my favorite political scientists from a bygone era, E. E. Schattschneider, who in 1960 cautioned, "The power of the people in a democracy depends on the *importance* of the decisions made by the electorate, not on the *number* of decisions they make."[3]

The following morning I found myself quoted in each paper. Both reporters, Fred Brown of the *Post* and J. R. Moehringer of the *News*, chose to accentuate my misgivings with the initiative process. Brown, the political editor for the *Post*, quoted me as stating that the citizen initiative is "needed as a safety valve, but not as a replacement for the legislative process," and that election day lawmaking "wouldn't be a problem if we actually had some real deliberation during the initiative process. . . but we have thirty-second sound bites on some very complicated questions."[4] Moehringer quoted me as saying, "Direct democracy means a simple majority of voters is going to be able to legislate, and James Madison had huge problems with the tyranny of the majority."[5] I could live with the portrayals of my observations, however fragmentary.

What unnerved me, though, was how each of the news-hawks used my comments as a foil to Douglas Bruce, the state's most celebrated defender, as well as practitioner, of direct democracy. Bruce is a reporter's dream, replete with a stinging tongue. In contrast to the comments of the "expert" political scientist who cautioned about the hazards of direct democracy, Brown quoted Bruce as saying, "Just wait and see all the brush fires I start." The juxtaposition between the dispassionate scholar and the "man of the people" was even more stark in Moehringer's column. On the heels of my remark on the dangers of a tyranny of the majority, Moehringer quoted Bruce: "If you're saying we have too many (amendments), you're saying we have too many choices. . . I think our opponents long for good old days when there was no Baskin-Robbins. You could only have vanilla, and you could have any car—so long as it was painted black."

An effective wordsmith, Bruce was accustomed to speaking on behalf of "the people." The fiery bachelor from Colorado Springs is known to distribute business cards with "Patriot" emblazoned beneath his name. (Prior to the 1995 bombing of the Alfred P. Murrah Federal Building in Oklahoma City, Bruce handed out cards with "Terrorist" inscribed under his name.) Bruce was, and still is, Colorado's unapologetic champion of direct democracy, whereas I, new to the daily practice of direct democracy, advanced only a detached, analytic perspective on the initiative process. As is often the case with the process of direct democracy, inflamed passion prevailed over more deliberative reason in the media's coverage.

Following my indirect public exchange with Bruce, I began to think more critically about the power of rhetoric in the initiative process, especially how the process of direct democracy has an intrinsic populist appeal. Direct democracy—also referred to by scholars as "direct legislation"[6] or "populist democracy"[7]—continues to be held by many observers to be a purer form of democracy than representative democracy. The initiative process is a form of democracy that theoretically embodies "the will of the people." The symbiosis of the initiative process and populist rhetoric becomes all the more intense when the substance of the ballot measure involves the taxing and spending powers of the state. The question of taxes seems to heighten the populist appeal of the initiative process.

## A Century of Direct Democracy

In 1898 the citizens of South Dakota became the first to amend their state constitution and adopt the process of direct democracy. The clamor for the citizen initiative across the Great Plains states arose out of the doctrines of the People's (or Populist) Party and other insurgent political organizations during the early 1890s. Rev. Robert W. Haire, a Catholic clergyman and an activist in the Knights of Labor, is generally given credit for devising South Dakota's scheme, whereby citizens would "expressly reserve to themselves the right to propose measures, which measures the legislature shall enact and submit to a vote of the electors of the State."[8] The initiative was prized by progressive reformers as a democratic device that would help clean up the spoils of highly partisan state governments. The reformers believed that state legislators were being unduly swayed by big business monopolies, most notably the railroads.

During the ensuing Progressive Era, eighteen other states (nearly all of them west of the Mississippi River) sanctioned the use of the initiative between 1898 and 1918. The use of the initiative soared during the Progressive Era, as government reformers used the citizen initiative to enact measures dealing with labor law, welfare, business regulation and taxation, and prohibition. The adoption of direct democracy, which included not only the initiative, but also the referendum and the recall of public officials, was seen by progressives as an "instrument of democracy" that could help return government back to the people.[9]

The use of the initiative, while still robust during the depression and New Deal era, slowly began to taper off in the 1940s. In 1954, for example, citizens managed to place only eighteen statewide measures on the ballots of the states permitting the initiative; in 1968, there were only ten ballot measures nationwide, down from the one-year high of ninety in 1914.[10] In terms of the geographic expansion of the initiative, only one state, Alaska, added the initiative to its state constitution between 1919 and 1967. Not until the early 1970s, with the blossoming of democratic participation spurred on by the civil rights and the women's movements, did citizens once again turn to the initiative as a policy-making tool in the states.[11]

Over the past century, direct democracy and the use of the citizen initiative has become permanently established in almost half of the states in the union. Citizens in twenty-four states (plus the District of Columbia) are allowed to propose either ordinary statutes or amendments to their state constitutions, which are then submitted to the voters for ratification.[12]

## State Adoption of Citizen Initiative, by Date

| | |
|---|---|
| 1898 | South Dakota |
| 1900 | Utah |
| 1902 | Oregon |
| 1906 | Montana |
| 1907 | Oklahoma |
| 1908 | Maine, Missouri |
| 1910 | Arkansas, Colorado |
| 1911 | Arizona, California |
| 1912 | Idaho, Nebraska, Nevada, Ohio, Washington |
| 1913 | Michigan |
| 1914 | North Dakota |
| 1918 | Massachusetts |
| 1959 | Alaska |
| 1968 | Florida, Wyoming |
| 1970 | Illinois |
| 1977 | District of Columbia |
| 1992 | Mississippi |

*Figure 1.1*   States with Citizen Initiative

*Figure 1.2*    Mike Keefe (Denver Post) editorial cartoon of Citizens as Policy Makers — "Who Do You Favor in the Legislature?"

The citizen initiative is a readily accepted practice in the states that have adopted it. According to public opinion polls, direct democracy is seen by a majority of people as a legitimate tool to propose and enact legislation as well as amendments to their state constitutions.[13] Once thought of as a supplement to representative democracy, the initiative process now plays a major role in the shaping and making of public policy in these two-dozen states.[14] Citizens, businesses, and interest groups in these states regularly use the ballot initiative as a way to circumvent their intransigent state legislatures. Furthermore, voters are often as interested or even more interested in ballot measures as they are in races for political office, although scholarly research generally finds that initiatives do not measurably increase voter turnout.[15] What is certain, though, is that the initiative process prompts citizens, rather than state legislators, to become policy-makers for a day.

## Proposition 13 and the Rise of Direct Democracy

The catalyst for the nationwide surge of citizen initiatives was unquestionably California's 1978 property tax cutting measure, Proposition 13. According to political scientist Jack Citrin, "Proposition 13 ushered in an era of plebiscitary government in California."[16]  The democratizing influence of Proposition 13, though, was not limited to California. The tax limitation earthquake in California sent aftershocks rumbling throughout the country.[17] Thomas Cronin, a prominent scholar of direct democracy, argues that Proposition 13 "triggered similar tax-slashing measures (both as bills and as direct legislation by the people) in numerous other states, and it encouraged conservative interest groups to use the initiative and referendum processes to achieve some of their goals."[18]  The measure heralded a new generation of direct democracy in the states. "[N]ot only did the California tax-cutting vote overshadow the candidate races and other propositions of the 1978 primary election season," writes political scientist David Magleby, a seasoned observer of the initiative process, "but its importance also grew as it received national attention."[19] Across the nation, the voice of the people would be heard. David Schmidt, an outspoken proponent of the initiative process, writes that, "the Tax Revolt has proven once again the wisdom of Thomas Jefferson's faith in the electorate."[20]

Since the passage of Proposition 13 (also known as Prop. 13), citizens and interest groups have increasingly turned to the initiative process to promote a variety of causes. In the two dozen (mostly western) states that permit the initiative process, voters now expect a handful, if not more, citizen initiatives to be on their ballots. "The populist spirit," according to Citrin, "animates the current era in American politics."[21] In 1996, citizens in twenty-two states voted on a combined total of ninety statewide ballot measures, the most since 1914.[22] In many states, initiative campaigns receive more public attention, and cost more, than even statewide races for public office. Californians, for example, voted on fifteen ballot questions in the 1996 general election, including three bond measures placed on the ballot by the state legislature. Voters ended up passing eight of the measures. Before the vote in California was even held, groups campaigning for and against the fifteen measures had raised more than $83 million in private contributions to advance their respective sides.[23]

In many states, anti-tax measures have been overshadowed by other contentious ballot initiatives. In the states with the initiative process, citizens are being asked to vote on an array of disparate, as well as divisive, issues. In the 1990s alone, citizens have voted directly on questions concerning school vouchers, gay rights, English as the official language, affirmative action, euthanasia, legalizing marijuana, term limits, crime victims' rights, abortion and parental notification, environmental regulation, gambling, child pornography, campaign finance reform, health care reform, welfare reform, and tort reform. In addition, voters have considered several bizarre issues, such as banning the use of animal traps, outlawing the hunting of lactating mother bears, prohibiting triple trailers, requiring warning labels on hazardous materials, and even the deregulation of the denture industry. The subject matter of a citizen initiative is limited only by the ability of petitioners to collect the required number of valid signatures to place the measure on the ballot.

While over half of all citizen initiatives are defeated at the polls, tax limitation ballot measures continue to achieve a high degree of success on election day. In 1996, voters in California, Florida, Nevada, and Oregon passed anti-tax citizen initiatives. That year, anti-tax measures were defeated in only two states, Idaho and Nebraska. Leaders of successful anti-tax measures—for example Barbara Anderson in Massachusetts, David Biddulph in Florida, Douglas Bruce in Colorado, Joel Fox in California, and Bill Sizemore in Oregon—have become major political players in their respective states. Deft in their ability to spin populist-sounding sound bites in their appeal for public support, these charismatic individuals command the attention of not only the media, but also the public officials of their states. As we shall see, tax crusaders are major power brokers in the political arenas of the American states.

## The Citizen Initiative Explosion

Why has there been such an explosion in the use of the citizen initiative in the twenty years since Proposition 13? According to numerous scholars, journalists, and practitioners of the initiative, the proliferation of ballot initiatives in the American states signifies a growing popular dissatisfaction with the institution of representative government. Citizen and special interest groups are turning to the ballot initiative in order to circumvent their state legislatures which are either hopelessly unresponsive or gridlocked by partisan politics. The citizen initiative, according to these observers, functions as a barometer of the popular discontent of "politics as usual." Advocates like to note that the initiative process—unlike the institution of representative government—gives citizens a genuine voice by bringing democracy down to its grassroots. It enables and even encourages people to become directly involved in the political process. By circumventing state legislatures, the citizen initiative allows for popular sentiments to be heard and acted upon directly by the people. It reduces the influence of the "special interests" who have gained—in many people's eyes—undue leverage over our elected officials. "The initiative process is the guarantee that the people will always have the last say in important matters in state policy," reasons Jim Shultz, the executive director of the Democracy Center, a voter advocacy group based in San Francisco.[24] By way of these ballot initiatives, proponents claim, the states have experienced a resurgence of activist, populist politics. The people are reclaiming what is rightfully theirs—government of and by the people.

Or so the story generally goes. While the rhetoric giving sustenance to direct democracy tends to consist of a patriotic blend of populist and democratic pronouncements, precious little is known about the actual mechanics of the initiative process. Compared with other sub-fields of political science, relatively few scholars have probed the inner workings of the initiative process. As a result, a host of questions, empirical and normative alike, have gone largely unanswered by students of direct democracy. How, for example, are citizen initiative campaigns run and what types of individuals, groups, and businesses contribute money and provide in-kind resources to initiative campaigns? What is the role of the author of the measure? Why are some ballot initiatives ultimately successful at the polls, and others not? And perhaps most important of all, if ballot measures, as proponents of the process like to extol, ostensibly empower "the people" to govern themselves directly, how participatory, grassroots, and democratic is the initiative process?

## Contesting the Conventional Wisdom

This book attempts to answer these and other questions by focusing on a single, though perennial, ballot question: the limitation of the taxing and spending powers of the state. More narrowly, it profiles three tax crusaders—Howard Jarvis in California, Barbara Anderson in Massachusetts, and Douglas Bruce in Colorado—and examines their efforts to rein in the taxing and spending powers of state and local governments through the initiative process. Although the three ballot warriors employed different strategies in waging their tax limitation campaigns, they shared a common passion, and rhetoric, of returning power back to the people. In each case, the tax crusader was able to successfully tap an ambiguous public mood with a populist message, and by using the initiative process, advance his or her tax limitation measure. Following intense campaigns, the three ballot measures resonated with a majority of voters on election day.

Conventional wisdom suggests that these and other citizen initiatives bent on reducing taxes are typically populist endeavors, stemming from ordinary people. Journalists and scholars who track and study tax limitation initiatives regularly suggest that the measures pit average taxpayers against the entrenched interests of government officials and public servants. As historian Michael Kazin writes, the tax limitation "movement as a populist insurgency rapidly passed into conventional wisdom—along with the language its organizers had used to describe themselves."[25] Tax limitation initiatives continue to be generally accepted as authentic forms of mass protest. Indeed, the three tax limitation initiatives I consider in depth won high levels of support at the polls. In each case considered here—Proposition 13 in California (1978), Proposition 2 1/2 in Massachusetts (1980), and Amendment 1 in Colorado (1992)—citizens favored by considerable margins to lower or limit their taxes. According to most observers, the passage of these initiatives reflects the spontaneous, populist spirit of direct democracy as envisioned by those who championed the radical process a century ago.

The core of my argument challenges this conventional view of tax limitation ballot measures. Through the three historical case studies, I attempt to uncover what is beneath such boilerplate. I argue that the process of direct democracy in the case of these three tax limitation measures was far less populist, grassroots-driven, and democratic than is generally assumed. While appearing on the surface to be populist endeavors, they lack many of the qualities of traditional populist movements. In all three states, a tax crusader, acting as a populist entrepreneur, maneuvered a tax limitation ballot initiative through the direct democracy process. Sensing the public mood, each collected signatures for a ballot initiative and offered it to the voters as *the* solution to the perceived problem of excessive taxation. Save for coming out to vote, citizens were not mobilized into direct political action in support of the measure once it had qualified for the ballot. While the tax crusaders swaddled their measures with populist rhetoric, their initiative campaigns were not grassroots or populist. Rather, I suggest they were more akin to "*faux* populist moments"—fleeting expressions of popular support for tax limitation initiatives crafted by entrepreneurial tax crusaders. These ballot measures, while buoyed by the populist-sounding rhetoric of a tax crusader, lacked the active participation and mobilization of "the people."

## Defying Tidy Causal Analysis

Although not the primary focus of the book, the three case studies provide some insight as to why some ballot initiatives are successful at the polls, and others not. Neither liberals nor conservatives have emerged to dominate the initiative process since the passage of Proposition 13, but the process has become more open to individuals, businesses, and interest groups equipped with considerable financial resources at their disposal. Money, though, by no means guarantees an electoral victory. As Cronin laments, "[e]xplaining outcomes over a broad range of issues and in diverse states is a challenge that defies tidy causal analysis."[26]

Relatively few scholars have tried to systematically probe the underlying causes for successful initiatives.[27] The principal reason for this gap in the scholarly literature is fairly obvious. The tremendous variation among the twenty-four states that permit the initiative—from the size and demographics of the state, to the state's petition requirements, to whether an initiative is statutory or constitutional, to the subject matter of the initiative, to the professionalization of the campaigns, to the media play, to disparities in aggregate campaign spending, to the number and levels of individual contributions made to campaign committees—inhibits data collection and quantitative analysis. In addition, the great variance among these independent variables makes it extremely difficult to generalize about their potential influence on the initiative process.

Instead, scholars have tended to focus their attention on the aggregate spending of initiative campaigns to determine whether or not measures are successful. All of the states require groups promoting or opposing ballot measures to report their campaign contributions and expenditures in a timely fashion. As such, scholars have found it convenient to analyze the amount of money collected and spent by groups rather than some of these more intangible variables that undoubtedly influence initiative campaigns.

With respect to campaign spending, money seems to matter more during initiative campaigns when it is spent by groups opposing ballot measures.[28] In one of the earliest quantitative studies on the topic, political scientist John Shockley discovered that by outspending the backers of the measures, nine out of twelve opposition groups were able to defeat pro-environment ballot measures, even though the measures were originally favored in the polls.[29] Examining more than two-dozen California initiatives from the late 1960s and 1970s, law professor Daniel Lowenstein found that one-sided spending by opponents of an initiative—even if the measure was supported in public opinion polls—led to the defeat of the measure ninety percent of the time. Disproportionate spending by the proponents of the measure, though, had much less of a positive affect on the election outcome.[30] Magleby's research on dozens of California initiatives between 1954 and 1982 showed that opposition groups spending as much as or more than the proponents of a measure were able to defeat the measure eighty percent of the time.[31] However, proponents spending twice as much as their opponents only succeeded in passing their initiative forty-eight percent of the time.[32] This disparity in the amount spent and expectant outcomes is important when examining the election results of ballot measures, as campaign spending between the proponents and the opponents is roughly equal only twenty percent of the time.[33] Betty Zisk's comprehensive examination of ballot initiatives in four states between 1976 and 1982 found an even stronger relationship between campaign spending and electoral outcome. Controlling for newspaper endorsements and other variables, the political scientist discovered that the higher-spending side won the election seventy-eight percent of the time.[34] As Cronin writes, "In short, although it would be incorrect to argue that corporate money in all cases was the most important factor in the success of defeat of initiatives, corporate lobbying had a powerful effect on public opinion and in a number of cases was a deciding factor."[35] In contrast, only a few scholars have discounted the relationship between campaign spending and the electoral success of a ballot initiative. A study by Schmidt of 189 statewide ballot initiatives between 1976 and 1984 found that campaign spending determined the election outcome only twelve percent of the time.[36]

Scholars have speculated about the influence of a host of other variables on the electoral outcomes of ballot initiatives, but only a few have tested their hypotheses empirically. Schmidt, for example, suggests that the strength of the initial public support for a measure, the credibility of the groups for and against the measure, and the strategies of the proponents and opponents are often more decisive in an initiative election than even campaign spending.[37] Cronin submits that grassroots endeavors, political endorsements, campaign organization, and tactical errors can influence the outcome of an initiative campaign.[38] Magleby, one of the few scholars who has empirically tested other variables besides money, finds that the single best predictor of how citizens are likely to vote is whether the measure approximates their own political ideology. He also notes that voters take into consideration "factors like the cost of the proposal, its perceived necessity, their feelings about the supporters or opponents, and confusion about the measure's costs and consequences."[39] Most recently, political scientist Ann Campbell has found that three variables—issue type, media coverage, and turnout—affected the outcomes of ballot measures in Colorado between 1966 and 1994.[40]

While some of these factors may be important in one initiative campaign, they may be completely irrelevant in another. The three tax limitation cases in this study demonstrate quite clearly that aggregate campaign spending, while important, was not a major determinant of why the measures ultimately passed. In two of the cases the proponents of the measures were actually outspent by their opponents, yet the voters overwhelmingly approved the tax limitations. The tax limitation initiatives demonstrate how money is not necessarily the only force behind the success of ballot initiatives. As we shall see, populist rhetoric and the mythos of tax limitation in this country, combined with the determined efforts of the tax crusaders to mobilize resources of vested interests, are powerful components in tax limitation campaigns.

## The Process of Direct Democracy

This study differs from other research on tax limitation ballot initiatives as it is primarily concerned with the *process* of direct democracy, not the substance or political ideology of a particular measure. This is not a book about the merits or drawbacks of tax cuts. I make no attempt to assess whether tax cuts are "good" or "bad" public policy. My concern lies not with how liberal or conservative or how progressive or regressive a given tax limitation measure is. Other scholars have written extensively about the fiscal, political, and sociological effects of these types of measures.

Rather, I focus on the procedural side of these tax limitation ballot initiatives. How does the process of direct democracy and the attending rhetoric of populism sway our understanding of citizen-initiated tax limitation measures? How does the deeply embedded tradition of tax revolts in this country influence the initiative process and foster populist rhetoric? Why are tax revolts in the states always assumed to be populist movements?

In answering these questions, I try to peel away the populist facade of each of these tax limitation measures. Documenting the activities of the three tax crusaders, I expose how they were able to court a myriad of political and economic interests to advance their measures. In particular, I examine the financial and organizational resources the tax crusaders relied upon to bolster their initiative campaigns. What I find may be somewhat surprising. The cases reveal how the three tax crusaders did not draw the bulk of their financial and organizational support from ordinary citizens and volunteers, as the conventional wisdom suggests, but rather from vested special interests with the assistance of top campaign consultants.

## Tax Revolts as "Critical Cases"

While by no means representative of all ballot initiatives, the profiles of the three tax crusaders and their tax limitation measures examined here can be used to shed some light on the overall process of direct democracy. The cases serve as what methodologists like to call "limiting" or "critical cases." In a statistical sense, the tax limitation measures are not "normal." Rather, they are likely to be statistical outliers—non-representative of the average citizen initiative. Yet, they are valuable cases for the very reason they are statistical outliers. If these initiatives, which are supposedly the most populist of all ballot measures, are actually underwritten by special interests, then other citizen initiatives using populist-sounding rhetoric become suspect. As such, these exceptional cases can be used to "confirm, challenge, or extend" current hypotheses about the initiative process, which can, in turn, help us to better understand the process and direct future research.[41] Because qualitative research tends to be "exploratory or descriptive," in-depth case studies that stress "the importance of context, setting, and subjects' frame of reference" can highlight complicated patterns or nuanced relationships that are frequently discounted or overlooked in more quantitative studies.[42]

The three tax limitation case studies offer sharp relief to the conventional wisdom associated with the initiative process in general, and tax revolts in particular. Unlike other types of citizen initiatives, which sometimes are backed by interest groups to protect government programs or to further "corporate self-defense," these "grassroots" tax limitation measures purportedly emanate from the people.[43] On the surface, they seem to be exactly the kinds of measures that the architects of the initiative process had in mind a century ago when they fought for the adoption of direct democracy. They are means by which the politically disenfranchised are able to reclaim the reins of their government. As such, tax limitation initiatives serve as critical cases in the sense that we can test the claims that the measures are grassroots, populist undertakings, pitting the common people against entrenched special interests and government forces.

## The Normative Implications for Direct Democracy

By analyzing the three tax limitation ballot initiatives through an historical lens we are able to evaluate normatively the process of direct democracy. The politics of direct democracy—as I tried to emphasize to the two journalists who contacted me several years ago—has both positive and negative aspects. Many scholars and practitioners argue that the proliferation of ballot initiatives in the states signifies a growing popular dissatisfaction with the institution of representative government. The initiative process, they say—unlike representative government—gives citizens a genuine voice by bringing democracy down to its grassroots. It encourages people to become directly involved in politics again. By circumventing our representative institutions, the initiative process allows for popular sentiments to be heard and acted upon directly by the people, thereby cutting out the "special interests" who have gained undue influence over our elected officials.

But direct democracy, critics point out, also has its pitfalls. While intended to alleviate many of the problems associated with the legislative process, it places tremendous demands on the voting public. Rather than being able to rely on various cues when voting for candidates running for public office—such as party affiliation, voting records, endorsements, name recognition, etc.—citizens must vote on what are often complicated ballot questions. Those who come out to vote are often not fully informed about the questions on which they are voting. Public debate is regularly reduced to sound-bite campaigns on TV and radio. In addition, voters are frequently uninformed about who is providing the financial backing and organizational support for a given measure. Rather than elevating public debate, the initiative process is often bereft of substantive deliberation and meaningful citizen involvement.

Furthermore, the rise of direct democracy may be contributing to the erosion of the public's trust in representative government. In his trenchant study of the decline of representative democracy in the American states, political scientist Alan Rosenthal suggests that, "participatory democracy" "has been growing in strength at the expense of representative processes." For Rosenthal, state government "is no longer conducted with the consent of the governed." Rather, it "is conducted with significant participation by the governed, and by those who claim to speak for the public's interest, according to a more populist plan."[44] Even some prominent practitioners of direct democracy, such as Jeanette Lona Fuen, think that the ballot measure process is "too often a repudiation of representative democracy." She argues that the initiative process "is being used by special-interest groups to promote single-issue agendas and to offer 'quick-fix' solutions to complex problems." Fuen, who has orchestrated dozens of successful statewide ballot measure drives, maintains that "the normal legislative process which, with all its imperfections, is far more likely to produce just, constitutional, reasonable, and work-able laws than is the ballot measure process."[45] As such, direct democracy may be subverting our institutions of representative government, and in the process, frustrating the public good.[46]

Through the prism of tax limitation initiatives, this book examines the nexus of direct democracy and populist rhetoric. It is not my contention that tax limitation ballot measures are representative of all citizen initiatives. However, an in-depth investigation of these three cases should not only improve our understanding of tax limitation citizen initiatives, but also the process of direct democracy. By reevaluating and reconceptualizing the three "tax revolts," casting them not as traditional populist movements but as carefully orchestrated *faux* populist moments, I hope to generate some critical discussion about the initiative process. It is important for citizens living in a democracy to be critical of their institutions and political processes, even ones that purportedly bring more power to the people. Direct democracy is but a process. As Theodore Roosevelt wrote in 1911, the initiative "is a devise and nothing more, is a means and not an end. The end is good government, obtained through genuine popular rule."[47] The citizen initiative may or may not lead to good government and genuine popular rule. That verdict is still out. What seems more certain, though, is that direct democracy should not be loosely prescribed as a panacea for all that ails our Republic, as it is not inherently any more democratic and representative than our current system of government. It is simply a different system.

# TWO

# TAXES, THE INITIATIVE PROCESS, AND THE LEGACY OF HOWARD JARVIS

From the fullest conviction, I disclaim every idea both of policy and the right internally to tax America. I disavow the whole system. It is commenced in iniquity; it is pursued with resentment; and it can terminate in nothing but blood.

*—Marquis of Grandby*[1]

Tonight was a victory against money, the politicians, the government. Government simply must be limited. Excessive taxation leads to either bankruptcy or dictatorship.

*—Howard Jarvis*[2]

## Introduction: The Incendiary Nature of Taxes

In the saga of American history, few political issues have proved to be as incendiary as taxes. Highly combustible, tax protests can be ignited by the slightest spark, and while rare, they are usually explosive. Tax revolts tend to flare up for a short period of time and then die back down. They are cyclical in nature. Alvin Rabushka and Pauline Ryan, two students of fiscal policy write, "Throughout history tax revolts have always been easier to initiate than to sustain."[3] While brief in duration, they nevertheless can have lasting effects. Like forest fires, which can instantaneously char the landscape, altering the ecosystem forever, tax revolts can engender permanent damage. And as with fires that sweep across the landscape, the lasting impact of tax revolts can be hard to determine. The resulting tax cuts and limitations can instantly decimate the public sector, incinerating expected governmental revenues overnight. But as with some natural conflagrations, they can also provide some hidden benefits. History suggests that tax revolts may foster new growth and opportunities by renourishing the delicate equilibrium between taxpayers and the state. The economic and political impact of tax revolts is both immediate and far-reaching, and largely cannot be evaluated until long after the burning embers have turned to ash.

Since the founding of the United States, the battle over taxes has lay at the heart of the American Republic. The tax revolts of the late eighteenth century continue to carry an important symbolic value in the nation's historical record. Protests against taxes, after all, are never solely fiscal in nature. They are also political. They are intimately tied to the ideal of representative governance. In the past, as in the present, political scientist Susan Hansen observes, "U.S. fiscal history illustrates that taxes respond to political incentives rather than to either political or economic theory."[4]

The current round of tax revolts, however, is different from the tax uprisings that transpired in the American states two centuries ago. Representative government in the United States is a given today. All Americans are guaranteed the right to elect a representative government. As such, elected officials, or those who are appointed by elected officials, determine the tax levels, assessments, and increases to be levied on the governed. Contemporary tax revolts no longer serve as proxies to bring about representative democracy; it is firmly institutionalized in the United States.

In a twist from the days prior to the creation of the Republic, tax crusaders now focus their attack on the principle of representative government. While bemoaning the level and amount of their taxes, they simultaneously take on the present system of government. Representative democracy, for these tax crusaders, is somehow not a sufficient form of governance when it comes to their hard-earned dollars. According to these enthusiasts for cuts in taxes and government spending, the people, not their elected officials, must be the ones who determine how much a government may tax and spend. Ironically, the same rhetoric once used by the founders to bring forth a new form of governance is being used by modern day tax crusaders to challenge the system of representative democracy. A more fitting declaration for many of these modern day tax crusaders, to paraphrase the Revolutionary maxim, might be, "No taxation, even with representation."

With the dawn of a new millennium in sight, the public outcry for smaller government and lower taxes appears to be getting louder across the

United States. Popular opposition toward taxes as well as government spending has become more robust, with greater staying power than in the past. Every year, countless numbers of enraged taxpayers can be heard clamoring to their local, state, or federal government officials for "less inefficient and ineffective government" and more tax relief.[5] From the well-publicized wrestling matches over the weighty tax code in Washington, D.C., to the annual wrangling over the redistribution of tax burdens in the states, to the equally fervent frays over bond issues for public schools at the local level, taxes have become a central concern to most Americans. While citizens might not know all the details of the various tax codes, they are not afraid to express themselves when they feel they are paying too many taxes.

As a result of this heightened citizen interest, combined with the use of the initiative process, the political arena in the American states has changed with respect to fiscal policy. The making of fiscal policy has become largely contingent on the demands of the public. In some states, citizens, and not their elected representatives, have become the *de facto* tax policy-makers. Tired of waiting for their elected representatives to debate and perchance reform the tax code, ordinary citizens have taken the fiscal matters of the state into their own hands. Alterations to the tax code are being made directly by citizens. Nearly a dozen states now require a majority of the electorate or a supermajority of the legislature to raise or create new taxes.[6] For example, the passage of Douglas Bruce's Amendment 1 in Colorado in 1992 bars legislators from raising or creating new taxes without the vote of the people. Complex formulas based on population growth and inflation rates drive the budgeting process. Backroom negotiations, steeped in the arcanna of accounting and hashed out between legislators and lawyers for special interests, are becoming less the norm. As journalist Fred Brown notes, "Deals no longer can be made in smoke-filled rooms," as smoking has been banned from the Capitol. "Colorado state legislators have little authority left," Brown writes with only slight overstatement.[7] In Oregon, Bill Sizemore's successful 1996 "Cap and Cut" ballot initiative, also known as Measure 47, severely restricts levies on residential property taxes and prevents the state from making up for the loss in property tax revenues with other taxes. By penning their own statutory and constitutional measures and petitioning signatures to place them on the ballot, anti-tax groups, like the one headed by Sizemore, have re-written state tax policy by putting their pet fiscal solutions to the direct vote of the electorate.

## Anatomy of a Ballot Initiative

While the particular statutes regulating the initiative process differ from state to state, campaigns for tax limitation ballot measures typically follow a similar pattern. As the campaign for limited taxes kicks off, often more than a year prior to the decisive election, a group requests permission from the state to circulate a petition. When a petition is filed, the proponents of the measure tend to hold a news conference announcing their intentions; their populist rhetoric, full of vibrato, resonates loudly over the free airwaves, albeit briefly. As the laborious collection of tens-of-thousands of signatures begins, average taxpayers who are disenchanted by the current tax structure or in favor of downsizing government, begin to contribute money to the anti-tax group, or even voluntarily go out to collect signatures. Usually, though, paid petitioners are recruited by the group to carry out the signature collection stage of the campaign.

As support for the measure builds, the backers of the measure seek to broaden their base of support by allying their citizen groups with vested business interests. Behind the scenes, with the assistance of professional campaign consulting firms, the tax crusader attempts to line up an array of financial and organizational resources to help "sell" the measure to the rest of the voting public. Landlords, real estate investors, small business owners, and occasionally larger corporations are contacted by direct mail for contributions to the group. Mailing lists are purchased from a variety of organizations to solicit funds from their members. In the waning weeks of the campaign prior to election day, the proponents of the tax limitation measure and their adversaries wage a thirty-second-sound-bite campaign on television and radio. Citizen interest in these fiscal ballot measures periodically supersedes the races for political office. Driven largely by emotion rather than deliberative analytical debates over the fiscal implications of the measure, anti-tax ballot campaigns are frequently discordant. The proponents, who argue in populist-sounding terms the need to downsize government and lower taxes, square off against their opponents, who focus on the specific cuts which might possibly result if the measure passes. The side left standing after the bloody campaign is crowned the victor.

If the ballot initiative is indeed successful at the polls on election day, the tax crusader behind the measure becomes an instant powerbroker in the corridors of the state Capitol. Fueled by the media's tendency to venerate the individual, the tax crusader's stature is only increased after the election. State legislators, envious—or perhaps fearful—of the imposing majority vote for the statewide measure, often kowtow to the demands of the author of the initiative. They often call upon the tax crusader to interpret the wording of his or her measure, or ask for advice on how to implement the alterations to the tax code. In a reversal of roles, state legislators often are the ones who try to modify the ballot measures authored by these enterprising, and highly influential, private citizens.

The playing out of this new scenario in the states has become more frequent then ever. In 1996, for example, David Biddulph, Bill Sizemore, and Joel Fox, established tax crusaders in Florida, Oregon, and California respectively, successfully persuaded voters to enact their own renditions of tax reform. Biddulph's measure, which was heavily financed by the Florida sugar industry, requires that the state of Florida have a statewide ballot question, which needs the approval of two-thirds of those casting votes, before any new tax could be added to the state constitution. In Oregon, Sizemore's measure, which was heavily funded by a Washington, D.C. advocacy group, Americans for Tax Reform, limits annual property tax increases to three percent, with only a few exceptions. Fox, the president of the Howard Jarvis Taxpayers Association, sponsored a measure in California requiring voter approval for all new local government taxes, and placing limitations on local fees, assessments, and charges. These anti-tax measures, decided on by the voters, are no less controversial than those in the past. They are simply becoming more commonplace.

It is important to note that these recent tax limitation initiatives are not solely concerned with fiscal policy. They are also inherently, if slightly indirectly, tied to the question of governance. Specifically, most contemporary anti-tax revolts signify a popular discontent with their system of representative government. Conventional wisdom suggests that the tax revolt embodies a legitimate form of protest against an undemocratic, unrepresentative government. Using the citizen initiative—a supposedly purer form of democracy—as their means, citizens are able to reclaim their government through these tax limitation measures. Steeped in the rhetorical tropes of the founding of the United States, this common view, while compelling, is often deceptive.

## An American Tradition of Tax Revolts

Calls for changes in the tax code and limits on taxation are not new in this country. There exists a long-standing tradition in the United States of citizens rising up against what they perceive to be unfair or excessive taxes levied by the state. Citing the Revolutionary War as a case in point, many Americans still broadly understand the United States as a nation founded by tax rebels. Sheldon Pollack, a historian of American tax policy, writes, "Popular resistance to tax increases is strong within the political culture" of the United States.[8]

The volatility of this popular resistance towards taxes is intrinsically tied to the ideal of democratic self-governance. While essential to the financing of the state, the question of taxes is not simply one of pocketbook economics. Rather, taxes in this country have come to symbolize the "sinews of power" of the sovereign state, be it local, state, or federal.[9] Tax collection for most Americans is an intrinsically political act. The payment of taxes on property, income, purchases, capital gains, or estate signifies to many people how state power must be attenuated, else personal freedom and liberty will be jeopardized. The question of taxation, then, is inherently entwined with the question of governance and political representation. In the words of Sidney Ratner, a chronicler of America's economic past, "taxation has always been intimately related to democracy."[10]

This connection exists for good reason. The tension between the payment of taxes and democratic governance is firmly rooted in the colonial and post-colonial history of the United States. As prelude to the Revolutionary War, American colonists rebelled against a series of taxes foisted upon them by the British. Resistance against the Crown's taxes—most notably the Sugar Act (1764), the Stamp Act (1765), the Townshend Act (1767), and the Tea Act (1773)—provided the stimulus and inspiration for economic as well as political independence. The Parliamentary legislation, which levied an assortment of duties, tariffs, and imposts on colonial imports and transactions, were used primarily to recompense the British for their military defense of the colonies. At the time, colonists perceived the taxes to be unfair as well as unjust. Eventually, boycotts and demonstrations by the colonists pressured the British to rescind most of the newly imposed taxes.

Today, historians generally concur that the revenues generated by the levies, which remained chiefly in the colonies, were comparatively modest and not terribly unjust. As historian Charles Adams writes, "If revolution is the consequence of oppression, then the American Revolution should never have occurred."[11] Yet a war did ensue. Although the colonial taxes were not economically inordinate, they were symbolic of a greater political injustice.

It is this political side of the taxation equation—the taxation of the colonists without their consent—that proved to be a major cause of the Revolutionary War. Most American school children are familiar with the worn tale of Samuel Adams in 1773 leading a band of patriots disguised as Native Americans to dump British tea into Boston Harbor.[12] The moral of the tale is that the country was founded by subjects of the Crown who successfully bucked, on principled grounds, the undemocratic taxes enacted by Parliament. The British government was not representing colonial interests. It had imposed taxes on the colonists without the consent of the governed. The battle cry of the day, "No taxation without representation," remains forever implanted in the American psyche.[13]

Of parallel importance to the colonists, though largely overlooked today, were the myriad taxes imposed internally by the colonies themselves. Despite the fact that a decade prior to the Revolutionary War colonists paid less taxes than the rest of the Anglo-European world, the burden of internal taxes was of immediate concern to most colonists.[14] "Unlike such temporary aberrations as the stamp tax or the Townshend revenue duties," historian Robert Becker writes, these internal taxes "had to be paid year after year, on the coasts and in the backlands, in good times and in bad, no matter what the state of English-colonial relations."[15] While the revenue laws of the colonies differed widely, they were particularly burdensome to the poor and politically powerless. Following the Revolutionary War, during the age of the Articles of Confederation, "rebel governments in all sections soon faced wide-spread popular opposition to tax collections, opposition that ranged from petitioning and remonstrating through tax withholding to attacking assessors and collectors, and rioting."[16] The cycle of "coercion-cum-resistance that stymied tax collection," historian Roger Brown writes, continued after independence. The "on-again-off-again" forcible tax collection by the fledgling states and federal government, according to Brown, "produced backlash and paralysis."[17] Tax revolts in the newly created states occurred frequently and were often debilitating.

One of the most celebrated uprisings that occurred during the Confederation period was Shays' Rebellion. This internal uprising pitted farmers, as well as laborers, mechanics, and artisans against Massachusetts state and local government officials. As established by the Articles of Confederation, states had to act as the revenue collectors for the impotent federal government. In Massachusetts, local officials were hard-pressed to collect outstanding debts and taxes following the war for independence, as numerous residents, especially in the central and western part of the state, were on the verge of bankruptcy and financial ruin.[18] In a letter to the *Boston Independent Chronicle*, an anonymous author decried the collection of public taxes. Calling on fellow citizens to flaunt the law, the essayist asked rhetorically:

> Can the People make bricks without straw? Will they not rather, through *necessity*, (as that is accounted the mother of invention) be reminded of, if not excited to *improve*, the first great law of nature, viz, *self-preservation*?[19]

In rural western Massachusetts, rebels took decisive action against the state (as well as private debt collectors) by blocking the doors of county court-houses so that civil and criminal cases could not be tried. When the Governor and the state legislature passed laws suspending *habeas corpus*, which allowed local sheriffs to seize property and hold debtors without a trial, as well as one making it easier to disperse rioters, rural residents took up arms and organized military units to defend themselves and their property.[20] In what turned out to be a violent bid to prevent foreclosures on debt-ridden land, a throng of armed men led by Daniel Shays, a former army captain, forcibly took over a federal arsenal in Springfield in January 1787. A month later, federal troops were able to finally suppress the uprising. But the federal government's slow response in quelling the rebellion accentuated the weakness of the Articles of Confederation and reinforced the clamor for a Constitutional Convention to grant more power to Congress and the federal government.[21] At the local level, though, many taxes and debts continued to go unpaid, and in Massachusetts, "it was very evident that the disaffection to government is by no means removed."[22]

Only seven years after the framers of the 1787 Constitutional Convention drew up a new constitution, which among other provisions granted Congress the power "to lay and collect Taxes . . . uniform throughout the United States," the federal government was faced with another tax rebellion. Swayed by the arguments of Treasury Secretary Alexander Hamilton, in 1791 Congress enacted an excise tax on the sale of whiskey, among other items, to raise additional revenue to pay off the federal debt which resulted from the war. "To many in America," Charles Adams writes, "Hamilton's excise was a betrayal of the revolution."[23] Rural distillers and swillers throughout Appalachia defied the tax. In western Pennsylvania, distillers and their thirsty patrons went as far as to tar and feather federal excise officers as well as burn their dwellings. By 1794, the Whiskey Rebellion was full blown. Civil unrest was so widespread in western Pennsylvania that President Washington, urged by Secretary Hamilton, called out the militia from four nearby states and led the troops himself into the region. Following the show of force, the tax rebels capitulated and the resistance was squelched without further bloodshed. Due largely to the perceived injustice of the excise, the tax on whiskey was later repealed under the administration of President Thomas Jefferson.[24]

## Inheriting the Revolutionary Struggle

More than two centuries after the founding of the United States, the colonial and post-colonial tax revolts continue to serve as grist for the mill for contemporary tax rebels. Howard Jarvis, the charismatic leader of Proposition 13, California's stunning property tax limitation measure of 1978, declared on election night, "Now we know how it felt when they dumped English tea in Boston Harbor! We have a new revolution. We are telling the government, 'Screw you!'"[25] The notion that the founders were just the first in a long line of vigilant tax rebels continues to be a powerful force in the rhetoric of contemporary tax revolts.

The question of taxation remains a delicate issue for governments. The sovereignty of the state can become attenuated if the public's perception of governmental action and services fails to match the state's level of appropriation. If the perceived disequilibrium continues, a tax revolt may not be far off in the making. Yet, as Supreme Court Justice Wendell T. Holmes once declared, "Taxes are the price we pay for civilization."[26] Fundamentally, the vitality of the state is dependent on its ability to legitimately usurp revenues. In particular, property taxes remain the cornerstone of local government, and by extension, state governments. Uniform property tax codes provide governments with a steady stream of revenue. They are also one of the biggest targets of tax crusaders.

With contemporary tax revolts, tax crusaders tend to couch their arguments against the expropriation powers of the state with the same rhetoric that was uttered during the founding. The press and many scholars often perceive these contemporary tax limitation advocates as modern day equivalents of Sam Adams and his band of patriots. Contemporary tax revolts—teeming with populist rhetoric and passion—are generally assumed to be fueled from the bottom-up, propelled by typical homeowners and taxpayers. As liberal political journalist Robert Kuttner writes, "Tax protest has a wonderfully American amateur tradition," in which ordinary folks, "without formal expertise in public finance, have haunted county courthouses, bitching about unfair assessments, and generally raising hell."[27]

# 207 years later, it's time for another Tea Party.

*Massachusetts.*
*Birthplace of America's First Tax Revolt.*
*Today, some call it "Taxachusetts."*

We pay higher taxes, but our services are no better than in most other states. Our property taxes are 70 percent above the national average. If you don't believe it, check your latest tax bill.

Our high tax rates hurt the elderly on fixed incomes, often driving them out of homes they have owned for years.

They hurt young couples, making home ownership almost impossible.

They hurt workers by discouraging businesses from expanding and creating new jobs in Massachusetts.

How concerned about all this is the Massachusetts legislature? Consider: Since 1932, our legislature has seen 125 proposals to limit taxes—and has killed every one of them.

Now we have a chance to speak out, to say to all the politicians and special interest groups on Beacon Hill: *"Enough!"*

We can do it by voting for Proposition 2½, a vital first step to reducing wasteful government spending in Massachusetts.

Proposition 2½ just may be our last chance to declare that We, the People of Massachusetts, want control of our future.

# Send a message to Beacon Hill: We want our taxes lowered. Now.

## Proposition 2½: Vote Yes on Question 2, No on Question 3.

*Figure 2.1* Campaign Ad for Proposition 2½, 1980 (Boston Tea Party). [Text recreated from Citizens for Limited Taxation campaign literature.]

Since the passage of Prop. 13, tax crusaders like Howard Jarvis have tapped into the public outrage. Capitalizing on the rhetoric of the founding, they romanticize these past tax revolts when promoting their tax-cutting agendas. They use populist-sounding bravado to attack the amount and levels of taxes that their fellow citizens must pay to money-grubbing, insatiable governments. Castigating the unjust taxing powers of the state, these tax crusaders focus on the tax burden that is placed on average citizens. The financial stress of taxes felt by citizens, of course, helps to fuel these tax revolts.

Yet contemporary battles over taxes, like those during the founding, are fought not only for economic reasons. Objections to the collection efforts of the state go beyond the fiscal side of the taxation question. As mentioned previously, tax rebellions are also highly political. The question of taxation is innately linked to issues concerning democracy and representation. Contemporary tax revolts in the American states are largely concerned with the question of democratic governance and political representation. Revolts against the taxing powers of the state, then, are intrinsically symbolic, as they challenge the supposedly oppressive and undemocratic nature of the state.

## The Legacy of Howard Jarvis

The progenitor of the current generation of tax crusaders is Howard Jarvis. Jarvis—the author of Proposition 13, California's momentous 1978 property tax limitation measure—opened the door for enterprising anti-tax ballot warriors in other states. At the time, Jarvis was a seemingly tireless, seventy-five-year-old semi-retired businessman living in Los Angeles with his wife Estelle and her sister. With the support of his slightly younger sidekick, Paul Gann, a retired car dealer and insurance salesman from Sacramento, Jarvis's ballot measure helped to rewrite California's property tax code. The initiative inspired enthusiastic citizens in other states. Following the June 1978 election, dozens of tax crusaders from around the country advanced copycat tax limitation initiatives in their respective states.[28] Jarvis's measure provided them with a technical as well as a strategic blueprint for their tax limitation endeavors. Virtually overnight, the triumph of the California measure confirmed the real possibility of using the initiative process to directly alter state taxation laws.

While California's initiative process had inspired a variety of tax-related ballot measures over the years, including several during the late 1960s and early 1970s, Prop. 13 was a watershed event in more ways than one.[29] The successful property tax limitation measure broke down the ostensibly impervious barrier between elected officials, who controlled and regulated taxes, and the ordinary people who paid them. In the months and years following the passage of Prop. 13, an increasing number of fiscal decisions in several of the states began to fall under the direct purview of the people via the initiative process. Bypassing state legislatures, new taxes and tax increases (and later, government spending measures) were put directly before the voters instead of being determined by their elected officials. Tax-weary citizens could decide for themselves their state's fiscal future.

Furthermore, the success of Prop. 13, known also as Jarvis-Gann, had national ramifications. As Jarvis declared shortly after his 1978 victory, "When Proposition 13 passed, we did not win the war on taxes. With Proposition 13, we won the first major battle in the war."[30] His brainchild served as the impetus for the wider tax limitation movement in the late 1970s and early 1980s. At the national level, only days after the passage of Prop. 13, Kansas Republican Bob Dole introduced four tax-cut measures into the Senate, including a constitutional amendment calling for the Federal Government to balance its budget every year. Representative David Obey, a Democrat from Wisconsin, groaned about how Prop. 13 caused "panic in this House." And the National Taxpayers Union, 45,000 members strong, launched a campaign in the states to petition for a national convention to amend the Constitution.[31]

Most significantly, though, Prop. 13 transcended the substantive issue of property tax limitation. Jarvis-Gann reinvigorated the use of the citizen initiative by legitimizing it. Jarvis, the perennial political underachiever, personified the underdog who was able to finally triumph against the established interests. Others, who had also fought to downsize government through the established legislative channels only to lose, were radiant with new hope. The initiative process offered ordinary citizens an opportunity to challenge, if not outright repudiate, their elected officials and the institution of representative government. Nearly twenty years after the measure, Jack Citrin, a political scientist from the University of California-Berkeley, commented perceptively that, "In the case of Proposition 13, the initiative process did fulfill its intended, populist purpose," as it "ushered in an era of plebiscitary government in California."[32] In retrospect, the paramount import of Jarvis's initiative was that it empowered citizens, however temporarily and imprudently, to act proactively, rather than wait for their elected officials to respond to their demands.

In 1978, Jarvis was no newcomer to the political cause of tax limitation. He had been waging a private battle against taxes his whole adult life. But it was not until he retired in 1962 at the age of fifty-nine that he became a professional gadfly. A self-described "pain in the ass," Jarvis considered himself to be "a rugged bastard who's had his head kicked in a thousand times by the government."[33] Impervious to criticism, he could dish it out as well as he could take it. During the 1978 campaign, Jarvis became well-known for the stand-up line he borrowed from the movie *Network*, "I'm mad as hell, and I'm not going to take it anymore!" The phrase would later become the title of his autobiography/tax limitation manifesto. Another expression Jarvis liked to sprinkle throughout his public talks was, "Death and taxes may be inevitable, but being taxed to death is not!" He claims to have coined the phrase after witnessing "a middle-aged woman drop dead at the Los Angeles County Hall of Administration in the very act of pleading about the prohibitive level of the property taxes on her home."[34] Ever the man of the people, Jarvis's outsider status helped him usher in a new era of citizen-inspired tax limitations which were piloted by a new breed of citizen-lawmakers. By placing tremendous pressure on elected officials via the citizen initiative in a handful of states, Jarvis led the way for direct democracy to dislodge representative democracy in the realm of fiscal policy.

With the passage of Prop. 13, Jarvis secured his place in tax limitation and ballot initiative lore. In the weeks following the election, his weather-beaten, beaming face graced the cover of *Time*, and he was featured in dozens of weekly magazines, including *Newsweek, US News and World Report, The Nation, The New Republic,* the *National Review, Harper's,* and the British *Economist*.[35] Jarvis became an instant, recognizable icon not only for conservative, anti-tax groups and citizens, but for middle-class American homeowners as well. As initiative scholar David Magleby writes, "Political commentators frequently argued that the passage of Proposition 13 signified a new move toward conservativism, a resurgent middle class, a tax-cutting tendency, and a message that the public desired less government."[36] Jarvis elevated initiative politics to a fashionable, almost celebrity level.

Although Jarvis hired the Newport Beach professional political campaign firm Butcher-Forde Consulting to do most of the fundraising and publicity for the initiative campaign, he remained the chief spokesman for his pathbreaking measure. Calling the state's tax system "grand felony theft," his opponents "liars," "dummies, goons, cannibals or bigmouths," and their arguments "a crock of manure," Jarvis generated his own publicity for Prop. 13.[37] After the victory, Bill Butcher commented on the key role Jarvis played during the campaign: "The focus was on him, not our campaign."[38] Jarvis's peculiar public appeal helped him to capitalize to the fullest degree on the democratic qualities of the initiative process. It was the undemocratic nature of government, as much as property taxes, that Jarvis railed against during his campaign speeches. In the process, he came to be viewed as the democratic savior for millions of Californians.

*Figure 2.2*  Paul Conrad (*Los Angeles Times*) editorial cartoon, Jarvis—"Give me anarchy—or give me debt"

While stubborn, Jarvis was no crank or demagogue.[39] He did not merely appeal to the base prejudices of the populace. Instead, he grasped and articulated for people many of their real economic and political concerns. During the 1978 campaign, Jarvis claims he:

found out a very startling thing: The people of this country didn't believe the politicians anymore. No matter what politician said what, nobody believed him. So I found out if you went out and told people the simple truth, they'll buy it. That's what happened with Proposition 13. We told them exactly what it was like and why. And they bought it.[40]

While Jarvis admitted he had an insatiable ego (he was fond of saying, "everyone is entitled to my opinion"), he claimed he was not motivated by political power, money, or grandeur.[41] Unlike his lesser-known co-sponsor, Paul Gann, Jarvis did not try to parlay his name recognition from Prop. 13 into political office.[42]

Jarvis, though, would profit munificently from his subsequent speaking engagements and book deal. After the election, he cashed in on his image as the defender of the middle class and champion of the initiative process. But during the campaign, he always maintained that he was never out for personal financial gain in his quest to lower taxes and downsize government. Indeed, Jarvis did not stand to make much money from resulting property tax cuts. Despite published accounts insinuating that he would realize great savings from his real estate interests, Jarvis did not have extensive property investments. His only property in 1978 was his modest two-bedroom home on North Crescent Heights Boulevard in West Los Angeles, valued at $80,000 in 1977, on which he paid $1,800 in property taxes. With the passage of Prop. 13, Jarvis's property taxes were reduced by about $600.[43] Either way, the retired millionaire had little difficulty paying his property taxes. "Hell, I can pay whatever my property taxes are. I'll just write a check," Jarvis would say. "Others, especially young couples who can't buy a place of their own, cannot do that."[44] Leona Magidson, a loyal supporter and long-time officer of Jarvis's organization, said of Jarvis, "He was the first human being I came across politically who I thought cared."[45] Jarvis's altruism, while real, was a by-product of his conservative politics bent on downsizing all levels of government.

## Beyond Proposition 13

It is important to recall that while Jarvis was the primary force behind the subsequent tax revolt that rumbled across the United States, the tax revolt did not happen overnight. Despite his pronouncements, Jarvis did not single-handedly bring about the fiscal limitation earthquake that rumbled through California in 1978. Fault lines of the California tax revolt appeared long before Jarvis's measure. Jarvis himself had been working on reducing the level of property taxes since the early 1960s, and had launched several unsuccessful petition drives prior to 1978. Others too had attempted to reign in property taxes in the Golden State. Los Angeles property tax assessor Philip Watson paid a San Francisco firm to collect signatures in order to place statewide initiatives on the ballot in 1968 and 1972,[46] but neither of his measures aimed at property tax relief won majorities on election day. In 1973, Governor Ronald Reagan advanced his own complicated tax and spending limitation initiative, but it also failed at the polls. Numerous tax limitation tremors predated Prop. 13, but it was not until election day that the anti-tax quake finally rocked California.

Across the country, citizens and state legislatures were also experimenting with tax limitation measures prior to Jarvis-Gann. In the late 1970s, a handful of states had passed tax and spending reform legislation, albeit not by citizen initiative. State legislatures in Colorado, Michigan, New Jersey, and Tennessee all restricted state taxes or government spending, but not with the flair seen in California in 1978. In 1976, for example, the New Jersey state legislature passed a bill tying state spending to the annual increase in per capita income (about ten percent a year), and restricted local spending to five percent annual hikes.[47] A year later, the Colorado legislature passed a law that restricted annual state spending increases to seven percent. In March 1978, Tennessee voters altered their state constitution with an amendment referred to them by the legislature limiting "the growth of appropriations from state tax revenues to the estimated rate of growth of the state's economy."[48] The vote in favor of the referendum, known as the Copeland Amendment, was sixty-four to thirty-six percent, although turnout was only seventeen percent of registered voters. Significant tax and government limitation efforts in other states predated Jarvis's measure.

But the passage of Prop. 13 in California proved to be the watershed event in the push for fiscal limitation in the states. Unlike the tax reforms in other states, Jarvis's measure, because it was a citizen initiative and was passed in the most populous state in the union, had national repercussions. Immediately following the vote, Jarvis started spreading his anti-tax message at the national level. On election day, June 6, 1978, Jarvis christened his new crusade, calling it the American Tax Reduction Movement. At once he embarked on a cross-country tour of dozens of cities, preaching the gospel of lower property taxes. As contributions to his national organization poured in from citizens and businesses alike, Jarvis bought chunks of television airtime to promote his property tax limitation ideas to a broader audience. His televised infomercials were aired across the country on 130 stations in the top 25 broadcast markets.[49] To many Americans, Jarvis was a national folk hero. He spoke for the ordinary taxpayers, long ignored by the lawmakers. He gave them a voice, elevating their personal financial burdens to the public dialogue.

As Jarvis was touting the merits of his initiative during his national tour, Prop. 13 clones were being replicated in dozens of states. Via ballot initiatives, legislature-sponsored referendums, and traditional legislative channels, tax limitation legislation was the hot political topic of the fall of 1978 and the spring of 1979. In November 1978, only five months after Proposition 13 passed, voters in twenty states considered tax or government spending limitation measures on election day.[50] The severity of the ballot questions ranged from transferring assessments from state to local governments, local property tax cuts, establishment of a "rainy day" reserve fund for state emergencies, and tying spending to inflation.[51] In the 1978 general election, voters in five of those states—Idaho, Massachusetts, Michigan, Missouri, and Nevada—approved tax limit initiatives. In 1979, twenty-two states passed laws limiting property taxes, eighteen reduced income taxes, fifteen lessened sales taxes, and a dozen cut or repealed a variety of other taxes.[52] The cuts in income and sales taxes alone exceeded $4 billion.[53]

While not all the subsequent tax limitation measures in California and in other states were successful, national public opinion polls discovered a discernable shift in attitudes towards taxes following Jarvis's measure. Immediately after the passage of Prop. 13, the news media conducted what seemed to be weekly public opinion polls on the subject of tax limitation, and more specifically, the reduction of property taxes. According to a *Newsweek/Gallup* poll, fifty-seven percent of Americans in a nationwide survey favored a measure to reduce or limit their property taxes, with only thirty percent opposing such a proposal.[54] Proposition 13 served as the turning point in the battle being waged by citizens against their governments on the question of taxation.

## Life After Proposition 13

As mentioned previously, though, the monumental success of Prop. 13 in no way guaranteed subsequent victories on tax limitation measures. Gann was able to guide a successful ballot measure in November 1979 restricting the expenditures of state and local governments to 1978–79 levels by tying the growth in appropriations to an index of population and cost of living increases. His measure, Proposition 4, known also as "Spirit of 13," won easily with seventy-four percent of the vote.[55] But less than a year later, in June 1980, Jarvis offered a sequel to Prop. 13, Proposition 9. The measure proposed cutting sharply the state personal income tax. The campaign for Prop. 9—also known as Jarvis II—was managed by Butcher-Forde Consulting, but Jarvis had lost some of his personal appeal. Far from his 1978 image as a tantalizing character, Jarvis was seen by many as a grating caricature of his old self.[56] The measure was defeated handily by the voters by a three-to-one margin.

Following the defeat of Jarvis II, some political pundits and scholars speculated that the tax revolt had finally "wound down" and "may have peaked."[57] Others saw the tax revolt in California as "distinctive," in part due to the particular "historical and structural elements" that made up the state's political context.[58] Indeed, there was a nationwide drop-off of victorious tax-limitation initiatives in the early 1980s. The tax revolt, somewhat ironically, seemed to be cooling off during the fall of 1980, just as the election of Ronald Reagan and the supply-side revolution was getting under way. In November 1980, five initiative measures that imitated Prop. 13 went down to defeat. Voters in Arizona, Nevada, Oregon, South Dakota, and Utah all rejected property tax limitation measures at the polls. Only voters in Massachusetts and Arkansas approved property tax reductions that year.[59]

Scholars and journalists were premature in collectively pronouncing the death knell of future tax limitation efforts in the states. Prop. 13 had sown seeds of tax revolt all over the country; it was just a matter of time before they would begin to germinate and grow for others to cultivate. Since the passage of Prop. 13, statewide revenue, tax, and bond ballot measures have topped all other types of citizen initiatives. Between 1978 and 1992, 105 of the 399 initiatives qualifying for the ballot in the states allowing the initiative were revenue-related, more than any other subject matter.[60]

One of the successful 1992 statewide initiatives propelled a new cycle of citizen involvement in state and local taxing and spending matters. Coloradans that year approved Douglas Bruce's creation, Amendment 1. Bruce's statewide measure required citizen approval of all new taxes and government spending for all of Colorado's political jurisdictions. Following Colorado's lead, citizens in two other states, Washington and Missouri, voted for initiatives mandating that the voters set the limits on state and local revenues and expenditures. In addition to voting occasionally on statewide ballot initiatives dealing with fiscal issues, citizens in these states are now required to approve any new tax or boost in the level of government spending. By deciding these matters at the polls, citizens—not elected officials—are directly deciding the parameters of state and local fiscal policy. To the surprise of many political pundits, the public support for citizen-led tax and government limitation measures is as strong as it was in the late 1970s.

## Jarvis's Progeny

While they all trace their lineage to him, some of today's tax crusaders who were inspired by Jarvis have come a long way from the roughly-hewn, acerbic curmudgeon. In 1978, Jarvis—who referred to himself as a "Jack Mormon," by which he meant, "I'm no goddam good. I drink vodka, smoke a pipe and play a little golf on Sunday"—was offensive to the point of ingratiating himself to the public.[61] But only two short years later, a majority of voters, disgusted by his insolence, overwhelmingly rejected his Proposition 9. In 1986, Jarvis died of a blood disease at the age of eighty-two. Three years later, his erstwhile partner, Paul Gann, also passed away. But a new generation of tax crusaders had already taken over the mantle of the tax revolt.

Of the current bevy of tax crusaders, Douglas Bruce of Colorado, a landlord and former prosecutor for the city and county of Los Angeles, most closely emulates Jarvis's confrontational style and bombastic rhetoric. Prior to the success of Amendment 1 in 1992, Bruce and his shell organization, the "Taxpayers Bill of Rights" Committee (TABOR), had failed on his two previous statewide attempts to limit taxes and government spending. Since his 1992 victory, Bruce has been unable to muster a majority for any of his subsequent ballot initiatives, including a 1996 petition rights amendment in 1996 in which a front organization sponsored his measure while he quietly worked behind the scenes.[62] His obnoxious demeanor during the campaigns has increased his name recognition, but it has come at a price. In 1995, nearly half of Coloradans held a negative view of Bruce.[63]

On the east coast, Barbara Anderson holds court as one of only a few female tax crusaders in the country. She has wisely and energetically led the anti-tax movement in Massachusetts for nearly two decades. In 1980, voters in Massachusetts approved a property tax limitation initiative placed on the ballot by Anderson's group, which among other provisions, reduced property taxes to 2.5 percent of the real property value. Originally a volunteer who worked the office phones and collected signatures for petition drives, Anderson has directed Citizens for Limited Taxation (CLT) since the summer of 1980. Taking over the organization only months before CLT's landmark property tax limitation initiative was to come to a vote in November, Anderson shepherded the measure to victory. CLT, which in November 1996 joined forces with Chip Ford's statewide activist network to become Citizens for Limited Taxation and Government (CLT&G), remains a force to be reckoned in the Bay State.

In addition to Bruce and Anderson, several other prominent descendants of Jarvis have made waves in the tax limitation business during the 1990s. Bill Sizemore of Oregon, David Biddulph of Florida, and Joel Fox of California, are the latest in a long line of enterprising tax crusaders who zealously use the initiative process to advance their tax and government limitation efforts. [64] Although differing in their styles and techniques, Sizemore, Biddulph, and Fox have struck terror in the hearts of their respective elected state officials. With an almost religious fervor, the three tax crusaders have unabashedly drawn on corporate or out-of-state financing to wage their crusades. Shunning the traditional channels of representative government to alter state fiscal policy, they have taken their pet fiscal solutions directly to the people for a vote.

While self-promotion and populist rhetoric are big parts of the initiative game, so too are financial and organizational resources needed to promote the campaigns. Although direct democracy is purportedly a process that is of the people, the financial and organizational support for these recent tax limitation measures is not always gleaned from the average taxpayer. In the case studies that follow, the actual process of these tax and government limitation campaigns are exposed, revealing the seamy and sometimes undemocratic side of the initiative process.

## The Nexus of Taxes and Direct Democracy

The tradition of popular tax revolts in the United States is strongly linked to the ideal of representative government. Because taxes and democracy are intimately entwined, individuals or groups can capitalize on the image of direct democracy as an uncompromised process. Proponents of direct democracy argue that the initiative process counters the supposedly unrepresentative, undemocratic state. The conventional wisdom, then, suggests that tax revolts are a democratic response to the unrepresentative usurpation powers of the state. Tax revolts are seen as a pure expression of democracy in action. They have come to represent the true sentiments of the people. Forged by populist-sounding rhetoric, tax limitation initiatives are as much about tax reduction as they are about the failings of the system of representative government.

Yet most contemporary tax revolts, while steeped in the populist rhetoric of democracy and participation, are no more democratic or participatory than the process of representative government. Once the rhetorical veneer is peeled away from most tax limitation initiatives, it becomes apparent that they are far less democratic and participatory than is generally assumed. In fact, with respect to tax and government limitation measures, there is little procedural difference between direct democracy and representative democracy. The organizational and financial support for most of these measures is highly concentrated. Sound-bite advertisements trump meaningful debate. Furthermore, contrary to the conventional view, citizen participation is largely contrived, as these measures are directed from the top-down. Professional campaign consultants have largely replaced volunteers, and populist-sounding rhetoric saturates the airwaves. The following chapter examines the link between the process of direct democracy and the populist tradition in the United States, providing the conceptual framework of *faux* populism to help inform the case studies.

# THREE

# POPULISM AND *FAUX* POPULIST MOMENTS

As opposed to the idea that society consists of a number of different and frequently clashing interests ... the populists adhered, less formally to be sure, but quite persistently, to a kind of social dualism: although they knew perfectly well that society was composed of a number of classes, for all practical purposes only one simple division need be considered. There were two nations. "It is a struggle," said Sockless Jerry Simpson, "between the robbers and the robbed."

—*Richard Hofstadter*[1]

Populism divides the political world into Us, the People, and Them, the professional politicians and bureaucrats who actually rule. Deeply suspicious of the politics of compromise, the populist's constant fear is that They will betray Us.

—*Jack Citrin*[2]

## Introduction: The Making of Conventional Wisdom

As discussed in the previous chapter, a government's tax collection powers and its political legitimacy are intrinsically linked. Tensions can easily arise in a state—which is purportedly democratic and representative of the interests of the governed—when citizens perceive that their elected officials are expropriating too many taxes. In such a case, the nexus can become highly sensitive, and a tax revolt is a possible outlet for the pent-up frustrations of a certain segment of the citizenry. The validity of this mass defiance is embedded in the country's political culture, as there is a long tradition in the U.S. of citizens rising up against the state over the question of taxation. Expressed as popular resistance to a government's taxing and spending powers, tax revolts are symptomatic of the perception that the state has taken an unrepresentative and anti-democratic turn.

While tax revolts continue to erupt in this country, especially in the states with the initiative process, the standard explanation for them has evolved over time. No longer, as was the case during pre-Revolutionary times, can tax revolts be understood as the manifestation of a desperate plea for representative government. Since the founding, the philosophical underpinnings of governance in this country have been firmly grounded in a system of representative democracy. With most substantive policy issues—welfare, health care, education, commerce, national defense, and foreign policy, to name a few—citizens rarely contest the legitimacy of the decisions made by their elected officials. Citizens may sometimes disagree with the policy preferences of their elected officials, but they nonetheless tend to deem the system of representative government to be a sufficient safeguard of their constitutional rights. With respect to these policy arenas, the legitimacy of the system of representative government seldom, if ever, comes into question.

But all bets are off when it comes to the taxing and spending powers of the state. With increasing frequency, it seems, citizens consider their democratically elected, representative government to be inadequate to determine fiscal questions of the state. Government by the consent of the governed, a fundamental tenet of this country, is no longer perceived to be an adequate form of governance. Prevailing in its stead is the notion that taxes (along with government spending) must be directly voted on by the people. No less than a popular vote will do. As Colorado tax crusader Douglas Bruce declared in 1994 in the midst of one of his many ballot initiative campaigns, "The petition really is the voice of the people."[3] Representative government, in the eyes of Bruce and other tax crusaders, has somehow failed to secure the consent of those who are governed.

As such, the modern-day battle over fiscal policy in nearly half of the states has taken on a populist hue. Tax and spending limitation efforts in the American states that technically arise from the citizenry (as opposed to elected officials) are conventionally understood by scholars and journalists as populist endeavors. This connection between taxes and direct democracy underpins the populist persuasion of modern-day tax revolts. Furthermore, resisting the taxation powers of the state evokes the colonial struggle of patriotic Americans rising up to fight the oppressive powers of an anti-democratic, foreign sovereign. It's the people against the state; it's "Us" against "Them." Battles over the taxation powers of the state summon the spirit of this apparent populist struggle. As scholar David Schmidt, an advocate of the citizen initiative vented recently, "Those who oppose direct citizen control of taxes and government spending forget the most important factor in this debate: it's *our* money."[4]

However, the basic function of taxation—the appropriation of money from the people by the state—only partly explains the predisposition of the public to generally understand tax revolts as populist endeavors. Equally powerful in the creation of this conventional wisdom is the means by which modern-day tax revolts occur. The initiative process is inherently understood as a populist endeavor. It pits the process of direct democracy against the entrenched institution of representative democracy. The initiative, after all, echoes the original Populist struggle of a century ago. It is "the people," and not the "professional politicians and bureaucrats," who control the ballot initiative. With respect to the conventional wisdom suggesting that tax revolts are rousing exhibits of populist politics, the seemingly purer democratic machinery of the initiative process has become as significant as the actual financial burden of the taxes in question.

This dual punch—the taut connection between taxes and representative democracy combined with the democratic seduction of the initiative process—seems to sway the conventional wisdom concerning contemporary tax revolts in the American states. Yet, this understanding is often misplaced because the actual process of the ballot initiative is not always closely examined. Most tax revolts in the states are neither populist nor movements. They are usually not *of*, and almost never *by* the people. While tax cuts may be *for* the people, it depends on how one defines "the people" and the public good.[5] To call tax revolt initiatives populist, though, belies the actual process of most of these measures.

## The Beleaguered Concept of Populism

Part of the reason why tax revolts are increasingly perceived as populist undertakings has to do with how the term populism is commonly understood. Over the years, students of populism have advanced numerous definitions. As a result, the concept has lost much of its analytic precision. For example, political observers routinely characterize Howard Jarvis, Barbara Anderson, and Douglas Bruce as populists, and their respective endeavors as populist movements.[6] As the case studies will reveal, though, Howard Jarvis and the other profiled tax crusaders lack many of the qualities of past populist leaders. Their new brand of populism falls outside the parameters of the populist tradition in America. It is more akin to what might be called "*faux* populism"—a populist rhetoric and message without "the people." To fill the theoretical gap and to better understand this alternative brand of populism, an analytic framework is offered that focuses on the forces that lead to successful *faux* populist endeavors.

Whether Jarvis, Anderson, and Bruce each presided over a populist movement or a *faux* populist *moment* [7] is more than a pedantic question of semantics. Labeling these initiatives carries enormous weight in terms of how the public perceives them. But defining and delimiting the concept of populism is no easy task. Scholars, journalists, and politicians have used the term to describe a variety of phenomena over the years. As David Laycock notes, in the vernacular, populism has come to connote "any folksy appeal to the 'average guy,' or some allegedly general will."[8] Indeed, "[t]he habit of branding as 'populist' everything from Bruce Springsteen to Rush Limbaugh to loose-fitting cotton trousers," historian Michael Kazin writes, results from the "glib" attempt "to capture the volatile tastes of the public."[9] In this broadest, and most watered-down sense, the three tax limitation initiatives did indeed share many "populist" qualities.

This sweeping understanding of populism, while frequently used, tells us little about the dynamics of the tax limitation campaigns. Equally problematic, however, are the more precise definitions of populism. While the term is historically rooted, the populist tradition in America most certainly transcends historian Lawrence Goodwyn's overly narrow definition of the concept. In his classic, but sometimes criticized examination of the Populist revolt of more than a century ago, Goodwyn argues that there are four sequential stages in the "democratic movement-building" of all populist endeavors: the movement forming, the movement recruiting, the movement educating, and the movement politicized.[10] This arduous, and perhaps idealized, process is necessarily democratic, according to Goodwyn. Populist movements, such as the one led by the agrarian radicals of the National Farmers Alliance and Industrial Union, Goodwyn contends, must ascend from the grassroots. As opposed to mere "shadow movements," populist uprisings have an "ethos," as they are educative and demand the active participation of the masses.[11]

To be sure, the concept of populism transcends the narrow margins of the radical agrarian movement and even the resulting People's (or Populist) Party of the late nineteenth century. Although the term was coined for the actions of these late nineteenth century insurgents, George Tindall points out, the "Populist spirit lived on after the People's Party."[12] Populism in America no longer solely signifies a regional championing of agrarian and democratic reforms by a group of agitated farmers and their working-class allies. The numerous mutations and reincarnations of so-called populist movements over the years, and the resulting number of incongruous interpretations of these movements, has weakened the concept. Indeed, the concept of populism, according to Isaiah Berlin, is vexed with a Cinderella complex:

> [T]here exists a shoe—the word "populism"—for which somewhere there exists a foot. There are all kinds of feet which it nearly fits, but we must not be trapped by these nearly fitting feet. The prince is always wandering about with the shoe; and somewhere, we feel sure, there awaits a limb called pure populism. This is the nucleus of populism, its essence.[13]

In shedding its distinctive historical origins—by "wandering about," as Berlin puts it—the concept of populism picked up much conceptual baggage, losing its analytic precision. As Christopher Lasch points out, "To speak of populism in such general terms admittedly carries the risk of imprecision."[14]

This interpretation, however, is nothing new. The concept of populism, as historian Richard Hofstadter noted over 40 years ago, has had "an ambiguous character" in the saga of American history.[15] A leading scholar as well as critic of the populist penchant of Americans, Hofstadter understood the pervasive resonance and appeal of populist ideology and discourse in American politics. Taking into account its ambiguous character, Hofstadter began to separate the term "populism" from its agrarian, egalitarian roots on the American prairie:

> By "Populism" I do not mean only the People's (or Populist) Party of the 1890s; for I consider the Populist Party to be merely a heightened expression, at a particular moment of time, of *a kind of popular impulse that is endemic in American political culture.*[16]

By chronicling other heightened expressions of popular impulses in the American political tradition, Hofstadter demonstrated how the populist ideal was not restricted to a particular time or place.

## The Changing Face of Populism

In losing its historic specificity, however, the concept of populism not only lost its temporal and spatial precision; it also surrendered its politics. Politically, there are no longer any congruent features of populism. The attempt "to label populism as either Right or Left," Margaret Canovan writes, "is a lost cause."[17] Concurring, Peter Wiles aptly characterizes populism as "a syndrome, not a doctrine."[18] The political ideology that drives a specific populist movement can be determined only by understanding its larger context. While some scholars insist that, "For coherency, and to keep faith with the origin of the term, the political should remain central to its meaning,"[19] the politics of populism is now (if not always) peripheral to the core meaning of the concept.

Historically, neither conservative nor liberal forces have had a monopoly on the populist vein of American politics. So-called populist leaders and populist causes have spanned the spectrum of political ideology. The "exaltation of this ambiguous 'people,'" as Canovan notes, "can take a variety of forms."[20] Political leaders—as ideologically diverse as Ignatius Donnelly, Tom Watson, William Jennings Bryan, Samuel Gompers, Father Charles Coughlin, George Wallace, Reverend Jesse Jackson, Reverend Pat Robertson, Ronald Reagan, Ross Perot, and Pat Buchanan—have spoken for vast numbers of common people, and in turn, have earned for themselves the populist moniker. These leaders have unquestionably served as political spokespersons for "the people." To identify them as populists, though, tells us little to nothing about "the people" for which they spoke or the political ideology which they advocated. Populists and their movements come in all shapes and sizes, stripes and colors. For the term to have political precision and meaning, it must be contextualized.

With respect to the political substance of populism, early scholars, including distinguished historians John Hicks and C. Vann Woodward, accentuated the radical egalitarian side of the late-nineteenth-century populists.[21] Writing in 1931, Hicks argued that these radicals observed two propositions: "one, that the government must restrain the selfish tendencies of those who profited at the expense of the poor and needy; the other, that the people, not the plutocrats, must control the government."[22] Populism, for these and other scholars, was the intellectual and political precursor of the Progressive Era. But subsequent scholars, led by Hofstadter, began to uncover a dark, authoritarian underside of early populist movements and their leaders. During the age of McCarthyism, revisionist historians and sociologists, including Hofstadter, Daniel Bell, and Seymour Martin Lipset, seized upon the dangers of the populist mind.[23] Hofstadter, writing in 1955, claimed that, "Populist thinking has survived in our own time, partly as an undercurrent of provincial resentments, popular and 'democratic' rebelliousness and suspiciousness, and nativism."[24] Other scholars, reiterating Hofstadter's skepticism of America's populist tradition, have characterized strands of populism as, "primitive xenophobia, intolerance, anti-urbanism and anti-industrialism."[25]

Running counter to the revisionists, some scholars have re-emphasized the positive, progressive side of the populist tradition in America. These scholars, including Norman Pollack, Gene Clanton, and most recently, Kazin, claim that the core of the populist heritage is "an insight of great democratic and moral significance."[26] This moral and democratic insight has served as a challenge to "prevailing attitudes" and has contributed "to an expansion of the conventional wisdom such as would eventually be conducive to a more creative social dialogue."[27] In celebration and defense of the rich populist legacy, counter-revisionist historian Norman Pollack argued, "It is this heightened awareness of the human condition in the late nineteenth century which gave rise to the Populist movement, and which served to define the outline of its thought."[28]

Each of these scholarly explications of the populist tradition in America brings a different interpretation of what the besieged concept substantively entails. As a result, the concept has become more imprecise and attenuated over time. A detailed historical record is needed to understand the substantive, political nature of a particular "populist movement." Without the historical context, the concept does little to help us understand the political aspirations or ideologies of so-called populist leaders and their followers.

## The Procedural Side of Populism

Although the substantive side of populism has become contested over the years, the concept remains a powerful signifier of popular discontent, protest, and radicalism. This is due to the fact that the concept of populism also has a vital, procedural side. The procedural side of populism, unlike the substantive side, has remained rather constant over time, place, and political ideology. It is this procedural side—the process of a bottom-up, political struggle pitting Us against Them—that still reveals whether or not a movement can legitimately be characterized as populist. Regardless of the political leanings of "the people" or their leaders, the process of populism indicates a mass outcry of a "common people" aimed at an established elite, their norms, and their practices. It signifies an unabashed defense of the common person. As Sociologist Trevor Harrison makes clear:

> [P]opulism constitutes an attempt to create a mass political movement, mobilized around symbols and traditions congruent with the popular culture, which expresses a group's sense of threat, arising from presumably powerful "outside" elements and directed at its perceived "peoplehood."[29]

The principled actions and activities of a common people, regardless of their substantive positions, largely define the concept. Other scholars have noted in passing this procedural side of populism. Paul Wilkinson argues that populism should not be regarded as "an elaborate ideology or indeed a comprehensive political programme; rather, it proclaims its faith in the essential virtues of the simple people and its suspicion of, or outright hostility towards, all elites."[30] Concurring, political scientist Allen Hertzke has remarked that, "One does not have to agree with populist prescriptions, or approve of their attacks on elites, to sympathize with their disquiet."[31] It is the active participation of the people and the direction of the protest—the process, not the substantive political prescriptions they espouse—that makes populist movements so attractive and powerful. From a procedural standpoint, then, the concept of populism still has analytic utility.

Central to the process of the populist tradition in America, then, is the directional flow of mass discontent and protest. Populism entails a grassroots, bottom-up form of protest and participation by the masses. While the political ideology of American populist movements has ebbed and flowed, as Hofstadter, Kazin and other scholars rightly argue, political eruptions on the American landscape, for them to be genuinely populist, must spring from "the people." Regardless of the political diversity of a so-called populist movement, the initial impulse of the movement, to be genuinely populist, must ascend from the people themselves. The leaders of the respective populist movements, of course, serve as the recognized spokespersons and standard-bearers of their movements. They mobilize, direct, target, and impart the will of the people to the appropriate audiences. But for a movement to be truly populist, it is the common people who need to be the source of the message. A populist message must be, in the words of Abraham Lincoln in his Gettysburg Address, "of the people, by the people, for the people." While perhaps not perfectly cohesive or coherent, a populist message and the resulting movement must be a collective and earnest effort of, by, and for the people; populist leaders simply convey the message to the powers that be.

Some scholars, while acknowledging the procedural side of American populist movements, have not fully appreciated its centrality to the concept. Instead, they have tended to concentrate on the particular brand of rhetoric used by populist leaders. And for good reason—the dualistic nature of populist movements leads naturally to sharp images and language. Hofstadter clearly delineated the binary relationship between movement leaders and their intended targets. In framing the substantive issues in an "us versus them" language, populist leaders usually try to exploit existing social, cultural, economic, or political chasms in society. "Although they [populist leaders] knew perfectly well that society was composed of a number of classes," Hofstadter noted in his classic study, "for all practical purposes only one simple division need be considered."[32] This "social dualism," as Hofstadter calls it, is a major trait of populist movements. According to Hofstadter, "In various phrases this central antagonism was expressed," from "[t]he people versus the interests," to "the public versus the plutocrats," to "the toiling multitude versus the money power."[33]

Most recently, Kazin has proffered a more rhetorical tack in his wide-ranging study of populist movements in the U.S. Focusing on the "persistent yet mutable style of political rhetoric" that has driven populist movements in America, Kazin analyzes the "tension between the social world of language users and the types of expression they employed."[34] Since the days of Andrew Jackson, Americans periodically have been drawn to what Kazin aptly terms the "populist persuasion." For Kazin, the thread running through the fabric of America's populist persuasion is the rhetoric used by populist leaders. Kazin defines populism as, "a language that extols the virtue of the hard-working, patriotic American majority and charges a succession of elites with benefiting their privileged friends and betraying 'the people.'"[35] While an "enduring irony of populism" is that the rhetoric of populism that "praises connections between anonymous people and mistrusts the palaver of elites has often been communicated most effectively by eloquent men who stand above the crowd,"[36] he argues that rhetoric was a major factor in the success of the populist movements which he documents. For example, Kazin notes that for two decades prior to the founding of the People's Party, "insurgents were nurturing a language of bitterness and betrayal."[37] But in order to succeed, Kazin argues, the Party needed to carve out a broad definition of "the people."

Kazin, while accepting the interaction of rhetoric and action, tends to overemphasize the importance of rhetoric in populist movements. While the centrality of persuasive speech by "eloquent men" may have been true a century ago, it is no longer the key variable determining the success of contemporary populist movements. Rhetoric, no doubt, is important in advancing populist causes, but men, and women, no longer need to be adroit wordsmiths in order to get their populist messages across to audiences. Rhetoric is only one of the many tools of so-called populist leaders; it is part and parcel of the larger sociopolitical process. Although a populist movement usually acquires an authoritative language or set of symbols, it is not the language or set of symbols that makes a movement populist. For a movement to be considered populist, the process must be from the ground up. A populist movement is not only for the people; it is also necessarily of and by the people. Rhetoric, then, is of secondary importance to populist movements. When it is used in populist movements, rhetoric is embedded in the upward process.

Many scholars, journalists, and politicians continue to fret over the imprecision and overuse of the term "populism." They claim the concept is rapidly becoming a hollow label, as it is used to lump together a wide array of supposed populist leaders and populist movements occurring in the U.S. Because of its loose usage, Lasch laments, the concept "seems compromised almost beyond hope of redemption."[38] Indeed, the term populism has lost the constitutive meaning it had when it was first used to describe the actions of the members of the People's Party and its antecedents. It is now impossible to define the concept in purely substantive terms. Yet, the procedural side of populism, which encompasses the rhetoric used by the leaders of populist movements, remains unequivocal. Grassroots protests "in response to a perceived threat to 'the people' and their social order,"[39] sprouting from either the left or the right side of the political spectrum, remain the essence of populism today.

## *Faux* Populist Moments

With this rather protracted discussion of populism as backdrop, I suggest—on procedural grounds—that the three tax limitation ballot initiatives can be better understood as *faux* populist *moments* rather than populist movements. *Faux* populism—defined here as a populist-sounding message without the political mobilization of "the people"—substitutes the ballot initiative for the deliberative process of Goodwyn's democratic "movement-building." While this process of movement-building need not be as comprehensive as Goodwyn's understanding, populist movements do require a relative degree of active participation by the masses. While the rhetoric used by the leaders of these alleged movements often approximates that heard during populist movements, procedurally, *faux* populist moments lack the mobilization and active participation of the citizenry. Instead, through the initiative process, ordinary citizens, such as Jarvis, Anderson, and Bruce are able to offer their fellow citizens populist-sounding solutions as antidotes to their societal problems. If their solution resonates with the public, citizens can become passive supporters of the measure. Although it echoes the original Populist struggle of a century ago and is inherently understood as a populist process, the citizen initiative is no guarantee of mass mobilization and participation. With the initiative process, citizens are merely asked to exercise their right to vote on election day. In no sense does this constitute a populist movement, except in the broadest, most popularized definition of the term.

For contemporary *faux* populist ventures to be successful, two necessary conditions must be present. First, an unequivocal (though usually latent) public mood must resonate among the populace. The public mood—understood collectively as popularly held sentiments—constitutes "the notion that a rather large number of people out in the country are thinking along certain common lines."[40] The public mood is real, but is poorly articulated; it is fragmented and ill-defined. Second, a populist entrepreneur who has sufficient charisma and organizational resources to capitalize on the amorphous, popular sentiment, must be able to channel and fashion the public mood into a coherent, popular message. Like John Kingdon's policy entrepreneur and Klaus Eder's moral entrepreneur, the populist entrepreneur, seizing an opportunity, taps into the public mood and couples his or her own pet solution to it.[41] The role of the populist entrepreneur, then, is to craft a popular message, place it on the ballot via the initiative process, and push it as *the* solution to the widely perceived public problem.[42] When the populist entrepreneur successfully taps the public mood, it is quite possible that a *faux* populist *moment* will occur.

Absent from *faux* populist moments is the active laboring and protest of the masses. *Faux* populist moments are fairly sterile. They are a far cry from traditional populist or even broader social movements, as they lack the "organized, nongovernmental efforts of large numbers of people to attain significant social and personal change."[43] With *faux* populist moments, common people do not organize themselves to promote change; mass organization of the common people is dropped from the equation. A *faux* populist moment, in terms of the collective commitment of its supporters, is a much more limited form of protest than a more conventional populist or social movement. With the *faux* populist moment, turnout on election day and more specifically, the vote for a popular initiative, supplants the mass movement of the common people.

The lack of visible protest in *faux* populist moments does not imply that the widely held sentiments of common people are unimportant. The public mood of the people, while vague, is identifiable. Because the public mood is real, the populist entrepreneur's efforts are readily legitimized after he or she is able to tap it. The popular sentiment, of course, may be perceived in a variety of ways; the populist entrepreneur is left with considerable discretion when interpreting, shaping, and packaging the ambiguous public mood into a popular initiative that roughly approximates the concerns of the people. Whether or not the populist entrepreneur is successful in that approximation is determined in the voting booth—the *faux* populist moment.

## From Populist Movements to *Faux* Populist Moments

As advanced in the preceding chapter, Howard Jarvis and the triumph of Proposition 13 ushered in this era of *faux* populist moments. An increase in the use of the ballot initiative in other states began immediately following the passage of the property tax cutting measure in California. Jarvis paved the way for future populist entrepreneurs. His measure unlocked the vast potential of using the citizen initiative once again to shape state public policy. In a way, Prop. 13 was as much about resurrecting the process of direct democracy as it was about reducing property taxes.

As such, Jarvis's 1978 measure is central to understanding the transformation from populist movements to *faux* populist moments with respect to tax limitation efforts, and the use of the citizen initiative more generally. Following Prop. 13, subsequent populist entrepreneurs began to realize how the process of direct democracy, rather than the actual substance of an issue, could provide the main thrust of an initiative campaign. Since Prop.

13, mass mobilization and grassroots support for tax limitation measures (and ballot initiatives more generally) have become almost secondary considerations of populist entrepreneurs. Citizen initiatives have built-in support, as the conventional wisdom suggests that they *must* be grassroots endeavors, emerging naturally from the people.

Much like political parties, which have evolved from "labor-intensive" party machines into "capital-intensive," technology-driven organizations,[44] initiative campaigns have become much more professionalized since the 1970s. This professionalization of the citizen initiative, Jack Citrin notes, has "facilitated the use of direct democracy by political entrepreneurs of all kinds."[45] Most initiative campaigns, far from being dependent on volunteers and grassroots support, have gone high tech. "Full-service consulting firms now draft and circulate petitions, collect signatures, raise funds through direct mail, prepare campaign advertising, conduct polls, and get out the vote," Citrin observes.[46] In 1996, for example, only one of Colorado's eight citizen initiatives was placed on the ballot by an all-volunteer corps of signature collectors. The other proponents of the measures either paid individuals to collect signatures, or hired an in- or out-of-state firm to amass the minimum number of valid signatures. One of the ballot measures, the Parental Rights Amendment, did not even originate in Colorado: It was sponsored, supervised, and almost entirely financed by a group based in Arlington, Virginia.[47] Like other ballot initiatives across the nation, the campaign for the Parental Rights Amendment was driven by the measure's campaign consultants, rather than by ordinary citizens.[48] Even Jarvis, the "author" of several tax limitation measures that followed the passage of Prop. 13, permanently hired a powerful consulting firm, Butcher-Forde Consultants, to collect signatures by mail and run the initiative campaigns.[49]

Across the country, initiative campaigns are no longer characterized by a groundswell of spontaneous popular support or mass outcry. Increasingly, volunteers and grassroots support for ballot measures are the exception, rather than the norm. With respect to citizen initiatives, *faux* populist moments are commonly displacing genuine populist movements.[50] This transformation was spawned by the tax limitation earthquake in California. Since 1978, so-called citizen initiatives, and especially tax and government limitation ballot measures, have become less and less the product of the people. Ironically, the tax crusaders themselves have been the first to comprehend this transformation. As Massachusetts tax crusader Barbara Anderson laments, people are not as willing or even able to volunteer for ballot campaigns. Compared with the late 1970s, she claims running an initiative campaign is, "a whole different world." Back then, according to Anderson, "a lot of our activists had one person working and the other person free" to "go out and get signatures on a petition drive."[51] Today, it is much more difficult to mobilize people. Douglas Bruce is even more candid in his assessment of citizen involvement in ballot initiatives today: "Basically, most people don't help; instead they sit there passively," and "all of the people who say they'll help out don't."[52] While their ballot initiatives may indeed be *for* "the people," fewer and fewer of them are generally *of* or *by* the people.

In the next three chapters, I directly challenge the conventional wisdom that tax revolts via the citizen initiative are populist endeavors. In the case studies that follow, I reexamine the procedural aspects of the three initiative campaigns, critically examining the popular support for each tax limitation measure. Using the conceptual framework of *faux* populism, I highlight the crucial, but frequently neglected role, strategies, and resources of the populist entrepreneur. I argue that the three tax crusaders depended on the financial and organizational resources of a narrow set of economic interests in order to generate more widespread support for their initiatives. As such, the evidence from the three cases brings into question much of the conventional wisdom surrounding the tax limiting measures, as they were far less grassroots and populist than is generally believed by scholars, journalists, and the broader public.

# FOUR

# PROPPING UP PROPOSITION 13

*Howard Jarvis, the United Organization of Taxpayers, and the Los Angeles Apartment Owners Association*

We are not geniuses. The people associated with me were citizens just on the same block as I was. We don't have any brilliant minds. All we had was guts. And when we started out we knew we were going to stay there till we won. We didn't care how long or how hard or how rough it was, we were going to stay there until we won.

—*Howard Jarvis*[1]

We're sending the whole country a huge message. We've been at this for 15 years. It's been like building the damn pyramids. But we've done it. The tax revolt is here, right now.

—*Howard Jarvis*[2]

## Introduction: The "Revolt of the Haves"

In the months preceding the June 6, 1978 primary election, Proposition 13, California's fractious property tax ballot measure, received almost daily media attention. Newspaper columnists from California and across the country swapped partisan barbs, debating *ad infinitum* the merits and faults of the initiative. Political and economic pundits calculated and recalculated the measure's possible effects and unintended consequences. Heated letters to the editor and sharp-edged political cartoons saturated the editorial pages of local newspapers. Opinion polls registered the public's sentiment toward the measure weekly. Shrill advertisements touting either the necessity or the destructiveness of the proposition interrupted regularly scheduled television and radio programs. Indefatigable Howard Jarvis, the monomaniacal, septuagenarian leader of the tax limitation movement, was seemingly everywhere. By election day, the proponents and the opponents of Prop. 13 had spent over two million dollars each on the measure.

Despite, or perhaps due to the immense media attention given to Prop. 13, sixty-nine percent of eligible California voters flocked to the polls on primary day to cast their vote on the controversial property tax limitation measure. The vote in favor of the 389-word ballot initiative was overwhelming. Californians supported Prop. 13 by a two-to-one margin. Sixty-five percent of those who turned out cast their vote for the measure. Commonly referred to as "Jarvis-Gann" for the amendment's co-authors, Howard Jarvis and Paul Gann, the initiative carried nearly every demographic group. Not surprisingly, homeowners supported Prop. 13 more than renters. Republicans were more apt to support Jarvis-Gann than Democrats. Support for Prop. 13 was greater among people with upper-bracket incomes, but declined among people with higher levels of education. Men and the elderly were generally more supportive of the measure, public employees widely opposed the measure, and whites were over three times as likely as blacks to vote for the property tax cut.[3]

After the passage of Jarvis-Gann, local government officials were forced to act swiftly. The measure was to take effect on July 1, only three weeks after it was passed by the voters. Prop. 13 required local governments to limit any *ad valorem* tax on real property to one percent of assessed valuation while scaling back assessed values of properties to 1975-76 levels, restrict increases in assessment to two percent a year except upon sale of the property, and prohibit any new state or local taxes without two-thirds voter approval. With their vote, Californians slashed property tax revenue in fiscal year 1978-1979 by an estimated fifty-seven percent. The annual revenue of local governments (cities, counties, schools, special districts) was reduced by roughly $6 billion.[4] Jarvis-Gann was a decisive property tax cut.

Over the past twenty years, dozens of articles and numerous books have examined both the causes and effects of the renowned property tax measure. Prop. 13 is probably the most-studied initiative measure in the history of the United States. The overarching significance of Jarvis-Gann far outstrips the immediate fiscal impact it had on the financial condition of the citizens as well as the state and local governments of California. Its

---

INITIATIVE CONSTITUTIONAL AMENDMENT—
PROPERTY TAX LIMITATION

Limits ad valorem taxes on real property to 1% of value except to pay indebted-
ness previously approved by voters. Establishes 1975-76 assessed valuation as base
value of property for tax purposes. Limits annual increases in value. Provides for
reassessment after sale, transfer, or construction. Requires 2/3 vote of Legislature
to enact any change in state taxes designed to increase revenues. Prohibits impo-
sition by state of new ad valorem, sales or transaction taxes on real property.
Authorizes specified local entities to impose special taxes except ad valorem, sales
and transaction taxes on real property. Financial Impact: Would result in loss of
local property tax revenues of $7 billion to $8 billion annually and a reduction in
state costs of about $700 million in 1978-79 and $800 million annually thereafter.

---

*Figure 4.1*   The Abbreviated Ballot Title of Proposition 13

symbolic import has grown to be much larger than its original fiscal purpose of reducing property taxes. For many observers, the passage of Prop.
13 in 1978 not only ignited a tax revolt in this country; it also ushered in a
rising tide of conservative populist rhetoric which inundated the national
conscience. "The collective impulse of Jarvis-Gann was populist," according to David Sears and Jack Citrin, two astute students of Proposition 13,
"in that it was hostile to established institutions and complex legislative
answers to rising taxes."[5] As for the authors of the measure, even scholarly
critics of the measure, such as James Pfiffner, have called Jarvis and Gann
"a pair of elderly populists."[6] The conventional wisdom that Prop. 13 was
the populist uprising that inspired a conservative crusade for lower taxes
and smaller government across the country endures today, twenty years
after the vote.

## The Conventional Wisdom

For their part, journalists have celebrated both the populist and conservative aspects of the tax limitation movement during the late 1970s in California. In their numerous essays and books, journalists generally have
lauded Prop. 13 as a grassroots, middle-class, popular revolt led by ordinary, small property-owning Californians. The monumental success of

Jarvis-Gann, many of these authors maintain, helped to pave the way for a seasoned proponent of tax cuts and former two-term governor of California to capture the White House in 1980. Elevating Prop. 13 to near mythic stature, these journalistic accounts have advanced the conventional wisdom that continues to envelop the tax cutting measure.

Liberal journalist Robert Kuttner offered one of the first extended investigations into the causes and consequences of the tax revolt in California. As the title of his notable book proclaimed, Kuttner viewed Proposition 13 as a *Revolt of the Haves*. The tax limitation movement in California was, according to Kuttner, "that rarest of political events, an authentic mass protest brought on by economic grievances."[7] According to Kuttner, Jarvis-Gann was inspired and championed by a populist cadre of middle-class taxpayers from across the state who collectively "adopted a what-the-hell attitude."[8] Although "Jarvis's legions were well fed, well off, mostly middle-class rebels," the California tax revolt, according to Kuttner, "recalled the mass movements of the Depression years."[9] Even renters loved Jarvis, as he had "assumed the populist mantle, while the state's liberal establishment came to personify the hated status quo."[10] Fed up with regressive property taxes and rising inflation, Californians of all walks of life attacked the problem head-on. While personally finding "the spectacle" of Howard Jarvis and Paul Gann "rallying the masses" somewhat "distressing," Kuttner nevertheless regarded Prop. 13 as a modern-day populist movement.[11]

Following Kuttner, a panoply of other distinguished journalists added to the conventional wisdom surrounding Prop. 13. With little hesitation, liberal and conservative journalists alike routinely anointed Proposition 13 as a cornerstone in the conservative movement. Taking a page out of Howard Jarvis's own handbook of pithy quotes, erstwhile political scientist turned *Wall Street Journal* journalist, James Ring Adams, remarked in his book, *Secrets of the Tax Revolt*, "The vote for Proposition 13 was to the Tax Revolt what Bastille Day was to the French Revolution."[12] Largely concurring with Kuttner on the events precipitating Proposition 13, Adams observed that the successful California uprising sparked a flame that quickly spread to other states. According to Adams, "excited taxpayers had risen in revolt against their established elites."[13] Jarvis-Gann would serve as a model for subsequent middle-class uprisings in other states, as the revolt was universal and not circumscribed by the economic factors found in California. Couching his argument in supply-side theory, Adams claimed that the supporters of Prop. 13 "cut across every special constituency in the state except for government workers," as "the excitement of Proposition 13 did not result simply from a mercenary calculation of costs and benefits."[14] For Adams, "The public had an innate sense that the tax burden had damaged the economy."[15] With the amendment, the people had spoken: "Voters discovered that they were right and their leaders were wrong."[16]

In their five-year retrospective of the California tax revolt, *Los Angeles Times* reporters Terry Schwadron and Paul Richter assert that Prop. 13 was "born of emotion and frustration."[17] Tracing the origins of the "tax revolt" to when "Ronald Reagan first announced his candidacy for governor of California," the journalists argue that the measure "transformed state and local government."[18] While the measure did not work exactly as its proponents had suggested, as Schwadron and Richter admit, neither "has it brought the dire consequences forecast by its opponents, who included most of the state's political establishment."[19] Nevertheless, they argue Proposition 13 "was a movement that would quickly influence other states and other populist efforts to cap tax spending."[20]

Others have written about the broader political ramifications of the tax cutting measure. According to a veteran journalist from the *Washington Post*, Thomas Edsall, Prop. 13 was a pivotal event which was readily capitalized on by the Republican party. In his important book, *Chain Reaction*, Edsall writes how the measure "split the electorate along lines that reinforced and widened the divisions that had already begun to appear over race."[21] Edsall argues provocatively:

> The tax revolt was a major turning point in American politics. It provided new muscle and new logic to the formation of a conservative coalition opposed to the liberal welfare state. The division of the electorate along lines of taxpayers versus tax recipients dovetailed with racial divisions. . . . The tax revolt provided conservativism with a powerful internal coherence, shaping an anti-government ethic, and firmly establishing new grounds for the disaffection of white working- and middle-class voters from their traditional Democratic roots.[22]

In short, Edsall argues that the tax revolt in California helped to drive a wedge between the Democratic party and its traditional base of working- and middle-class supporters.

Somewhat more subdued in his analysis, conservative political analyst Kevin Phillips has observed that Prop. 13 played more of a cameo role in the conservative revolution. In his book, *The Politics of Rich and Poor*, Phillips writes, the "abstract theories" of supply-side economics advanced in the 1970s were "fanned by populist successes during the late 1970s."[23]

According to Phillips, "California's Howard Jarvis had started a small national prairie fire in 1978 with his Proposition 13 'tax revolt.'"[24] The tax slashing measure, Phillips argues, unquestionably advanced the conservative political agenda in America.

A panoply of other journalists have offered a variety of interpretations of the success of Prop. 13. Liberal journalist Anthony Lewis, a columnist for the *New York Times*, wrote, "The citizenry thumbed its nose at government because of burdensome taxes, and Howard Jarvis and his Proposition 13 epistle were prophetic."[25] Tom Wicker, also a columnist for the *New York Times*, commented that Prop. 13 symbolized a "new revolution" in American politics, representing "a massive rejection of liberal government as it had developed in the post-New Deal era."[26] Writing in the *Saturday Review*, Carl Tucker charged that Jarvis-Gann was a vote for "control over government's purse strings."[27] Neo-conservative Irving Kristol opined that the property tax cut exemplified the victory of "economic growth in a free society" over "the allocation of income and wealth by government in a stagnant economy."[28] Concurring, Charles Crawford alleged that, "What happened is not so much a tax revolt as an anti-government big spending revolt."[29] Journalist Joseph Kraft, writing in the *Los Angeles Times*, on the other hand, equated the populist underpinnings of Prop. 13 with an expression of "middle class hedonism."[30]

These journalistic accounts have perpetuated the conventional wisdom that the California "tax revolt" was a conservative populist uprising which mobilized millions of Californians. Over the years, Prop. 13 has come to symbolize much more than a simple ballot question reducing property taxes. As William Baroody, publisher of *Public Opinion* noted:

> A referendum by its very nature is like a public opinion poll: the public is asked to say—yes or no, up or down—whether it supports a single idea. . . .
> Since the voters were answering only a single question, however, their response lends itself to many different interpretations.[31]

In the case of Prop. 13, though, there *is* a general consensus among journalists concerning the larger meaning of the measure. The conventional wisdom suggests that Prop. 13 was a populist uprising spawned by the people. The underlying assumption of most journalistic accounts is that the property tax limitation measure was propelled by middle-class property owners, and that Jarvis and Gann were genuine populists. Upon closer scrutiny, though, the specific underlying causes of this "populist revolt" are much less clear. While in a manner far less sensationalist than journalists, scholars too have explored the different causal aspects of the tax revolt.

## The Causes of Proposition 13: Scholarly Accounts

Academic research probing the causes of Proposition 13 has tended to reinforce the conventional wisdom advanced by journalists—that the passage of Proposition 13 was a sweeping populist uprising. Scholars have arrived at this conclusion because they have concentrated exclusively on two causal factors of Prop. 13. First, scholars have focused on the palpable public mood in California. Millions of Californians decried their rising property taxes and their idle state and local governments. Second, scholars have identified the presence of community-based, grassroots organizations which presumably sustained the initiative campaign. Scholars, though, have generally neglected the actual process of the campaign for Prop. 13, including the crucial role played by Howard Jarvis, the chief architect of the measure, and his support organizations.

## The Public Mood

Analyzing data collected from public opinion polls prior to the June 6, 1978 election, several scholars have shown that citizens were concerned with two issues: 1) rising property taxes and 2) frustration with the inadequate response by government officials in dealing with escalating property taxes. This volatile public mood among Californians, these scholars maintain, precipitated the passage of Prop. 13.

### Rising Property Taxes

The first aspect of the public mood which purportedly triggered the widespread support for Prop. 13 was that a majority of Californians believed that their property taxes were becoming prohibitively high.[32] The dramatic increase in tax assessments as well as the collective clamor for lower property taxes by California's property owners are well documented. Scholars have shown that the rational, economic self-interest of property owners led many to strongly support the tax limitation measure. Voters calculated their anticipated tax savings with the passage of Prop. 13 and acted accordingly.

The predicament of excessively high property taxes was not a new occurrence for most Californians. The groundswell of support for Proposition 13 was a long time in the making. Beginning in the mid-1960s, homeowners were becoming increasingly disgruntled, if not outraged, with their escalating property taxes.[33] In 1966, the state legislature tried to reform an admittedly inequitable property tax system by passing a law requiring all property to be reassessed systematically so as to conform to current market levels. The bill, AB 80, charged county tax assessors with setting property values uniformly at twenty-five percent of the market value by the 1971-72 fiscal year.[34] In the 1970s, though, a listless economy combined with rampant inflation eroded people's real incomes, simultaneously causing property values to rise. Because local governments did not reduce their property tax rates to offset the increase in homeowner assessments, property taxes too escalated at dizzying rates.[35] According to Jack Citrin and Frank Levy, "Inflation fed the public resentment that culminated in the passage of Proposition 13."[36]

Comparatively, property taxes and other taxes in California were indeed higher than in other states. Just prior to the passage of Prop. 13 in 1978, average "property taxes in California were fifty-one percent above the national average."[37] Furthermore, during the 1970s the overall tax burden falling on Californians was also well above the national average.[38] In fiscal year 1975-76, for example, California state and local governments took in close to $21 billion in taxes, with a per capita tax rate of $965. That year, property taxes alone accounted for approximately forty-one percent of the total tax revenue for state and local governments, which was five percent higher than the average for the rest of the states.[39] With local governments required to reassess property every three years, economist William Oakland noted soon after the election that homeowners were facing "property tax bills that were doubling or tripling without a corresponding increase in their income flow."[40]

Echoing Kuttner's analysis that Jarvis and Gann's ballot initiative was the beginning of the revolt of the haves, scholars have probed extensively the socioeconomic base of support for Jarvis-Gann using survey data. While Prop. 13 is generally viewed as a broad-based tax revolt among the masses who were bent on reining in excessive property taxes, some groups of people were more animated about their rising property taxes than others. In particular, "homeowners at all levels of income were more likely than renters to see themselves as benefitting from the property tax cut promised by Proposition 13."[41] Also not surprisingly, the "support for Proposition 13 increased with the size of one's anticipated tax reduction."[42]

Using survey data from 1978, David Sears and Jack Citrin found even more generally, "the more convinced the voter was that he was paying too much in taxes, the more likely he was to support" Jarvis-Gann.[43] In particular, residents living in Southern California who were "[m]iddle-aged, white, fully employed, affluent male homeowners were the greatest enthusiasts for it."[44] However, the survey data also indicated that not everyone supported Prop. 13, even though it might have been the rational, self-interested course of action. Ironically, those who were the "most economically vulnerable"—"elderly homeowners" and "those on low incomes feeling most squeezed by inflation"—demonstrated little support for the tax revolt.[45] Overall, though, Sears and Citrin found the forthright "preference for reduced taxes, especially among the affluent," was the major economic driving force behind the success of Proposition 13.[46]

Although for different reasons, the rational expectations of voters supports William Fischel's interesting analysis of the underlying base of support for Jarvis-Gann. Fischel argues that the popular support for Prop. 13 stemmed from the loss of local control over schooling after the California Supreme Court's *Serrano v. Priest* decision in 1972. In that decision, the Court ruled that the use of local property taxes to finance public schools violated the equal protection of children guaranteed by the state constitution. As a result of the decision, the funding of public education was detached from revenue generated by local property taxes. Fischel reasons that residents, following the *Serrano* ruling, desired to have their property taxes cut since the financing of their children's public education was no longer directly tied to their rate of taxation.[47] While this may have been an impetus for the support of Prop 13, public opinion polls failed to capture this line of logic.

Questions, though, continue to linger with respect to the supposed rational, self-interested motivation of those who supported the tax cutting initiative. In an interesting, but rarely cited study drawing on data from California's fifty-eight counties, Stanford political scientist Richard Brody found "no consistent relationship to a county's level of support for" Prop. 13, except for the percentage of owner-occupied homes in the county.[48] While Jarvis-Gann failed to muster a majority of votes in only three of the fifty-eight counties, Brody found no clear relationship between a county's support for the measure and its population, regional location, public school population, or residents' ability to pay taxes. In fact, Brody discovered some highly counterintuitive results. Most notably, Brody found "growth of per-capita county taxes between 1970 and 1977" was "*negatively* related to support for Proposition 13," as well as "counties with higher tax rates tended to be less enthusiastic about 13 than those with lower rates."[49]  With respect to county-level support of Prop. 13, Brody's unequivocal conclusion was, "it is not clear what voters were voting for or against when they supported it."[50]

*Unresponsive Government*

The second aspect of the public mood which bolstered the support of Proposition 13 was that a majority of Californians were infuriated by the slow response of their state and local governments in dealing with the property tax crisis. According to several scholars, Prop. 13 sounded the alarm of the average California homeowner's anger toward not only excessive property taxes, but also unresponsive government. Following the election, political pollster Mervin Field wrote, "There were clear signs that the public wanted to see large-scale cutbacks in government services, some well-paid bureaucrats out of jobs, and visible demonstrations that waste was being eliminated from government spending."[51] Fed up with public officials who were perceived to be inattentive and inefficient, the vote for Prop. 13 was a way for citizens to send a direct message to the state legislature and to Governor Jerry Brown. "Proposition 13 was not the first successful action in the grassroots uprising," Jack Citrin writes, "but as the most dramatic and best publicized it came to symbolize the public's disgruntlement and its desire for cheaper and humbler government."[52]

This public mood among Californians did not appear overnight. During the 1970s, a growing number of Californians came to view their state and local governments as increasingly wasteful and unresponsive. With property taxes on the rise, local governments were able to steadily boost their coffers. Concurrently, state revenues were also soaring. In 1978, the state was sitting atop an estimated budget surplus of $5.7 billion. By some accounts, the surplus would have eclipsed $10 billion if Prop. 13 had not passed.[53] Rather than providing some property tax relief, though, state officials in Sacramento were squirreling away the surplus funds for a rainy day. But in the interim, many taxpayers felt they were getting soaked.

For many Californians, the unproductive 1977 legislative session proved to be the last straw. Several property tax bills were introduced into the legislature during the year, but that fall, "the legislature adjourned in well publicized disarray, unable to agree on any new property tax relief."[54] As Eric Smith and Jack Citrin have noted, Jarvis-Gann gained tremendous support because of "the inability of state government to provide meaningful tax relief despite the existence of a huge surplus in its treasury."[55] After years of listening to the prattle coming out of Sacramento, "the people" decided to lower their property taxes themselves.

Polling data from 1978 clearly displayed that a majority of citizens thought their state and local governments were inefficient as well as unresponsive to the escalating property tax problem. In the months preceding the June election, one of the foremost independent political pollsters and public opinion analysts in California, Mervin Field, tracked public opinion pertaining to the role of government and the level of property taxes. Field found that in May 1978, a substantial majority of the public was sympathetic to three of the principal arguments put forth by the proponents of Prop. 13. Specifically, over seventy percent of the public agreed:

- Property taxes are so high many homeowners can't afford to live in their own homes.
- Local governments can get by on a lot less money.
- Proposition 13 is the only way to send a strong message to the government that people are fed up with high taxes and too much government spending.[56]

In contrast, only one of the arguments advanced by the opponents of Jarvis-Gann, according to Field's polling, resonated strongly with the public. Over sixty percent of those polled agreed with the statement, "property taxes cut by Proposition 13 would have to be replaced by other taxes."[57]

The extent to which Californians were striking out against their public institutions when they voted for the measure remains somewhat ambiguous. The vote for Prop. 13, as shown by the journalistic accounts, was broadly interpreted. As William Baroody perceptively warned shortly after the election:

> It is especially easy for commentators with an ideological bias to come to radically different conclusions: those on the left can persuasively argue that Californians were only seeking a cut-back in government waste, while those on the right can say with equal force that the public wants to roll back parts of the Great Society.[58]

While public opinion polls measured sizable animosity towards "government costs, waste and inefficiency," Californians did not express a particularly strong desire to downsize government or public services.[59] In fact, one survey revealed voters actually favoring an increase in expenditures on governmental services.[60]

A close examination of Field's survey research cautions against a broad interpretation of the anti-government sentiment of Californians in their support of Prop. 13. Public opinion polls carried out just prior to the June election indicated that the vote for Prop. 13 was not cast against government in general. According to Field, "While there were numerous expressions of 'let's get rid of government' at Proposition 13 rallies, the majority of voters do not appear to have been indicating such a revolutionary desire."[61] Rather than calling for the abolition or even the downsizing of government, Californians more narrowly wanted their state and local government officials to be more responsive to their concerns over the mounting taxes on their property.

## Grassroots Community Organizations

The second major causal explanation for the passage of Proposition 13 advanced by scholars underscores the initiative's grassroots underpinnings. Two scholars in particular have focused on the myriad of local homeowners associations and taxpayers organizations existing in California prior to 1978. Approaching the topic with different research methodologies, Jack Citrin and Clarence Lo have offered assessments of the role activists and their organizations played in the mobilization of popular support for the property tax slashing initiative. While acknowledging the catalytic importance of higher tax assessments and the growing bitterness towards government among many Californians, Lo and Citrin both argue that Jarvis-Gann ultimately passed due to the surge of political activism by middle- and upper-class citizens. They contend that the leaders of Prop. 13 surfed on the organizational crest provided by the numerous preexisting, decentralized, community-based, tax limitation organizations and homeowners associations.[62]

In his many writings on the subject, Citrin, a University of California-Berkeley political scientist, thoroughly credits the importance of rising property taxes and the prevalent perception of unresponsive governments for the passage of Jarvis-Gann. A theme found in his writings that is equally strong, though, is that Proposition 13 was a genuine middle-class, populist uprising. Extrapolating from his own as well as Mervin Field's public opinion survey data, Citrin argues that the "tax revolt" was a spontaneous, decentralized, "popular movement."[63] Using a military analogy, Citrin writes:

> Impatient with the ordinary processes of legislation, angry citizens took matters into their own hands to propose far-reaching and enduring restrictions on the authority of elected officials to tax and spend. Like bands of guerrilla army in the process of formation, state and local units of tax rebels sprung up independently and operated with relatively little coordination.[64]

With little evidence other than public opinion polls to support his claim, Citrin nonetheless asserts that the tax revolt had not "developed a central command structure," as the "relationships among the various organizations dedicated to reducing the size of government tended to be informal and spasmodic."[65]

Arguing that the leaders of the tax rebels consisted of "political outsiders," Citrin contends that they "recruited mainly from groups on the fringe of the dominant institutions in American society."[66] The organizational "core" of the "grass-roots" movement, according to Citrin, was Jarvis's United Organization [sic] of Taxpayers, which "grafted their campaign onto local taxpayer and homeowner associations."[67] Utilizing the ballot initiative, the tax rebels were able to wage a successful campaign against "the virtually united opposition of the state's political elite."[68] According to Citrin, by circumventing the unresponsive political system in its dual assault on property taxes and government programs, Prop. 13 "represent[ed] a successful translation of mass opinion into public policy."[69]

In contrast to Citrin's rather thin empirical research on the social and organizational dimensions underlying Prop. 13, Lo, a sociologist, bases his research on over a hundred interviews he conducted with community activists who participated in the making of the "tax revolt." In his book, *Small Property Versus Big Government*, Lo presents extensive documentation to support his inquiry into the social origins of Prop. 13. He argues that the tax revolt "was a face-to-face social process," in which the "activists in the tax protest movement were the stewards of the great American Middle Class."[70] "The tax revolt was made by a multitude that left no annals," Lo maintains, as it "was a revolt of communities against big government and the bureaucratic interest groups associated with it."[71]

Like Citrin, Lo advances that the success of Jarvis-Gann can be traced to the largely undocumented and unheralded work carried out by thousands of people throughout California who had assembled in hundreds of community associations. Lo hails the tax revolt as a "popular movement" which arose from the labors of these unsung heroes. "Countless small meetings and discussions among neighbors," Lo writes, "formed the ideas that shaped the political direction of the tax revolt."[72] The drive for petition signatures to place the measure on the ballot, for example, was "sustained by homeowners groups and other community organizations."[73] Suburbanites forged the way.

Early on, according to Lo, the tax limitation movement in California "had no direction."[74] During the late 1960s and early 1970s, tax protests "flared up," but they lacked "multistrata alliances."[75] As the tax limitation movement gained headway, though, control of the ballot initiative drifted up the socioeconomic ladder. The tax revolt, according to Lo, became more and more dominated by "suburban businesses and professionals who used their skills, resources, and influence in their communities to organize a campaign directed against the higher levels of government and other corporatist institutions."[76] By election day, "homeowners in upper-middle-class locales and the leading small businesses in those communities worked together and developed common interests."[77] "Proposition 13 succeeded," according to Lo, "because a multistrata alliance had emerged between homeowners and local landed elites."[78] Jarvis did not lead, but had behind him "a grassroots movement."[79]

Celebrating these small property owners who supposedly made Proposition 13 a reality, Lo documents the emerging sense of political efficacy felt by many ordinary homeowners. These predominantly middle- and upper-class homeowners who allied themselves with small community business people "came together around common beliefs about the unresponsive power of government."[80] "The participants in tax protests," Lo writes, "hoped to recapture their power as citizens."[81] The June 6 initiative allowed property owners not only to lash out against unresponsive government elites who were excessively assessing their properties, but actually to set their own property tax levels. "Tax policy was not being made by the politicians," Lo argues, "but by a social movement."[82] The people, in defiance of the special interests and government officials who were largely opposed to Jarvis-Gann, would not be thwarted.

Throughout the campaign for Prop. 13, the "populist" struggle for property tax reform was led by volunteers. "The tax revolt movement that succeeded in putting Proposition 13 on the ballot," Lo claims, "was not professionally managed."[83] Rather, he contends:

> From the early protests in the 1950s to the gathering of a million and a half signatures that placed Proposition 13 on the ballot, none of the leaders of the movement drew a salary. The movement was a shifting coalition of small

groups of homeowners and taxpayers. The groups maintained only a tenuous connection to an umbrella group, the United Organizations of Taxpayers, and directed their own community activities to reduce property taxes.[84]

Lo claims that it was not until after the passage of Jarvis-Gann that "paid political consultants and advertising agencies" dominated the movement.[85] For Lo, the small, decentralized groups of ordinary citizens—not "Howard Jarvis, the media-appointed hero of Proposition 13," and his United Organizations of Taxpayers—were the ones who led the drive for Prop. 13.[86]

## Tapping the Public Mood: Howard Jarvis, Populist Entrepreneur

Digging beneath the surface of the conventional wisdom unearths how Prop. 13 was not a spontaneous, mass uprising. There was a potent public mood, but as scholars have revealed, it was not monolithic, as journalists have generally assumed. Nor was Prop. 13 the natural outgrowth of the community-based citizens groups, as Lo, Citrin, and scores of journalists have claimed. While the numerous unheralded homeowner and tax limitation associations did indeed give the tax limitation cause a sense of depth, they were not central to either the organizational or financial effort that placed Prop. 13 on the ballot or insured its success at the polls. Prop. 13 was a well-orchestrated, top-down ballot initiative campaign. Jarvis-Gann did not constitute a populist movement. Rather, Howard Jarvis, the engineer of Prop. 13, successfully detected the widespread but diffuse public mood and crafted a ballot initiative which enabled citizens to vent their collective anger.

Scholars and journalists who have championed the populist underpinnings of Prop. 13 have tended to neglect in their analyses the crucial role played by Jarvis and his two support organizations—the United Organizations of Taxpayers (UOT) and the Los Angeles Apartment Owners Association (LAAOA). Jarvis, through these two organizations, was able to tap into the very real and negative public mood over rising property taxes and unresponsive government. As populist entrepreneur, Jarvis successfully captured the palpable public mood and offered his pet initiative—which he had been peddling for over a dozen years—as the solution to the property tax problem. As a result, the process of the actual campaign for Jarvis-Gann was far less populist, grassroots, and community-based than is assumed. Proposition 13 was not, as Jarvis was fond of saying, "a people's movement."[87] Ordinary people were only nominally involved in the campaign for Prop. 13. Rather, vested commercial property interests—particularly apartment owners and realtors—were the key to the organizational and financial success of Jarvis's initiative.

The conventional wisdom regarding the extremely negative public mood in California prior to the June 6, 1978 election is well-founded. The scientific polling done before the election recorded the general disgust of citizens for rising property taxes and unresponsive government. The *Serrano* decision and the loss of local control over public education very well might have added fuel for middle- and upper-class support for Jarvis-Gann. In addition, the growing number of local tax limitation and homeowners associations, even though they were not central to the organizational or financial success of Proposition 13, surely indicated the displeasure of many middle and upper middle-class homeowners with the property tax situation. The public mood was ready, and Howard Jarvis, playing the role of populist entrepreneur, was ready to prime it.

## The Rise of Howard Jarvis

Jarvis was no political neophyte in 1978. Earning close to a million dollars from a number of successful industrial ventures he developed in southern California, Jarvis retired from the world of business in 1962.[88] Fond of saying how he "made a whole shitpot full of money during the Depression and I've always worked my ass off,"[89] Jarvis and his wife Estelle nevertheless lived in a modest house in the Fairfax area of Los Angeles, near Beverly Hills. Just as he was retiring, Jarvis entered the world of politics. Although as a younger man he had dabbled in Republican party politics, in 1962 he made a primary bid for the Republican nomination for U.S. Senate. Jarvis wound up losing the race by 100,000 votes. He would later lose his two other bids for public office. In 1970, Jarvis lost a statewide race for State Board of Equalization (Jarvis claims friends of then Governor Ronald Reagan urged him to run), and in 1977, he came up short in the primary for Mayor of Los Angeles.[90] Jarvis claims he ran for public office his final two times purely in order to further his tax limitation agenda.[91]

Jarvis, of course, would not leave his mark in California as an elected official, but as one of their most vociferous critics. Although losing the primary election in 1962, Jarvis gained valuable name recognition in conservative political circles. Because of his reputation in the area as a "[l]ife-long activist for lowering taxes," some of his Los Angeles neighbors recruited him that year to help establish and then become State Chairman of a new citizens group, the United Organizations of Taxpayers.[92] According to Jarvis, his neighbors "felt they were paying too much. They asked me to help them write the by-laws for this organization . . . . So the more I got into the tax situation, the more I liked it. I felt somebody had to do this."[93] The group met once a month at the home of Leona Magidson, who would later become the treasurer of the organization during the Prop. 13 campaign. In 1965, Jarvis and the members decided to incorporate the group. Local tax groups were encouraged to affiliate themselves with the UOT. Tax limitation became an obsession for Jarvis. "I'm doing it," Jarvis professed patriotically, "because I've had a very successful and happy life in this country and a great many have not. I'm doing it because nobody else had either the brains or the guts or the money to do it . . . . I'm determined to do this before I kick off and go across."[94]

Jarvis and the United Organizations of Taxpayers (which served as a loose umbrella group and clearinghouse for other taxpayers associations in southern California) launched its first property tax limitation initiative campaign in 1968. The group, though, failed to collect enough signatures to place the measure on the ballot that year. In 1971, the group launched its second unsuccessful campaign to collect signatures to place their initiative on the ballot. During those early years, several members of the UOT worked on other campaigns aimed at lowering taxes at both the state and local levels. They also contested several Los Angeles ballot measures, and worked on (after their own measures had failed to qualify) unsuccessful tax limitation initiatives written by Los Angeles County tax assessor Philip Watson in 1968 and 1972. In 1973, Jarvis and others in the organization supported Governor Ronald Reagan's unsuccessful revenue limitation referendum, Proposition 1.[95] During this period, Jarvis enhanced his reputation as a tax rebel. In 1970, the Los Angeles Times noted his prominence: "Jarvis in the past five years has become the chief spokesman for a large group of disgruntled California property owners who are convinced, simply, that they pay too much of the cost of government."[96] While their own ballot initiatives were frustrated, Jarvis and his band of loyal followers were not dissuaded. "All we had was guts," Jarvis claimed. "And when we started out we knew we were going to stay there till we won. We didn't care how long or how hard or how rough it was, we were going to stay there until we won."[97]

After a four year hiatus from being directly involved in a statewide tax limitation ballot initiative, Jarvis and the UOT launched its third initiative

*Figure 4.2*   Howard Jarvis in action. (A *Los Angeles Times* Photo)

campaign in 1976. Between October 1976 and March 1977, Jarvis and his supporters gathered over 500,000 signatures, but came up short of the 557,000 valid signatures required to place the measure on the June 6, 1977 ballot.[98] During the 1976-77 signature collection campaign, the UOT was not a financially viable organization.[99] Based on the monetary contributions it received between January 1976 and March 1977, the group only had slightly more than 4,000 members paying the $5 membership fee.[100] The group received a total of only $22,053 in membership fees over a fourteen month period, but received additional financial support from the Los Angeles Board of Realtors Political Action Committee, which contributed $350 to the UOT, and the Los Angeles Apartment Owners Association, which "independently" spent $5,600 on advertisements promoting the initiative.[101] Jarvis claims in his autobiography:

> I never got a nickel . . . nor did any other officer or director. Neither did anyone else who was associated with us . . . . Not only did I never receive a nickel for my work, I spent about $100,000 out of my own pocket over the fifteen

years. I wore out two cars driving around the state and spent thousands of dollars on motels and meals while I was traveling around and leading the drive to lower taxes. And I bought typewriters, a press to print news releases on, stamps—you name it.[102]

But during the unsuccessful 1976–77 campaign, the UOT paid at least one person $90 to stuff envelopes, paid a public relations consultant $4,415 to "place [an] ad" in the *Los Angeles Times*, and reimbursed Jarvis $450 for some of his travels.[103]

Although they failed to place their previous three property tax limitation initiatives on the ballot, Jarvis and the core members of the UOT remained undaunted. In June 1977, following the UOT's third failure to collect enough signatures to qualify for the ballot, Jarvis and his followers "had a meeting and cried in our beer and were so damn disgusted, decided we wouldn't start on a new one [initiative campaign] until the next day. The next day we started on Proposition 13."[104] An aide of Jarvis's called Paul Gann, a former car and real estate salesman residing in Carmichael, a suburb of Sacramento, to see if he and his organization, the People's Advocate, wanted to join forces. The next day Gann flew to Los Angeles to meet with Jarvis and talk strategy.[105] Gann, who had incorporated his organization in 1974, had not been involved in property taxes until 1976.[106] In 1976 and 1977, Gann and his supporters in northern California failed to collect enough signatures to place their property tax limitation measures on the ballot. But the People's Advocate was over 10,000 members strong and had a solid organizational base in northern California.[107] With both Gann and Jarvis failing to collect enough valid signatures on their own, the two tax crusaders, who had differences of opinion with respect to tax limitation and very different personal styles, reluctantly joined forces.

After settling on the language of Jarvis's 389-word initiative that was to become Prop. 13, Jarvis and Gann rarely coordinated their efforts. On July 6, 1977, the two organizations began to circulate petitions independently of one another in order to meet the December 2, 1977 deadline for the submission of petitioned signatures. Needing valid signatures from 499,846 registered voters (which was eight percent of the previous vote for Governor), Jarvis hoped that Gann and his organization would be able to collect 150,000 signatures from the fifty northern counties in California, while Jarvis and his group would collect 500,000 from the eight southern counties.[108] Jarvis claims to have contributed $1,000 a week to Gann and his organization to help him in his effort to collect signatures; the UOT's financial records, though, reveal that it contributed a total of only $5,000 to Gann's People's Advocate between June and December 1977.[109] While some money did change hands, for the most part it was true that Jarvis and Gann did not communicate with each another during their separate drives to collect signatures. According to the soft-spoken Gann, "We just each went our own way," and did not "divide up the chores."[110]

In the northern part of California and in the Central Valley, Gann and the People's Advocate successfully gathered over 150,000 valid signatures. They relied on "people writing in, volunteering, calling, phoning day and night. Volunteering to circulate petitions, do anything they can do."[111] But the organization also welcomed the assistance of the business community to gather signatures. According to Gann:

> I had chambers of commerce all over the State of California helping me, I had real estate people in every section of the State of California. In fact, they make the difference, believe me—small business and real estate. Those people . . . who were out there selling that property, were the people that had taken that petition [around]. And they obtained signatures and signatures and signatures.[112]

Perhaps even more important than the chambers of commerce was the role various apartment owners' associations played in getting their tenants to sign the petitions. As the coordinator of Gann's petition drive in the Central Valley explained, "What really put across Proposition 13 was the apartment owners' association . . . . [T]hey gave money and they had meetings and they got people to sign petitions and really, I think that's what put it across."[113]

In southern California, Jarvis and his United Organizations of Taxpayers ran the show. Jarvis was a frequent guest on talk radio and wrote a newspaper column entitled "The People Must Know" which he sent out unsolicited to 140 publications.[114] On the radio and in his column, he urged people to sign and circulate the petitions and return them to headquarters by the filing date, December 2, 1977. Jarvis gave hundreds of speeches, held press conferences, and wrote fund-raising letters for the UOT.[115] During the campaign, Jarvis said:

> I didn't comprehend this during the 15 years we worked on 13. I didn't comprehend the size it was going to be. I was running around the track like a horse with blinders on. If I had known it was going to take 15 years, if I had known it was going to take $100,000 bucks out of my pocket, then I might have been too chicken to have gone on.[116]

He recruited volunteers—"most of them women"—to circulate the petitions. "I was able to cross the state and get twenty women in San Jose and twenty-three in Oakland and eighteen in Pasadena and thirty in Palm Springs and eleven in Santa Monica and twelve in Culver City to go out and collect signatures every day."[117] Jarvis served as "the political strategist, the media man, the copywriter and the janitor. I was the driver of the tractor."[118] Refusing to pay people to collect signatures, Jarvis even enlisted his wife Estelle to organize a "crew of women to gather signatures. She would pick them up in her car every day, make their lunch, and take them to a supermarket where they stood outside and got people to sign our petitions."[119]

Over the course of the campaign, Jarvis did not think much of his co-author, Gann, or his organization, the People's Advocate. Jarvis claims he and Gann "never had an argument or a bad word during the 13 campaign, but I became aware of his capacities."[120] Calling Gann a "Johnny-come-lately who arrived on the scene after I and the other members of the United Organizations of Taxpayers had done all the heavy work," Jarvis claimed that "We would have won with or without Paul Gann."[121] In fact, it turned out that the UOT did collect more than enough signatures on its own to place the measure on the ballot. An aide to Jarvis commented on election night, "We thought we needed the 150,000 votes [Gann's] group could deliver in petition signatures. We alone got a million names and we didn't need him at all."[122] When the signatures were finally tallied by the Office of the Secretary of State in late December, 1977, the two organizations had collected 1,263,698 valid signatures, the most ever for a California ballot initiative.

## The Campaign for Proposition 13

In early 1978, soon after Jarvis and Gann qualified their tax limitation initiative for the primary ballot, the state legislature began to take notice of the rising support for property tax reform. During the previous session, the highly partisan state legislature missed several opportunities to push through property tax reform. Senator Peter Behr, a liberal Republican from Marin County, north of San Francisco, became the unlikely legislative redeemer. The author of the "dark-horse property-tax bill that languished in committee while lawmakers fought over other relief plans," Behr's property tax relief bill had died in committee the previous year.[123] But in January, Behr's bill found support among legislators who wanted a measure that could counter Jarvis's property-tax initiative. Behr's bill proposed to raise homeowner property tax exemptions, thereby reducing property-tax bills by half. It also included a revenue limit on cities and counties and a 5 percent transfer tax on the sale of owner-occupied homes.[124] Governor Brown spoke in favor of Behr's bill, calling it "the only glimmer of hope left" for property tax relief in 1978.[125]

Despite the urgency, the bill did not move through the legislature smoothly. The California Association of Realtors comprised of 116,000 members mounted a strong campaign against Behr's bill. The realtors argued that the tax on home-sales profits would severely hurt their sales. Behr's bill "sparked the biggest 'red alert' in the group's history," according to lobbyist Dugald Gilleis, prompting the association to send letters to its 25,000 real estate brokers "asking them to get in touch with their legislator and urge opposition."[126] After intense deliberation and several amendments, both the Senate and the Assembly narrowly passed Behr's bill by slim two-thirds majorities. In early March, Governor Brown quickly signed the bill, which was then referred to the citizens for their approval. Behr's bill, which was listed on the June 6 ballot as Proposition 8, was praised by the legislature and Governor Brown as a moderate alternative to Jarvis's more extreme measure.

As the campaign for Prop. 13 heated up in the spring of 1978, with Jarvis and Behr sparring with each other at public forums, the media began to cast Prop. 13 as a grassroots, populist endeavor, and Behr's bill as the establishment's long-overdue response. While often critical of the actual substance of Jarvis's tax limitation measure (the property tax cut would devastate schools and public services), the media tended to paint a positive picture of the overall initiative process that Jarvis was heading. Headlines in the influential *Los Angeles Times*, which had editorialized against Jarvis's measure from the start, touted Prop. 13 as "Grass Roots," a "Rebellion," and a "Revolt" spawned by the people.[127] In a study of the headlines and subheadings in the *Los Angeles Times*, sociologist Herman Turk found "by the end of April the large size and visibility of California's property taxes were cited, as were public figures claiming widespread anger at taxes and at wasteful spending by government," and in the month of May "carried the themes of high taxes, taxpayer unrest" and "the large volume of activity and support that had gotten the initiative on the ballot."[128] One week prior to the election, according to Turk, the *Times* paid tribute to the 1.2 million people who had signed the petition.[129] Instead of focusing their attention

*Figure 4.3*   Paul Conrad (*Los Angeles Times*) editorial cartoon, Jarvis—"I'm mad as hell"

on the actual process of the campaign being waged by Jarvis, the media increasingly referred to Prop. 13 as a genuine populist tax revolt.[130]

Journalists also stressed the populist rhetoric of the outspoken, irreverent author of Proposition 13 who was energizing the public mood. Jarvis, like the substance of his initiative, was criticized personally at times by the media, but generally he was championed as the great protector of homeowners. The media devoured Jarvis's colorful style. "I've made a pledge to a bunch of poor taxpayers," Jarvis often said, "and we're never going to quit."[131] Jarvis called the Behr bill "a fraud." "Instead of returning the power to the people by having it in writing in the constitution how they will be taxed," Jarvis screamed, "the Behr Bill just returns the whole thing to those clowns who have been bungling it for years. And the whole thing starts all over again."[132]  Behr admitted that he could not match Jarvis's "rhetoric," and accused his opponent of "never discussing facts."[133]  Jarvis, in response, called Behr, a "senile old man,"[134] and referred to the League of Women Voters and Common Cause, both opposing Prop. 13, as "phony left-wing fronts."[135]  Calling himself a "pain in the ass" and "a rugged bastard who's had his head kicked in a thousand times by the government,"[136] Jarvis's self-deprecating raillery diffused the media's attention away from the actual operation of the pro-Prop. 13 campaign. Featuring Jarvis in a story less than a month prior to the election, Ronald Soble, a staff writer for the *Los Angeles Times*, wrote:

> At first glance, it would seem that Jarvis has a rag-tag approach to stumping for his cause. He carries a few notes in a briefcase. He is in the habit of making last-minute connections for transportation to engagements and, indeed, does not even show up for some. And, he claims, there are times when he forgets what group he is addressing until just minutes before he speaks. Much of this is a facade. . . . For all of his homespun style, Jarvis should not be sold short. [137]

Although they provided a rich portrait of Jarvis, journalists neglected to probe very deeply the operations of Jarvis's two well-oiled machines, the UOT and the LAAOA.

## Jarvis's Organizational and Financial Base #1: The United Organizations of Taxpayers

While his populist rhetoric was crucial for tapping into the public mood against property taxes, Jarvis and his two organizations played key roles in the orchestration of the successful campaign. In 1978, Jarvis variously claimed that the United Organizations of Taxpayers had signed 120,000 to 200,000 dues-paying members (each paying the $5 membership fee), which included people who belonged to other tax limitation associations.[138]  During the signature collection phase of the campaign, the UOT had relied on volunteers from these community-based groups to collect the million-plus signatures. Jarvis claimed that the UOT had not "asked for money, but contributions [were] coming in daily. None of them [were] over $50," as "we were going to try our damndest to get people voluntarily to send in a million dollars."[139] Jarvis also declared that the reliance on volunteers continued throughout the rest of the campaign, as he touted the organization's reliance on "1 million hours—voluntary, non-paid help—extending 15 years."[140]

Contrary to the conventional wisdom (fostered by Jarvis and perpetuated by the media and scholars) that the "tax revolt movement" was comprised of volunteers and "was not professionally managed,"[141] the UOT did operate as a professional organization. Jarvis equipped it to raise an enormous amount of money for the passage of Prop. 13. Soon after the Secretary of State's office had validated the signatures and placed the measure on the ballot in January, the UOT became a well-oiled fundraising machine. Jarvis's various pronouncements frequently contradicted the committee campaign statements that the UOT filed with the state. For example, during the signature collection phase of the campaign, Jarvis claimed the UOT "spent about $28,500 and we finished with $13,000 in the bank."[142] In actuality, between June 28 and December 30, 1977, the UOT received monetary contributions of $49,584, and spent (running up a deficit) $50,442.[143] Conflicting with Jarvis's public assertions, the UOT did rely on professional assistance during their signature collection campaign. While polishing up the UOT's populist facade, Jarvis hired a Van Nuys fund-raising organization, Romagen Corporation, to publicize the signature-gathering campaign. Between June and December 1977, Jarvis's UOT paid Romagen $22,466 to get their message out to the potential voters.[144]

With less than five months to go before the election, Jarvis kicked the UOT's fund-raising efforts into high gear. On February 7, 1978, Jarvis established the "Yes on 13 Committee" as a special purpose committee to raise money in support of the initiative. Under the auspices of the UOT, with Jarvis serving as its treasurer, the Yes on 13 Committee operated out of the office of the Los Angeles Apartment Owners Association.[145] Jarvis hired an accountant, Julius Glazer (who surprisingly received no mention in Jarvis's autobiography), to run the day-to-day operations of the Yes on 13 Committee. Again, contrary to claims made by Jarvis to the press that the campaign was being run entirely by volunteers, Glazer was paid a handsome sum of $37,802 by Yes on 13 for "accounting services" rendered during the late stages of the campaign.[146] Jarvis also drafted Roland Vincent, a former stockbroker for Paine, Webber who had run Alabama Governor George Wallace's 1976 presidential bid in California, to head the media and advertisement side of the operation.[147] Vincent contracted the services of Media & Marketing Affiliates, based in Newport Beach, to carry out most of the radio and television advertisement blitz. During the three months prior to the election, Yes on 13 paid Media & Marketing Affiliates $425,000 to produce and air television and radio spots.[148]

To generate a constant stream of revenue for the Prop. 13 campaign, Jarvis relied heavily on soliciting contributions through mass mailings. Rather than running the operation in-house with volunteer labor, Jarvis turned over the fund-raising and promotional operation to four private groups: Romagen Corporation; Below, Tobe & Associates; The America Group; and Butcher-Forde Consulting. The UOT paid Romagen, which had worked for Jarvis during the signature collection campaign, $114,581 between January and June for its direct mail services.[149] The Yes on 13 Committee paid Below, Tobe & Associates, a firm providing mailing services for commercial advertisers, $184,000 to raise funds and publicize Proposition 13 during April and May.[150] Although it failed to report its expenditures, the UOT, on behalf of Yes on 13 Committee, also paid Below, Tobe & Associates $140,000 between April and June 1978 for its fund-raising mass mailings.[151] In the two weeks prior to the election, Yes on 13 paid The America Group, based out of Anaheim, $23,889 for its computerized mailing service. Finally, Jarvis hired the Newport Beach firm, Butcher-Forde Consulting, to generate numerous fund-raising letters for Prop. 13. Jarvis alleged in his autobiography that:

> Butcher and Forde didn't charge us a nickel for their services—not a nickel. I met them through the campaign of State Senator John Briggs for Governor in late 1977. John Briggs was one of the first major candidates to endorse 13. Butcher and Forde thought they could piggyback John Briggs on the campaign for 13—or vice versa. They could send out mailers for both John Briggs and Proposition 13 at no extra cost—except the price of paper.[152]

According to the financial records, though, Yes on 13 paid Butcher-Forde $29,350 late in the campaign for their radio and TV production services.[153] In addition, Butcher-Forde received hefty commissions from the television and radio stations for bringing Jarvis's business to them.[154] Scratching Senator Briggs's back, Yes on 13 also made a contribution of $7,839 to Citizens for Senator Briggs in March.[155] More significantly, though, Jarvis failed to report to the California Fair Political Practices Commission (CFPPC) that the Yes on 13 Committee indirectly paid a total of $84,479 to its consultants in expensive advertising commissions. Over the course of the campaign, Yes on 13 paid $16,896 to Media & Marketing Affiliates, $22,114 to The America Group, and $45,469 to Butcher-Forde in advertising commissions.[156] Despite Jarvis's claims that "Butcher and Forde gave us a great deal and we didn't have to pay them at all for what they did,"[157] Jarvis hired a variety of experienced consultants to help run his campaign.

Contracting with professionals to handle the mass mailing fund-raising paid off well. While there were thirty-two official groups campaigning and raising money for Prop. 13, the bulk of the money was raised by Jarvis's two groups, the Los Angeles-based Yes on 13 Committee and the UOT. The two committees collected $2,022,308, which was eighty-nine percent of the total amount raised for Prop. 13. In comparison, Gann's People's Advocate took in only $136,480 (six percent) of the total raised in support of the measure. Jarvis's Yes on 13 Committee raised $1,580,433 in contributions over the four month period prior to the election.[158] Contributions made to Yes on 13 accounted for sixty-nine percent of all contributions made to the thirty-two official groups which campaigned and raised money for Prop. 13. Between April 24 and May 22, and May 23 and June 30, the Yes on Committee received $534,912 and $744,038 in contributions respectively.[159] Contributions from close to 10,000 individuals (primarily Los Angeles residents) and businesses (primarily rental agencies and apartment owners from Los Angeles) poured in to the Yes on 13 office; checks ranged from $25 to $250, with an occasional check for $1,000. The UOT also raised a substantial amount of money in the form membership dues. During the campaign, the UOT amassed $441,875 in small contributions made by 50,000 new or renewing members.[160] But once again contrary to Jarvis's claims that the opposition was out-spending his side, the supporters of Proposition 13 raised a total of $2,279,567 and spent $2,152,874, whereas the opponents of Prop. 13, led by the Los Angeles No on 13 Committee, raised a total of $2,120,931 and spent $2,000,204.[161]

## Jarvis's Organizational and Financial Base #2: The Los Angeles Apartment Owners Association

Equally crucial in the campaign for Prop. 13 as the UOT and the Yes on 13 Committee, but playing a shadow role, was the Los Angeles Apartment Owners Association. In the late 1960s and early 1970s, Jarvis became known in the area as a perennial gadfly. He made frequent appearances at

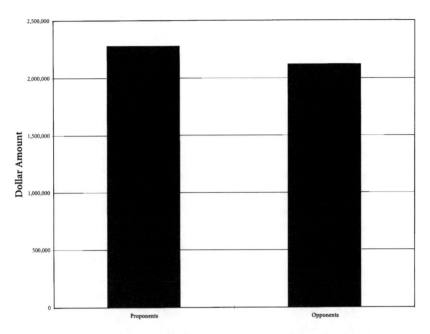

*Figure 4.4* Total Campaign Contributions, Principal Committees Supporting and Opposing Proposition 13, January 1—June 30, 1978

City Council meetings in Los Angeles and Pasadena, testifying primarily against proposed property tax increases.[162] The Apartment Owners Association took notice, and in 1972 hired him as the executive director of the organization.[163] According to Jarvis, the association, which was losing about $1,500 a month, approached him to head the organization. Jarvis reluctantly accepted. He claims not to have taken a salary until 1974; at that time, the association paid him $1,700 a month.[164] Jarvis was much more than, as James Ring Adams asserts, a "part-time lobbyist" for the organization.[165] As Executive Director, Jarvis successfully lobbied the state Legislature to defeat a rent-control bill, and persuaded the Los Angeles City Council to vote against several ordinances that would have placed tight restrictions and the increase costs of apartment owners.[166] More importantly, Jarvis rejuvenated the organization and put it on solid financial footing. When he took over the association in 1972, it had 1,100 members; by 1978, Jarvis had boosted the membership to 5,000 (out of a total of 64,000 apartment owners in Los Angeles).

As Executive Director of the LAAOA, Jarvis worked closely with the membership. Not surprisingly, throughout the campaign opponents of

Prop. 13 tried to paint him as a pawn of apartment owners. In the weeks leading up to the election, Jarvis vehemently denied the accusations:

> They say I'm an apartment owner and I stand to make millions off this proposition. Well, I don't own any apartments, never have. They're a lousy investment. The truth is, I don't stand to make one dime off this amendment and anybody who says different is a liar.[167]

According to Jarvis, he "never discussed the present amendment with anybody in the apartment industry. It was none of their business. This is the United Organizations' amendment, not the Apartment Association's."[168] Jarvis claimed that "while we were in the process of gathering signatures in 1977, the members of the apartment association asked me if I would like them to put some money in the campaign, and I said no."[169]

The evidence, though, directly contradicts Jarvis's assertions. The two organizations Jarvis directed were closely tied together. From the beginning of the campaign, Prop. 13 was run out of the offices of the LAAOA (as was the case two years earlier when Jarvis failed to collect enough signatures to place his 1977 initiative on the ballot). According to committee campaign statements filed by the UOT with the state, the organization received $3,500 in 1976 and $2,100 in 1977 in "non-monetary contributions" from the LAAOA for office space it provided.[170] During the signatures collection campaigns in 1976 and 1977, the Apartment Owners Association ran advertisements in the *Los Angeles Times* which reproduced the ballot initiative petitions, and urged the public to tear them out, collect signatures, and send them to the UOT. According to the UOT's own filing with the CFPPC:

> This non-monetary "contribution" or benefit [from the LAAOA] was made or conferred totally independent of the United Organization of Taxpayers, Inc., but is reported and included herein for purposes of complete disclosure. (In other words, the UOT had nothing to do with the running of this ad and had no control over it of any kind.)[171]

Claims notwithstanding, a cozy relationship existed between Jarvis's two organizations. During the spring of 1978, the Yes on 13 Committee was also run out of the LAAOA. According to Charles Betz, a Board Member of the UOT:

> The Apartment Association was deeply involved in Proposition 13. Howard Jarvis was the director of the Apartment Association of Los Angeles County

and used that as one of his bases to raise money and to conduct the campaign .... They made large contributions; they solicited their membership for contributions.[172]

The LAAOA not only contributed office space to the UOT; it also supplied Jarvis with a ready-made base of financial support.

As Executive Director, Jarvis made full use of the membership of the LAAOA to financially support his campaign for Proposition 13. In January 1978, Jarvis hired his primary campaign consultants Butcher-Forde to launch a mass mailing to all the apartment owners in California, "asking for a contribution of one percent of their gross annual revenues from rent," which he claimed they would recoup after the passage of his measure.[173] The computerized mailing generated over $120,000 in contributions to the Yes on 13 Committee.[174] Jarvis and Butcher-Forde also mailed numerous fund-raising letters to the 5,000 apartment owners belonging to the LAAOA, soliciting financial contributions. According to Jarvis, the average member of the LAAOA owned eleven units, with the members owning a combined total of more than 50,000 units.[175] In a letter addressed to the members of the LAAOA dated April 3, 1978, Jarvis claimed that if Prop. 13 was defeated, "we are the big losers." On LAAOA letterhead, he asked the apartment owners to contribute $1 million to the Yes on 13 Committee. The amount of each contribution, Jarvis implored, should be made according to a sliding scale based on the number of apartment units owned:

> If you own from 2 to 5 units, I suggest a donation of $25. For 5 to 10 units, $50 would be appreciated. 10 to 15 units demands $100. For 25 units or more, a contribution of $250 would be fair. This might seem like a lot to ask, but it is peanuts compared to your annual tax savings under Proposition 13.[176]

Jarvis's fund-raising letter also included a chart detailing the expected property tax savings for people who owned property worth between $250,000 and $5,000,000. Although Prop. 13 had no provision mandating apartment owners to pass some of their property tax windfalls to their renters, Jarvis emphasized that the apartment owners should try to "convince your tenants that lower property taxes mean lower rents. Renter votes could decide this election."[177]

Soon after Jarvis sent out his letters of solicitation, a steady stream of money from Los Angeles apartment owners began to flow to the Yes on 13 Committee. Thousands of contributions in the amounts of $100 and $250 were mailed into the Yes on 13 Committee, along with over $166,000 in

APARTMENT OWNERS ASSOCIATION
551 S. Oxford
Los Angeles, California

OCT 23 1978

April 3, 1978

The average rental owner pays property taxes equal to 3% of the value of his or her property.

Proposition 13, the Jarvis-Gann Amendment, would permanently reduce this unreasonable tax rate to 1% of the market value of your rental property. If Proposition 13 is defeated, we are the big losers.

Don't think that it will be easy to pass Proposition 13. Powerful public employee unions and other tax spending special interests plan to spend 1 million dollars on a sophisticated propaganda campaign to defeat Proposition 13.

To win, we must spend at least one-third as much as our opponents. That's ONE MILLION DOLLARS. You can help us by sending your maximum contribution to YES on 13.

If you own from 2 to 5 units, I suggest a donation of $25. For 5 to 10 units, $50 would be appreciated. 10 to 15 units demands $100. For 25 units or more, a contribution of $250 would be fair. This might seem like a lot to ask, but it is peanuts compared to your annual tax savings under Proposition 13.

In addition, convince your tenants that lower property taxes mean lower rents. Renter votes could decide this election.

Believe me, Alberta, this is our last chance to permanently reduce property taxes. Your maximum contribution to YES on 13 is needed today!

Sincerely,

HOWARD JARVIS
Chairman, YES on 13 Committee

P.S. Tie is growing short, Alberta. Please send your check to YES on 13 now.

# Proposition 13:

**Your Last Chance for Property Tax Reform**

| If Your Property is worth | Your 1977 Property Tax was | Proposition 13 will reduce your Taxes to | Each year you will save* |
|---|---|---|---|
| $5,000,000 | 150,000 | 50,000 | 100,000 |
| $3,000,000 | 90,000 | 30,000 | 60,000 |
| $1,000,000 | 30,000 | 10,000 | 20,000 |
| $ 500,000 | 15,000 | 5,000 | 10,000 |
| $ 250,000 | 7,500 | 2,500 | 5,000 |

*Figures based on California average property tax rate of 3% of the market value of property. In addition to reducing this rate to 1%, Proposition 13 limits annual assessment increases to 2%.

*Figure 4.5* Howard Jarvis' fundraising letter to members of the Los Angeles Apartment Owners Association, April 3, 1978. [Original letter on file with the Institute of Governmental Studies, University of California, Berkeley.]

contributions which were over $1,000 each. In addition to the contributions made by the individual members of the Apartment Owners Association, the organization itself contributed $31,068 to the Yes on 13 Committee (two separate checks for $15,534 each).[178] Of the $166,853 in contributions to the committees in support of Prop. 13 that were $1,000 or more, only $13,505 (8%) came from citizens groups. The balance came from apartment owners and associations, industrial parks, and realtor associations.[179] Contrary to Lo's assertion that "Jarvis tapped relatively small donors,"[180] Jarvis, with the assistance of the crack campaign consultant Butcher-Forde, targeted much of the fund-raising strategy directly at prosperous apartment owners. With his populist-sounding bluster the focus of the media's attention, Jarvis quietly tapped the financial support of the Southern California landed gentry.

## Conclusion: Proposition 13—A Faux Populist Moment

The downplaying of Jarvis's role in the campaign for Proposition 13 by scholars is certainly understandable. On more than one occasion Jarvis was known to trumpet loudly his messianic role "as instigator and implementer of this movement."[181] While his megalomaniacal pronouncements, such as, "I guess nobody chose me to lead the parade. I guess I chose myself. If I hadn't done it, I don't think anybody else in California would have done it. Nobody . . ."[182] were indeed wearisome and should be taken with a grain of salt, Jarvis was the primary force behind the campaign for lower property taxes. Without Jarvis's leadership, and perhaps more importantly the financial resources and organizational support of the LAAOA, Proposition 13 would not have been a success on election day, much less have been on the ballot in the first place. Due to the highly centralized nature of Proposition 13 and the solid financial backing of the apartment owners, the initiative can be best understood as a *faux* populist *moment*.

In the traditional sense, then, Proposition 13 was not a populist movement. The renowned California ballot initiative, while hugely successful at the polls, lacked many of the qualities associated with populist movements. With the exception of the efforts of some small, disjointed homeowners and taxpayers associations, the campaign for Prop. 13 did not emanate from the active toiling of the masses. Rather, tax crusader Howard Jarvis, acting as populist entrepreneur, successfully tapped Californians' amorphous anger toward their rising property taxes and their unresponsive state and local governments. He toiled for them. In this sense, Prop. 13 was not a grassroots, educative form of protest; it did not stem from the active participation of the masses. While populist in its rhetoric, Prop. 13 was centrally orchestrated from above. Contrary to most accounts, Jarvis did not draw his financial support from ordinary taxpayers. Rather, he relied heavily on corporate property interests for his organizational and financial backing. These particular realities of Prop. 13 diverge notably from the widely held conventional wisdom shared by most journalists and scholars.

The conflation of public opinion and social action, which has led to the widespread notion that Prop. 13 was a grassroots, populist revolt of middle- and uppermiddle-class Californians, is problematic. Positive public opinion for a ballot measure is not equivalent to social action. As political scientist Michael Engle perceptively writes:

> [O]ne must first reject the concept of public opinion as somehow spontaneous, self-generating, and self-organizing. Revolts of any kind do not organize themselves and political ideas and directions do not arise out of the random whims of individuals. The success of Proposition 13 rested on a particular set of political circumstances in California in 1978: a competent and experienced set of organizers with a clear special interest; a rapidly rising property tax; a fairly large statewide conservative political base; and a huge unused state surplus.[183]

The considerable showing of public support for the ballot initiative did not constitute a populist movement. Rather than a spontaneous mobilization of the masses, populist entrepreneur Jarvis was able to successfully tap the public mood and couple his pet solution, Proposition 13, to the perceived problem. Utilizing the organizational and financial resources of his two associations, Jarvis was able to manufacture substantial popular support for his measure on the June 6 ballot.

# FIVE

# GOING HIGH TECH

*Barbara Anderson, Citizens for Limited Taxation,*
*and the Massachusetts High Tech Council*

We couldn't have done it if Proposition 13 hadn't
passed in California. . . . Massachusetts is not as
adventurous as California. Certainly, the big argument we used was, "California did it, and they didn't
fall into the ocean."

            —*Barbara Anderson* [1]

           The real issue wasn't money, it was control and atti-
           tude. People were fed up with the attitude of the gov-
           ernment toward them. Then, suddenly, it all changed,
           like when a 70-pound weakling stands up and punches
           the bully. He gets respect.

                        —*Barbara Anderson* [2]

## Introduction: Feeling the Aftershocks of Proposition 13

On November 4, 1980, a record number of voters donned their rain gear
and trudged to one of Massachusetts' 2201 polling places. Eighty-three
percent of the state's registered electorate turned out to vote in the state,
one of the highest percentages in the nation that year. In addition to electing Ronald Reagan as the country's new President, citizens of the Bay State
approved a controversial ballot measure reducing and then limiting local
levies on property taxes. Voters passed the statutory measure, known as
Proposition 2 1/2, by a wide margin of fifty-nine to forty-one percent. Of

the 2.4 million citizens who turned out to vote, more than 1.4 million marked their ballots for the property tax cutting and limiting measure. In one fell swoop, citizens directly reduced their state's overreliance on property taxes.

With no statewide elections for political office that year, the citizen-initiated measure overshadowed every other race, including the presidential election. Even though the race for the White House was too close to call in Massachusetts on election night—Reagan ended up squeaking out a razor-thin, 3,458-vote victory over President Jimmy Carter in the traditionally Democratic-leaning state—most citizens were focusing on the vote tally for Proposition 2 1/2. Indeed, 400,000 more people voted for Proposition 2 1/2, listed on the ballot as Question 2, than cast their vote for Reagan.[3] By turning out in record numbers on that windy and rainy election day, voters were voicing their deep concern over the state's high dependence on property taxes.

The vote for Proposition 2 1/2 (also called Prop. 2 1/2) cut across numerous demographic, political, and economic lines. According to one pre-election survey, property owners, registered Republicans and Independents, self-identified conservatives, non-public sector employees, high school graduates, and men all favored the measure. Those with some college education and those between the ages of forty-five and sixty-four supported the measure even more strongly. The measure was generally opposed by public sector employees, students, college graduates and post graduates. Support for the measure increased as personal income increased.[4] Of the 351 cities and towns in the state, a majority of citizens in only sixty-five localities voted against the measure. Support for the property tax cut was equally strong in rural and urban areas, small villages and large cities, and eastern and western parts of the state.[5]

Modeled roughly after its predecessor in California, the Massachusetts initiative placed an overall cap on state and local property tax levies. As its name implied, Proposition 2 1/2 limited property taxes to 2.5 percent of the "full and fair cash value" of a given property based on its 1979 assessed level. Taking effect on July 1, 1981, the measure forced towns and cities with tax levies greater than 2.5 percent in 1979 to roll back their property tax levels by fifteen percent each fiscal year until they attained a 2.5 percent level. Once a municipality was in compliance with the prescribed rate, the measure restricted future annual property tax levies to 2.5 percent of the assessed value, unless two-thirds of a given community voted to override the measure in a local referendum. Communities with property tax rates less than 2.5 percent were able to raise their levels, but no more than 2.5 percent a year.[6] The statute also had a no-growth provision. In its original language, the measure did not allow for any exceptions to the 2.5 percent limit even if the taxable property in a community was expanding due to population growth or new construction projects.

It is important to note that the measure included a number of provisions that were not directly related to the reduction and limitation of property taxes. Among its sundry provisions, the measure slashed the auto excise tax by 62 percent (from $66 per $1,000 to $25 per $1,000). It limited the assessment on municipalities by other governmental entities, such as counties, to four percent annual increases. It banned communities from charging fees for municipal services exceeding the actual cost of the services provided. It entitled tenants to deduct 50 percent of their annual rent from their state income taxes. In addition, the measure included some provisions unrelated to tax issues. Prop. 2 1/2 called for limits on public schools by restricting the fiscal autonomy of local school boards. Equally important, it permitted local officials to reject unfunded state mandates. Finally, the measure banned compulsory binding arbitration of municipal contracts with police and fire personnel.

Thoroughly frustrated by their high rate of property taxes, Bay Staters secured property tax relief for themselves by approving the controversial measure. A few years after the passage of 2 1/2, property taxes in Massachusetts were brought into line with the rest of the nation. The trade-off, of course, was that their local governments had less revenue for services. Unlike California, Massachusetts did not have a state budget with a $5.7 billion surplus. As a result, numerous public employees were laid off, teachers in the public schools either lost their jobs or had larger classes and extramural activities were eliminated, public libraries and swimming pools closed or reduced their hours, and fire and police departments downsized their staffs. Local governments would have to learn to cope with fewer taxpayer dollars. It was a conscious decision made by those who voted for Prop. 2 1/2. As the leader of Prop. 2 1/2, Barbara Anderson, declared following the passage of the tax limiting measure:

> We want some control over the money we have earned, some limit on how much the government can take from us, some appreciation for the amount we share with the less fortunate, some respect from the people we elect to public office. . . . We feel good that Proposition 2 1/2 is going to cut property taxes and perhaps make government in general more efficient. We do not feel guilty about anything.[7]

INITIATIVE PETITION FOR AN ACT LIMITING STATE
AND LOCAL TAXATION AND EXPENDITURES

The proposed law would limit certain taxes, and change laws relating to school budgets and compulsory binding arbitration. It would impose a limit on state and local taxes on real estate and personal property equal to 2 1/2% of the full and fair cash value of the property being taxed. If a locality currently imposes a tax greater than 2 1/2% of that cash value, the tax would have to be decreased by 15% each year until the 2 1/2% level is reached. If a locality currently imposes a tax of less than 2 1/2%, it would not be allowed to increase the tax rate. In either situation, a city or town could raise its limit by a 2/3 local vote at a general election. The proposed law would provide that the total taxes on real estate and personal property imposed by the state or by localities could never be increased by more than 2 1/2% of the total taxes imposed for the preceding year, unless two thirds of the voters agreed to the increase at a general election.

The proposed law would provide that the total taxes on real estate and personal property imposed by the state or by localities could never be increased by more than 2 1/2% of the total taxes imposed for the preceding year, unless two thirds of the voters agreed to the increase at a general election.

It would further provide that no law or regulation which imposes additional costs on a city or town, or a law granting or increasing tax exemptions, would be effective unless the state agrees to assume the added cost. A division of the State Auditor's Department would determine the financial effect of laws and regulations on the various localities.

The proposal would limit the amount of money required to be appropriated for public schools to that amount voted upon by the local appropriating authority. It would also repeal the law which provides for compulsory binding arbitration when labor negotiations concerning police and fire personnel come to an impasse. In addition, the petition would provide that no county, district, or authority could impose any annual increase in costs on a locality of greater than 4% of the total of the year before.

The proposed law would also reduce the maximum excise tax rate on motor vehicles from $66 per thousand to $25 per thousand, and it would allow a state income tax deduction equal to one half of the rent paid for the taxpayer's principal place of residence.

*Figure 5.1*   The Abbreviated Ballot Title of Proposition 2 1/2

*Figure 5.2*  Barbara Anderson in her office. [A *Boston Globe* photo]

Proposition 2 1/2, according to Anderson and other supporters of the measure, was direct democracy in action. Citizens would have to live with the consequences, guilt or no guilt.

Barbara Anderson was one Bay Stater who was not the slightest bit contrite following the passage of the controversial measure. And for good reason. She was the primary force behind the measure during the final stages of the campaign for Proposition 2 1/2. It is safe to say that tax limitation in Massachusetts would never have come to fruition if it were not for the yeoman-like effort of Anderson and her zealous compatriots who staffed a small citizen-led organization, Citizens for Limited Taxation (CLT). During the summer of 1980, only a few years after she had joined the organization as a volunteer, Anderson was promoted from secretary to Executive Director of the group. She took over the reins of the struggling organization in July, 1980, four months prior to the vote on the measure. Yet with an incredible amount of perseverance and skill, the greenhorn Anderson was able to elevate the initiative process in Massachusetts to a new height.

Bringing to the campaign a self-effacing, disarming style, Anderson, a former YMCA swimming instructor, would sincerely describe her credentials for running the tax limitation campaign as having "a degree in water safety instructorship from the Red Cross."[8] She was an average citizen who could bring to the campaign the true voice of "the people." Leading the band of "grass-roots people," as one political scientist referred to CLT,[9] Anderson quickly became the darling of the news media. Able to effortlessly spew out Jarvisesque sound bites that resonated with populist undertones, she stressed during the campaign how her concerned group of citizens, in contrast to the special interests and the state government, were working in the best interest of the people of the Commonwealth. "Our fight is not mainly about money," the fiery Anderson would say. "It's about control. *They* [the state legislature] have to learn once and for all that it's *our* government."[10] Under her vigilant and determined leadership, Anderson was able to reinvigorate CLT in its crusade for Proposition 2 1/2. More than a decade after its passage, columnists continued to refer to her as a "savior," praising her as "the high priestess of the commonwealth's most powerful bloc of voters, men and women wage earners, who are sick and tired of being ripped off by avaricious politicos who ply their shameful trade at all levels."[11]

Equally critical to the success of Prop. 2 1/2, though downplayed by the press during the campaign, was the burgeoning computer-related industry and its bountiful financial contributions in support of the measure. In particular, the Massachusetts High Tech Council (High Tech) and its eighty-six member firms were key players in the fall campaign for the tax limitation measure. High Tech, a lobbying organization established in the late 1970s by a consortium of high technology companies, footed nearly all the bill to broadcast Prop. 2 1/2 to the public. According to Anderson, the measure would not have passed without the money raised by High Tech.[12] High Tech and its member companies, though, were not only the financial underwriters of the campaign. Howard Foley, the activist president of High Tech Council, conspired with CLT to fund a parallel campaign in support of Prop. 2 1/2. Late in the campaign, Foley and his organization contracted with a New York City stalwart political consulting firm to engineer the advertising blitz that pushed the measure to victory. Joining forces, Foley and Anderson became "full partners" in the drive for property tax cuts and limitations,[13] although Foley knew that politically, Anderson was "heads and shoulders above all of us in this arena."[14]

As partners, CLT and High Tech skillfully maneuvered Proposition 2 1/2 through Massachusetts's intricate citizen initiative process. Overcoming both procedural and perceptual obstacles, the proponents of the tax cuts strategized with one another throughout the fall campaign. In public, Anderson and the handful of paid staffers at CLT touted their populist credentials. Simultaneously, Foley and the high technology firms worked quietly behind the scenes, greasing the legislative wheels, raising much needed cash, and saturating the airwaves with radio and television spots. The media, fixated by the measure's populist persuasion and the possibilities of direct democracy, glorified Anderson and her citizens organization and hyped the grassroots angle of the campaign.

A closer look at the political process of the triumphant measure, however, reveals how CLT and the state's high tech business elites operated behind what can be best understood as a populist facade. Prop. 2 1/2, despite the populist overtones, was a carefully orchestrated ballot initiative run by a savvy tax crusader and her high tech allies. But at the time, the measure was portrayed as the outgrowth of a grassroots uprising of the people. Rebuffed countless times by the state legislature, the only recourse for the angry taxpayers was to take their pet solution on property taxes directly to the voters. If their fellow citizens failed to support Prop. 2 1/2, CLT asserted it was unlikely that real property tax relief would ever come to pass in Massachusetts. All citizens had to do was come out to vote on election day for a ballot initiative which was designed and championed by their fellow middle-class homeowners. Or so it seemed.

## Proposition 2 1/2: The Second Generation

At the time of its passage, many observers perceived Massachusetts's Proposition 2 1/2 as a natural extension of California's Proposition 13. The *Wall Street Journal*, editorializing in favor of the Bay State's "second-generation tax limit," called the measure a "grass-roots tax revolt" advanced by "an inarticulate horde of taxpayers and homeowner groups." Like their compatriots who were trying to advance similar tax limitation ballot initiatives in six other states that year, the self-styled tax crusaders in Massachusetts, the editors grumbled, were up against the likes of Democratic and Republican legislative leaders, good government groups, unions, and even business groups. In particular, the *Journal* criticized the disinclination of many businesses to join the citizen-led effort. "Business sits on the sideline or allows itself to be whipped glumly into the opposition," the editors lamented, while the "public is trying to regain some control over its government."[15] Although of the people, businesses had an obligation to get behind the measure.

Like Proposition 13, the editors of the *Journal* saw the tax limitation initiative in Massachusetts as having national implications. The great tax revolt that started in California two years earlier was supposed to sweep across the nation. But the citizen uprising over rising taxes seemed to be floundering after Jarvis's initial success when he barnstormed the country promoting his brand of tax relief. In June 1980, Jarvis's ballot measure aiming to slash the personal income tax in California, Proposition 9, was defeated by a three-to-one margin. CLT's Proposition 2 1/2 gave defenders of tax cuts a glimmer of hope that the revolt was still alive. The editors of the *Journal*, along with other fiscal conservatives, argued that if such a restrictive measure could pass in a traditionally liberal state like Massachusetts, it could pass anywhere.

The local press cast the campaign for tax limitation in epic proportions. The influential *Boston Globe*, whose editorial board came out against Proposition 2 1/2, nevertheless ran a series of favorable news stories about the measure. Reporters analyzed the numerous components of the measure, detailing the various savings taxpayers would realize if the measure was passed. The headline of one *Globe* article rang out, "Prop 2 1/2: It's time to forget all those doomsday cries."[16] Another proclaimed Prop. 2 1/2 to be a battle between the "pros" and the "enthusiasts."[17] Walter Robinson, the well-respected senior statehouse reporter for the *Globe* who covered the issue, wrote just a month prior to the election that, "the political tussle over Proposition 2 1/2 appears to be an uneven match." Robinson described how the sponsor of the measure, Citizens for Limited Taxation (CLT), with its "tiny staff of political neophytes and a shoestring budget" was up against the formidable "'Vote No' on 2 Committee," "a team of political professionals funded by a six-figure budget and supported by several powerful unions and groups that included the League of Women Voters and the Council of Churches."[18] Robinson commented on how the organizational and financial resources of the two campaigns could not have been more disparate. CLT was working out of a "cramped, 200-square-foot office over a Tremont street pizza parlor," and counted on contributions "principally from individual taxpayers, who sometimes sen[t] in $2 crumpled up in an envelope." In a campaign marked by reportedly stark contrasts, the well-heeled opponents of the measure had all the riches of a professional staff and large campaign contributions, and were preparing to embark on a strategy of "vertical organization," in which they would wage "351 separate campaigns," or one for every city and town in the Commonwealth.[19] The under-dog tax crusaders, the *Globe* relayed, faced an uphill battle against the usual entrenched special interests and government officials.

Also prior to the election, Boston's more conservative counterpart to the *Globe*, the *Boston Herald American*, ran several editorials in strong support of the measure. Denouncing the "scare fiction and scary facts" allegedly being disseminated by the enemies of Proposition 2 1/2, the paper railed against "the bureaucracy and special interests" who were trying to derail the initiative.[20] Commenting on the "sleazy" tactics of the opposition, the editorial staff urged citizens to rely on "reason" rather than "fear" when deciding how to vote on election day.[21] Somewhat surprisingly, the reporters for the *Herald American* tended to be more evenhanded in their coverage of the campaign. One reporter for the daily chronicled the "gross exaggeration" that radiated from both camps regarding the possible effects of the measure.[22] Indeed, after the election, several "Vote No" spokespeople told one reporter they felt the *Globe*'s news stories were slanted and had unfairly "endorsed the concept," while stories in the *Herald American* were more balanced in their coverage.[23]

As with California's Proposition 13, it was apparent well before election day that the ballot measure would be one of the most important citizen-initiated measures since the initiative process was first introduced in Mass-achusetts in 1918. Edward F. King, who in 1974 had established the conservative, anti-tax group, Citizens for Limited Taxation—the group that five years later would lead the charge for property tax limitations—boasted, "It is by far the most ambitious attempt to govern by referendum" in the history of Massachusetts.[24] Those covering the issue agreed. The *Globe* called the measure, "the most sweeping ballot question in the state's history," and "the dominant Massachusetts campaign issue this fall."[25] The *Herald American*, more subdued in its coverage of the measure during the campaign, called Prop. 2 1/2 after its passage, "the most drastic tax limita-tion proposal in Massachusetts history."[26] For more than six months, the print media, along with talk radio and local television stations, closely cov-ered the ongoing developments of the measure.[27]

## Scholarly Accounts and the Conventional Wisdom

Since the passage of Proposition 2 1/2 scholars have devoted a fair amount of attention to the fiscal impact of the statutory measure. Most hold that the nor'easter was more disruptive for Massachusetts than the Proposition 13 earthquake was for California.[28] Unlike California, the Bay State had no budget surplus from which it could offer relief to the state's 351 cities and towns. For fiscal year 1981, localities in the Bay State faced a $1.3 billion reduction in their property tax revenues.[29] The measure forced nearly every city and town to trim its budget, but it hurt older and poorer municipalities the most. Most of the municipalities that had historically low property values had over the years raised their property taxes well above the 2.5 percent level to pay for services. The year Proposition 2 1/2 passed, residents living in 192 of the state's 351 cities and towns paid property taxes in excess of 2.5 percent a year; in forty-eight of those municipalities, the levies exceeded 3.5 percent of assessed property valuations.[30] The measure drastically cut the budgets of these municipalities. Immediately following the passage of the measure, for example, the annual property tax receipts in Chelsea declined from $24 million to $3.5 million. Boston's revenues from property taxes were cut by 71 percent.[31] By fiscal year 1982, state revenues had dwindled by a total of $311 million from 1980 levels, or 9.3 percent.[32]

For many scholars and journalists, the significance of the measure extends beyond its stringent tax limitation features and economic impact on the state. Proposition 2 1/2, for these observers, serves as a symbolic expression of the people lashing out against their unresponsive government. As with Proposition 13, Prop. 2 1/2 is frequently understood as a populist uprising. Political scientist Jack Citrin writes, "Proposition 2 1/2, like Proposition 13, is both a source of tangible benefits and a symbol of the 'people's' victory over the 'politicians.'"[33] Concurring with Citrin, James Ring Adams, a conservative journalist who has training as a political scientist, argues that the 1980 initiative was born out of "[f]rustration with the commonwealth's high tax burden," as it "spread from property owners to aggressive new members of the business community."[34] Drawing parallels with the American Revolutionaries who fought the British two hundred years earlier over the issue of taxation without representation, Adams claims that the Massachusetts legislature was intransigent, as it "failed to represent the people."[35] By these accounts, Proposition 2 1/2, like its California cousin, was a victory of, by, and for the people.

To some extent, of course, the populist interpretations advanced by Citrin, Adams, and others hold a grain of truth. It is incontrovertible that voters supported Prop. 2 1/2 by a three-to-two margin. Proposition 2 1/2 proved to be a powerful antidote relieving a clear problem of the state's unbalanced tax structure. Property taxes in many localities were excessive. As in California, voter displeasure with escalating property taxes was palpable. Prop. 2 1/2 hit a tender nerve felt by many homeowners. The authors of the measure successfully tapped into the public mood and offered the citizens of Massachusetts their own home remedy for what they perceived to be ailing the average taxpayer.

But to characterize the campaign as a spontaneous populist uprising which was led by a group of disorganized and over-matched citizens glosses over the details. Contrary to conventional views, the Massachusetts "tax revolt" was not a populist movement in any traditional sense of the word. During the campaign for Prop. 2 1/2, there were no spontaneous mass demonstrations by people in favor of the measure, only a few collective clamors by outraged homeowners over their exorbitant property taxes, and nary a display of local support to rein in government spending. In contrast to the local eruptions by taxpayer and homeowner groups against property taxes in California, there was only a sprinkling of local homeowners associations and taxpayers groups in Massachusetts that were united in support of the measure. These groups, it turned out, were not major players during the campaign. It was not so much a battle between David and Goliath, as the press and scholars would have us believe; it was more akin to Goliath versus Goliath.

The campaign for Proposition 2 1/2 was indicative of a *faux* populist moment. The tax crusaders, especially Anderson, were portrayed by the press as a grassroots band of volunteers whose financially insolvent organization, Citizens for Limited Taxation, was held together by "chewing gum and bailing wire."[36] Yet CLT had considerably more firepower than the media reported. As with Prop. 13, this small group of dedicated individuals was able to successfully tap the widespread anxiety expressed by many homeowners over their high property taxes. After drafting their rambling ballot initiative, the populist entrepreneurs offered it to the voters as their take-it-or-leave-it palliative. Equipped with populist-sounding rhetoric and the substantial financial help from a few key sectors of the business community, the savvy tax crusaders waged six months of "guerrilla warfare" to advance their initiative.[37] To an even greater degree than in California, ordinary citizens in the Bay State remained removed from the initiative process until election day—the realization of the *faux* populist moment.

## The Road to Proposition 2 1/2: Overdependence on Property Taxes and Legislative Inaction

The Massachusetts tax structure at the time Proposition 2 1/2 was placed before the voters could best be described as unbalanced. The state had not systematically revised its system of state and local taxation for over fifty years. A 1954 report conducted by the Fiscal Survey Commission concluded that Massachusetts's system of taxes "is somewhat like a building with a Gothic foundation, a Renaissance frame, and an Elizabethan facade."[38] The lack of a systematic tax blueprint for the Commonwealth, compounded by the smattering of idiosyncratic changes that modified the tax code over the years, made the state's system of taxes extremely complex and unevenly distributed. Despite its disorder, the tax system in Massachusetts had preserved its solid foundation—the property tax. In 1980, Massachusetts's cities and towns relied on the property tax for fifty-three percent of their total revenues, a higher percentage than every other state save Alaska.

During the 1970s, Massachusetts was tagged with the disparaging label, "Taxachusetts." The moniker was not without credence, but it had as much to do with the uneven dependency on property taxes as with the overall tax burden. In 1980, Massachusetts ranked forty-second among the states with respect to its balanced use of taxes. A 1978 U.S. Bureau of the Census survey found that Massachusetts ranked second in terms of its per capita property tax collection and fifth in its state individual income taxes per $1000 of personal income. That year, local property taxes were seventy percent higher and personal income taxes were sixty-eight percent above the national average.[39] Prior to the passage of Prop. 2 1/2, statewide property taxes averaged 4.7 percent for all classes of property, and 3.5 percent for residential property only. Businesses, on average, were being taxed at a slightly higher rate than homeowners.[40] Particularly hard hit were the residents of the cities and larger towns in the state; in 1980, Massachusetts's cities had 160 percent less per capita property value than its small towns. As a result, the average property tax levy in cities was three times higher than in small towns.[41]

But Massachusetts's comparably high dependency on local property taxes as its primary revenue source was offset somewhat by its relatively "underdeveloped" sales tax of five percent, its five percent flat income tax, and its lack of user fees.[42] In 1980, Massachusetts's general sales tax was nearly fifty percent below the national average. In terms of the overall tax burden, in 1980 Massachusetts's state and local taxes were nine percent above national average.[43] Nevertheless, its inordinate reliance on property taxes created the perception among many residents that "Taxachusetts" was an appropriate label for the state.

Reforming the unbalanced tax system seemed to be a perennial topic of discussion on Beacon Hill. The state legislature, officially called the General

Court, had a long history of tax reform attempts, but an equally long record of tax reform failures. Nearly every year the legislature made at least one attempt to reduce the state's dependency on the property tax. Legislators, between 1932 and 1980, introduced 126 legislative proposals "calling for some form of limitation on local property taxes or on local or state expenditures."[44] None of the proposed bills, though, was ever signed into law. The General Court also named five different state commissions between 1927 and 1970 to make recommendations on how to overhaul Massachusetts's tax system. All five commissions recommended the used of other taxes— especially the sales tax—to offset the heavy burden placed on the property tax. But the reports fell upon deaf ears once they made their way to the legislature.[45] The state's high dependence on the property tax endured.

Using the initiative process, citizens made various attempts to alter the state's tax code. In 1936, forty-four years before the successful passage of Proposition 2 1/2, a remarkably similar ballot initiative was proposed by a group of citizens. Through the petition process, a group of citizens collected enough valid signatures to place a measure on the ballot that would have limited property tax increases to 2.5 percent of the "full and fair cash value" of a given property. Citizens, however, were never given the chance to vote for the measure. In 1937, the Supreme Judicial Court invalidated the measure before it was placed on the ballot due to "procedural defects."[46]

Subsequent citizen initiatives to alleviate the state and local dependency on the property tax also failed. On three separate occasions in the late 1960s and early 1970s, a coalition of 12,000 dues-paying citizens and liberal public interest groups collected enough valid signatures to place a question on the ballot that would have replaced the state's flat income tax with a progressive income tax. The measure would have had the effect of easing the heavy burden placed on the property tax by increasing the income tax on wealthy individuals. Robert Kuttner, in his well-documented book *The Revolt of the Haves*, documents the grassroots effort of Massachusetts Fair Share, the group behind the progressive tax reform. Voters, though, did not find the prospects of a graduated income tax attractive. They soundly rejected Fair Share's proposed income tax initiatives in 1968, 1972, and 1976, each time by a larger margin than the previous attempt.[47]

In 1978, the legislature finally offered homeowners assistance by placing an advisory referendum on the November ballot. Aligned with Boston Mayor Kevin White, Fair Share successfully lobbied the legislature to place a property tax classification amendment to the state constitution to the vote of the citizenry. Property owners in major cities, such as Boston, had been paying much higher taxes as a result of a 1974 ruling by the Massachusetts Supreme Judicial Court. The decision, known as *Sudbury*, required all local jurisdictions to assess property at its full market value, which had the effect of raising property taxes. Many municipalities, including Boston, resisted the high court's ruling. The proposed 1978 constitutional amendment asked citizens if the legislature should annul the court's decision and maintain the current rate of assessment for homes at approximately forty percent of value, with commercial and industrial property assessed at fifty and fifty-five percent of value, respectively.[48] Voters approved the advisory referendum by close to a two-to-one-margin.

In 1979, the legislature provided additional property tax relief to taxpayers. Feeling pressure from the newly elected governor, conservative Democrat Edward J. King (no relation to Edward F. King, the founder of CLT), the legislature passed a law giving temporary property tax relief to homeowners. For a two year period, the law provided a four percent cap on the rate municipal, county, and regional governments could spend over their budgets from the previous year.[49] In its first year, the statutory limit lowered statewide property taxes by approximately $33 million, translating into an average reduction of the property tax levy of nearly one percent.[50] While the measure provided temporary relief to some Massachusetts homeowners, many were ready for something more.

## The Ripening Public Mood

Prior to the passage of Prop. 2 1/2, the overall public mood existing in Massachusetts toward government and taxes did not seem to be nearly as negative as it was in California two years earlier. This was not surprising, as the fiscal situation in Massachusetts was very different from the one out west. In California, prior to the passage of Proposition 13, property taxes in some localities were doubling every three years. In contrast, property taxes in Massachusetts in 1980 actually declined by an average of 1 percent, and in 1979, increased by only 2.1 percent. Unlike Massachusetts, California's property values had become rapidly inflated during the mid-1970s, which in turn increased the annual property taxes homeowners had to pay. In Massachusetts, local property tax levies were much higher on average than those in California, but residential property was not being assessed at its full market value (despite the *Sudbury* decision) and property values were not inflated. As a result, property taxes in Massachusetts were not rising at the phenomenal rates seen in California.

Public opinion polls conducted prior to the election tracked citizen attitudes towards taxes and government.[51] While upset, Bay Staters in general were not outraged by the taxes they paid. A private poll conducted by the Massachusetts Teachers Association in March 1980, found that sixty-three percent of those polled backed a property tax limitation measure comparable to Prop. 2 1/2.[52] Two months later, a survey conducted by the Center for Studies in Policy and the Public Interest at the University of Massachusetts-Boston, found that seventy percent of the respondents believed that their property taxes would rise in 1980. Furthermore, "a majority felt that their property taxes were too high considering the services their local communities provided."[53] Yet, the survey also found citizens believed that government spending could be cut, but that "only limited cuts are possible without affecting services."[54] Only eleven percent of those polled said local governments could cut their taxes and spending by twenty percent or more without eliminating services; nearly half (forty-nine percent) said local governments could cut their taxes and spending by ten percent without affecting services.[55]

Public enthusiasm for Prop. 2 1/2 waned some over the summer, and by the fall there was an even amount of support and opposition for the measure. In early October, less than a month before the general election, a *Boston Globe* poll found that voters favored the initiative, "but they have little understanding of the issue."[56] When asked if they were for a property tax limitation measure, forty-four percent of the 500 voters polled who said they were certain to vote and who always vote on ballot questions replied "yes," whereas forty percent opposed such a measure. The remainder did not know how they would vote. But, when voters were asked if they supported Proposition 2 1/2 without being told what the measure entailed, only twenty-five percent of the voters supported the measure, with thirty-six percent opposing it. An additional twenty-two percent of voters did not know how they would vote on the measure, and seventeen percent had never heard of it. A few weeks later, in mid-October, a second *Globe* survey of likely voters found forty-nine percent favored, forty-three percent opposed and seven percent were undecided about the measure. Most of the shift in support of 2 1/2 came from "men, Republicans, self-described conservatives, and voters older than forty-five."[57]

Of those who supported the measure and were concerned about their high property tax levels, the polls revealed that most citizens were not

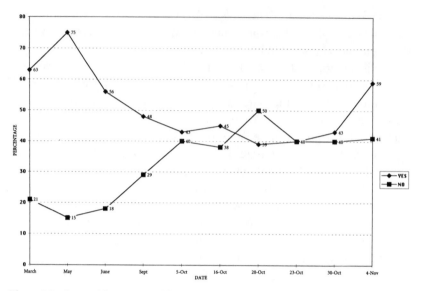

*Figure 5.3* Proposition 2 1/2 Public Opinion, 1980

clamoring to downsize their state or local governments. While a standard explanation for the motivations of disgruntled taxpayers, downsizing government did not seem to resonate among Massachusetts voters.[58] Rather, polling data revealed that citizens were becoming increasingly fed up with the disproportionate balance of state and local revenues derived from the property tax. As Sherry Tvelt Davis argues, "Massachusetts voters were frustrated with high taxes and a recalcitrant legislature that refused to enact tax reform or tax relief."[59] Cities and towns relied heavily on the property tax: It was virtually their only own-source revenue. Voters were concerned about their rate of taxation, especially with regard to property taxes, but they did not express a high level of anger towards government. As Davis points out:

> [I]n several surveys conducted prior to the election, Massachusetts voters indicated that they were satisfied with local officials and services. Many expressed deep apprehension about local service cutbacks. Most did not believe local governments were wasteful or corrupt.[60]

But by the fall of 1980, many citizens viewed Proposition 2 1/2 as their only chance to exert control over taxes and expenditures and to "send a message" to the legislature for tax reform. In this sense, the Massachusetts "tax revolt" was steeped in similar logic as the one Jarvis had led.

## The Rise of Citizens for Limited Taxation

Similar to the situation in California, where it took Howard Jarvis fifteen years to place a property tax limitation measure on the ballot, the quest for a citizen-inspired property tax reform transpired slowly and erratically in Massachusetts. The general consensus among citizens of the Bay State was that something had to be done to the state's inequitable and unbalanced tax system. Public opinion polls documented that citizens wanted some type of tax relief. As late as the summer of 1980, though, two questions continued to linger: What kind of tax reform would emerge, and who would be able to deliver it to the voters?

The group ultimately responsible for offering the public a property tax reduction and limitation ballot measure was an unseasoned but zealous group, Citizens for Limited Taxation (CLT). The grassroots group, like Jarvis's United Organizations of Taxpayers, started out unassumingly. It was born when "a handful of conservative friends organized a group in 1973 that hoped to light the match" to reduce the overall tax burden in Massachusetts.[61] Edward F. King, an arch-conservative Republican businessman from West Roxbury, a suburb of Boston, founded the organization. King was not unfamiliar with the initiative process. In 1968 and 1972, he worked as the front man for a phony grassroots group created by two of the state's most powerful business organizations. The Associated Industries of Massachusetts (AIM), representing over 2,000 traditional industrial manufacturers, and the Massachusetts Taxpayers Foundation (MTF), a public policy think tank supported financially by the general business community, hired King to lead campaigns against two progressive income tax measures placed on the ballot by Massachusetts Fair Share. The president of MTF at the time, Richard Manley, claims the business associations left "no fingerprints" in their financial support of the opposition campaigns that King lead.[62]

It was during the 1972 campaign that King decided to form his own group to fight taxes. He told a reporter with the *Boston Globe* he came up with the idea to create a tax reduction citizens group, "when he was putting in one fifteen-hour day after another stumping the state against the graduated income tax."[63] In 1973, after Massachusetts voters soundly defeated the second graduated tax initiative that he worked against, King called his close friends together. Among them were Don Cassidy, a friend of King's from umpiring little league together who later succeeded him as Director of CLT, and neighbor Pauline Zywaski.[64] Casually, and then more formally, the close group of friends started talking about Massachusetts's taxes, and soon after decided to establish CLT. In 1974, the group officially became an unincorporated business and registered as a non-elected political committee with the Office of Campaign and Political Finance. Like Jarvis's UOT, King decided that CLT should have a Board of Directors control the agenda of the organization. Although King claimed that his "nonpartisan" organization was "a collection of people with disparate backgrounds, occupations and income levels who share belief that taxes in Massachusetts are too high and must be knocked down," there were no registered Democrats on the Board of Directors.[65] Between 1974 and early 1978, when he voluntarily stepped down as Director of CLT to run in the Republican primary for Governor, King presided over the organization with a heavy hand. Over that period, King claims, "I ran the show. It was pretty much a one-man operation . . . what I said went."[66]

In their effort to lower taxes in the state, King and his small band of loyalists turned to the same initiative process that was used, albeit unsuccessfully, by the progressive tax reform group Fair Share. In 1975, King headed up the group's first bid to limit in governmental spending. The group collected signatures for a ballot measure that would have amended the state constitution by capping state expenditures. According to King, volunteers during his petition campaign collected more than 50,000 signatures, just short of the 55,644 valid signatures needed to qualify the measure for the ballot. "It was a real heart-breaker," King recalled in 1980, on the eve of the passage of Proposition 2 1/2.[67]

Then, in the fall of 1976, CLT spearheaded a defensive campaign against yet another graduated income tax proposal placed on the ballot by Massachusetts Fair Share. Fair Share's measure had the full backing of dozens of liberal public interest groups and the state legislature's Democratic leadership. CLT, through King's contacts, had the substantial financial support of the business community,[68] and was able to help defeat the measure at the polls by a three-to-one margin, "practically eliminating it as a political issue."[69]

As the principal group in the campaign against the graduated tax, CLT quickly gained a reputation around the state as a conservative grassroots organization bent on checking taxation and government spending. CLT's stature was enhanced by an editorial written by *Boston Herald American* columnist Warren Brookes following the defeat of the 1976 graduated income tax initiative. Brookes, an erstwhile businessman and reclusive journalist, often opined in the *Herald* about the fiscal merits of limiting property taxes. The writings by Brookes and others in the Boston area made Massachusetts "one of the intellectual centers of the new doctrine" of supply-side economic theory.[70] Brookes especially liked to tout the grass-roots efforts of CLT, and suggested that readers interested in doing something about taxes join CLT. One of those most eager to heed Brookes' call was a redheaded lifeguard and self-professed "housewife" from the coastal town of Marblehead, Barbara Anderson.[71]

## CLT and the Evolution of Proposition 2 1/2

A more unlikely heroine of the tax limitation movement in Massachusetts could not have been scripted. Anderson first became interested in reducing taxes when, in the mid-1970s, she and her then-husband, Ralph Anderson, returned to Massachusetts after having lived out-of-state. Anderson felt a huge "culture shock" when she moved back to the Bay State. At the time she thought to herself that something was "terribly wrong here."[72] Taxes, in her mind, were much too high, and on top of that, Fair Share was advocating yet another graduated income tax, which she and her husband strongly opposed.[73]

Anderson began working for CLT as a volunteer shortly after reading Brookes's call to arms. After another summer of lifeguard duty, Anderson joined CLT in the fall of 1977. She collected signatures in the Marblehead area, as CLT tried for a second time to place a measure to limit state spending on the statewide ballot. The constitutional amendment initiative, known as the King Amendment, was named after CLT's director at the time, Edward F. King. It aimed to limit state spending by the ratio of state expenditures to personal income averaged over the previous three years.[74] With help from individual members of the Republican and Libertarian parties as well as its own volunteers, CLT collected 86,771 valid signatures during the fall, more than enough to advance it to the second step the constitutional amendment initiative process.[75] During the petition drive, Anderson stuffed envelopes at CLT's Boston office and personally collected 4,800 signatures.[76] Anderson, along with Francis "Chip" Faulkner, who was also a CLT volunteer in 1977, collected more signatures during the drive than anyone else.[77] At the time, the *Wall Street Journal* ran a story extolling the efforts of King and CLT, and wondered out loud if Massachusetts might be the first state to limit taxes through the initiative process.[78]

Before the King Amendment was placed on the ballot for the voters it had to make its way through a specially convened joint session of the state legislature.[79] During the 1978 Constitutional Convention, or "Con-Con" as it is known on Beacon Hill, the legislature voted in favor of the King Amendment. However, prior to the vote, the Democratic leadership made a technical change to the amendment during the "third reading" stage of consideration.[80] The amendment excluded local aid from the state tax and spending cap, which at the time accounted for a substantial portion of the state budget. As Anderson recalls, the legislative leadership took CLT's amendment "into a back room, and made a tiny technical change which basically destroyed it. . . . That was our first lesson in politics as a young, fledgling organization, which is *never, ever* trust the legislative leadership."[81] CLT disavowed the King amendment after the changes were made to it, and filed a suit in the Supreme Judicial Court to have the original wording restored.[82]

Despite the legislative leadership's duplicitous action which made the King Amendment impotent, 1978 would turn out to be a pivotal year for proponents of tax limitation in the Bay State. On June 6, Howard Jarvis declared victory in the first battle in the war on property taxes. The success of Jarvis's tax slashing measure had a national impact. Immediately following the passage of Prop. 13, Jarvis launched his American Tax Reduction Movement and headed east to tout the merits of his measure to tax limitation activists in other states. Jarvis gave hundreds of speeches and made an infomercial that was broadcast across the country. Although his infomercial never aired in Massachusetts (the Boston TV stations boycotted it), Jarvis still managed to make his presence felt in the Bay State.

CLT's fortunes were profoundly affected by Jarvis's victory in California. Commenting in 1978 on the eve of the Prop. 13 vote, Don Feder, the new Executive Director of CLT, told the *Wall Street Journal*, "There is a synergy in the taxpayers' movement."[83] Prop. 13 had a major effect on CLT, as it steered the organization away from limiting spending to cutting property taxes. "We were watching Proposition 13 very carefully through the spring of 1978," Feder remembers. "We were thinking that if this goes over well in California—which is a fairly liberal state—perhaps we should try it in Massachusetts."[84] Following Jarvis's lead, CLT immediately recalibrated its strategy from one of advocating spending caps to one of placing limits on property taxes. But CLT would embark on its new property tax limitation strategy without its founder. Ed King stepped down as Director of CLT as the tidal wave of taxes was cresting across the nation, and enthusiastically threw his hat into the 1978 Republican primary for governor. His friend from the little league baseball diamonds, Don Cassidy, replaced him as Director, and Anderson became CLT's new full-time secretary.

After the passage of Jarvis-Gann, a few members of the legislature were also feeling optimistic about the possible impact Prop. 13 might have in Massachusetts. Only three days after the passage of Prop. 13, four Republican state representatives introduced a 2.5 percent property tax limitation initiative into the Massachusetts General Court.[85] Along with his fellow representatives, Rep Andrew Natsios (R-Holliston) penned a bill patterned on Jarvis's measure and introduced it into the House.[86] On June 29, 1978, CLT's fiery Executive Director Don Feder testified before the Joint Committee on Taxation in favor of the bill. During the hearing, Feder caustically asserted that "most of what government does is not only unnecessary, but actually interferes with the productive endeavors of its citizens."[87] He then asked rhetorically if government really provided any services that were "necessary." Reading off a list of examples, Feder asked the members of the committee:

- Is an Olympic size swimming pool for the new high school an essential service?
- Is busing an essential service?
- Is Mayor White's limousine an essential service?
- Are municipal tennis courts an essential service?
- Are the highest welfare payments in the United States, ninety percent above the national average, an essential service?
- Are lavish public pensions an essential service?
- Is a new city hall an essential service?

Feder's animated testimony failed to make a positive impression on the Democratic leadership in control of the House and Senate. By the end of July, the House leadership foiled three separate attempts to bring Natsios's bill to the House floor. Instead, the House voted 222 to twenty-three for the watered-down version of the King Amendment, an amendment CLT no longer supported. "The legislature tried to pretend that California didn't exist and that Howard Jarvis had never been heard of," Anderson recollects.[88]

Defeated, Natsios and the handful of Republican lawmakers decided to change their strategy and look for help outside of the legislature. Later that summer, the Holliston Republican contacted CLT to ask the group to help him draft a second version of the tax limitation measure. The idea was to circumvent the legislature and, as in California, take a property tax limitation measure directly to the taxpayers of Massachusetts. CLT agreed, and its staffers quickly drew up the group's first property tax limitation initiative petition, which became known as Proposition 2 1/2.

In early August, abiding by the rules guiding the initiative process, the group filed its statutory initiative with Attorney General Francis X. Bellotti. Bellotti unceremoniously struck down the ballot proposal as unconstitutional, citing a provision in the proposed measure that would have returned a percentage of state tax revenues to cities and towns. He ruled that the state constitution prohibited appropriation bills to be placed on the ballot before the voters.[89] CLT shrugged off the decision. If Bellotti had approved the measure, it would have been extremely difficult to gather signatures that fall, as most political activists were already tied up with political races. In addition, the measure would not have been placed before the voters until 1980. Rather than becoming despondent, CLT learned from Bellotti's decision, and began preparing a revised ballot initiative to bring to him in 1979.[90] By then Natsios and his fellow Republicans had decided to work on their own legislative proposal, so CLT "went it alone."[91]

Even though CLT's ballot measure was struck down by the Attorney General, the issue of tax cuts remained a hot topic during the fall of 1978. In September, to the surprise if not shock of most observers, incumbent Governor Michael Dukakis was defeated at the polls in the Democratic primary in a huge upset by "ultraconservative" Edward J. King.[92] By some estimates, the heavily favored Dukakis was ahead in the polls by nearly twenty percent the morning of the primary. At the time King was the executive director of Massport, the state agency overseeing the operation of Logan Airport in Boston. In the primary, King had run an uninspired campaign until he started hammering home the issue of high property taxes.[93]

King's victory over Dukakis had serious ramifications for the property tax limitation cause in Massachusetts. In the opinion of journalist Warren Brookes, there was "only one over-riding reason for the stunning upset of Michael Dukakis by Edward King: taxes—and in particular, property taxes."[94] The King campaign, he noted, "was dead in the water" until he started to stress the issue of property taxes. Analyzing the primary results, Brookes found a strong correlation between cities and towns that voted for King and those with high property taxes. In "the seventy-five most heavily taxed cities and towns, with property tax rates of $42 per thousand and up," according to Brookes's study, "Dukakis lost to King fifty-five percent to forty-five percent,"[95] matching King's overall statewide margin of victory.

In an effort to boost his showing heading into the general election against Republican nominee, Francis Hatch, King sought the backing of Howard Jarvis. Although a registered Republican, Jarvis agreed to champion the conservative Democrat's tax reduction proposal, the centerpiece of his otherwise rather lackluster campaign. King's proposal, dubbed "Massachusetts 13," was anything but original. It was a near replica of Jarvis's Prop. 13. Taking advantage of Jarvis's national popularity, as well as the public outcry in Massachusetts over the television blackouts of Jarvis's infomercials, King asked Jarvis to tape a television spot for him. Hamming it up in front of the camera, Jarvis extolled the merits of King's "Massachusetts 13" tax-rollback plan, testifying in the ad, "If Ed King can not do it in Massachusetts, my name is not Howard Jarvis."[96] King ended up winning the general election in November easily, defeating his Republican opponent by more than 100,000 votes.[97]

In addition to electing a new, more conservative governor, voters passed a non-binding advisory question placed on the ballot by the General Court. The referendum directed the legislature to take immediate action to reduce property taxes, increase state aid to localities, and provide for separate assessments on residential and commercial property. Following his inauguration, Governor King successfully steered a substantial tax and spending limitation proposal through the legislature. Although the "zero-cap" tax bill he originally submitted was rejected by the legislature, the amended law limited local property tax and spending increases over the following two fiscal years to four percent.[98]

Meanwhile, CLT was busy drafting a new property tax limitation measure. Heeding the advice of Warren Brookes and Howard Jarvis, CLT hired a respected tax lawyer, Morris Goldings, to help draft a revised measure to limit property taxes to 2.5 percent of the real assessed value of a given property. The inspiration for the new measure, Anderson insists, came from Warren Brookes: "Warren was the father of 2 1/2 . . . the man who came up with the concept of 2.5 percent."[99] To build support for its initiative, CLT asked Jarvis to stop in Massachusetts during his American Tax Reduction Movement speaking tour. On October 15, 1978, Jarvis spoke to a couple hundred people in Newton, a suburb west of Boston. Though he was suffering from laryngitis, the California millionaire told the audience:

> You look like middle-class people to me. And I'm a middle-class guy. . . .
> Although taxes and death are inevitable, being taxed to death is not
> inevitable. . . . You don't have to be a subject in the United States, you can be

a citizen. . . . Thirteen proved, by God, the will is there and we're going to do it from Maine to California. . . . We're going to take it to the politicians and shove it right in their ear. We proved (in California) it does make a difference when you say what you want.[100]

At the rally, Jarvis met with CLT leaders Don Feder and Ed King and helped them put together the ideas for the upcoming 1979 petition drive. CLT "conferred with him from the beginning . . . he was wonderful," Anderson remembers. "He advised us and actually saved the petition for us, because the advice he gave us, which we took, accounted for a large part of the victory." Jarvis recommended against freezing property tax assessments and to "give something to renters so we don't have this civil war between tenants and landlords after it passes."[101]

In December 1978, Don Feder unveiled CLT's new version of Proposition 2 1/2. The group decided it would submit its measure as a statutory initiative as well as a constitutional amendment initiative. Other than the fact that one of the measures would become a law, amendable by the legislature, and the other would become an amendment to the Constitution, CLT's two ballot initiatives were identical.

As mentioned earlier, CLT's ballot initiative was not limited to the reduction and limitation of property taxes. Other tax-related provisions were added to the draft as CLT continued to revise it during the spring of 1979. In particular, CLT decided to include a provision that would slash the auto excise tax by sixty-two percent. Anderson, who was working as CLT's paid secretary at the time, recalls that the auto excise tax cut was a fairly late addition to the measure:

> That came from our trying to put together a coalition to help us do the petition drive. The auto dealers in the state were planning a petition drive to cut the auto excise tax . . . they were going to abolish it. . . . So we met with them.[102]

Elliot Savitz, CLT's chief fundraiser, set up a meeting between Don Feder and an officer with the Massachusetts State Automobile Dealers Association (MSADA), Arthur Bent. As Anderson recalls, Savitz "explained the facts of life of how tough it is to do a petition drive, particularly if you're a business organization, how difficult it is, how you need a 'grassroots' organization to do it."[103] CLT was able to negotiate a deal with MSADA, agreeing to put the auto excise tax cut in its petition "if they [MSADA] wanted to help fund our drive instead of doing their own." That summer,

MSADA contributed $20,000 to CLT in preparation for their petition drive.[104]

Later that spring, CLT tacked on two more provisions to its tax limitation measure. The provisions concerned school board autonomy and mandatory binding arbitration for police and fire employees. CLT decided to add the provisions after Anderson, filling in for Feder, attended a hearing at the state house and heard testimony given by Joel Pressman, the mayor of Chelsea. Pressman complained about how he could not cut his city's property taxes because he was controlled by the school board committee and by the police and fire unions, which could indirectly raise property taxes with impunity. The provisions were directed to the cities and towns to give them sharper teeth if Prop. 2 1/2 eventually became law. At the time, CLT also threw in provisions calling for the elimination of unfunded state mandates, the abolishment of a "temporary" 7.5 percent income surcharge and a ten percent tax on unearned income, and a resolution calling on the Legislature to vote for a Balanced Budget Amendment to the U.S. Constitution.[105] CLT's leaders hoped to broaden as much as possible the appeal of the group's tax limitation measure.

With the draft of the measure set, CLT suffered its first major setback during the spring of 1979. Don Feder, CLT's Executive Director, made a shocking series of public comments following a scheduled press conference in which he denounced Governor King's failure to veto the four percent cap on local spending and taxes in favor of his original zero-cap proposal. With his assistant Chip Faulkner at his side, Feder was quoted by reporters as personally favoring the elimination of "most public services, including schools, libraries and fire departments," as well as advocating the elimination of "public works and having roads and streets privately owned and maintained." With Faulkner trying to bridle him, Feder continued to vent, saying local expenditures could be cut by eliminating "teachers and administrators; summer school; home economics; sex education, gym classes" as well as "unneeded facilities like swimming pools; uniforms for bands and athletic equipment."[106]

Faulkner was in disbelief as Feder continued to speak off-the-cuff. Faulkner remembered how he had, "never seen reporters scribble notes so furiously."[107] "We got more publicity on that day than we've every gotten in our history," Anderson recollects. "It was chaos." CLT spent "two years trying to live that down," Anderson recalled, as during the campaign for 2 1/2 "the quote was thrown back at us."[108] Feder's term as CLT's Executive Director came to an end shortly thereafter, just as the momentum into the petition drive was getting started. Although he was not forced to resign by the Board of Directors, Feder went on vacation to the state of Washington soon after the incident and decided to move there permanently. "He'd had enough by then," Anderson recalls.[109]

After Feder's outburst, the financial standing of CLT, if not its public perception, floundered. Over the summer of 1979, the press was reporting that CLT had between 4,000 and 7,000 members.[110] In actuality, Anderson says the group had "something like 2,000 by the time we had gotten rid of everyone who had died or left the state."[111] Members of CLT included dues-paying individuals as well as volunteers interested in lowering taxes in the Commonwealth. Again, contrary to press reports, CLT's finances were also dwindling. One *Globe* article reported CLT had a $100,000 budget in 1979, "the vast majority of which was raised from small donors giving $25 and $50."[112] In fact, the organization was running in the red. When staffer Greg Hyatt replaced Feder as Executive Director in late July 1979, CLT was $18,000 in debt.[113] Hyatt, a Yale graduate who had recently earned his law degree from Boston University, had little experience with ballot drives. Much of the work ended up falling on the shoulders of Anderson and Faulkner, who were also inexperienced at running an initiative campaign. Without the help of Massachusetts's rapidly growing high technology sector, and the ability of Anderson to make inroads into the business community, CLT's property tax limitation measure would most likely have failed.

## Wiring the High Tech Community

Working independently of CLT, two powerful business interest groups were simultaneously lobbying the state legislature for a series of tax reforms. Howard Foley, President of the upstart Massachusetts High Tech Council (High Tech), and Heinz Muehlmann, Chief Economist of the Associated Industries of Massachusetts (AIM), directed the effort. In the early 1970s, the two men worked together at Jobs for Massachusetts, Inc., after Foley hired Muehlmann as the organization's chief economist. Jobs for Massachusetts was a "closed-door forum" where business and labor leaders met with government officials to "iron out problems," and to hash out "private deals."[114] Foley and Muehlmann both left Jobs about the same time in late 1977 to establish High Tech, which was comprised of twenty-seven founding members. Soon after helping to set up High Tech,

Muehlmann left to take the position at AIM. The two designed High Tech to serve as an umbrella organization that would represent the growing number of technology and computer firms in Massachusetts. These businesses, according to Foley, had "different needs" than the traditional manufacturers represented by AIM.[115] Almost one hundred emerging, high value-added companies demanding highly skilled laborers would soon be represented by High Tech. The bulk of the firms were concentrated along Route 128, Boston's outer beltway, Massachusetts's version of Silicon Valley. In contrast, AIM represented over 2,000 traditional industrial manufacturers in the state.

The high tech and the traditional industries did not always agree on legislative lobbying tactics or on public policies. As Muehlmann remembers, the creation of High Tech "left bad blood between the old guys and the new guys."[116] High Tech was chiefly interested in having the state lower its property taxes. Because the computer industry was geographically flexible but heavily reliant on costly human capital, firms were able to shop around the country in search of the most lucrative location to set up shop. Foley was understandably concerned with the state's image of Taxachusetts. "When people see the taxes in this state," Foley told a reporter, "it scares them. It's as simple as that."[117] According to Foley, the employers who High Tech represented were unable to attract highly skilled employees because of the state's high income and property taxes.

The two industrial sectors did manage to come together in 1979, primarily because of the close relationship between Foley and Muehlmann. During the spring of 1979, Foley and the High Tech Council, in conjunction with Muehlmann and AIM, approached the newly elected Governor King with an innovative "state public policy" proposal called the "Social Contract."[118] The non-binding, implicit understanding focused on the correlation of the relatively high costs of doing business in Massachusetts and the ability of private sector to create jobs. The document stated:

> If tax rates are reduced, jobs and hence tax revenues in Massachusetts will over time actually increase so that the Commonwealth will have greater financial resources to address its social problems and public responsibilities.[119]

Specifically, High Tech's "eighty-nine members would generate 60,000 new high tech jobs over the next four years if the state government reduced the overall tax burden by thirteen percent."[120] Concerned about job creation, Governor King was more than willing to work with the emerging, though already powerful, high-tech industry. But the legislature was less willing to negotiate, especially with respect to reducing income taxes or the property tax burden.

During the summer of 1979, High Tech, AIM, and the Massachusetts Taxpayers Foundation (MTF) met to discuss their own tax limitation proposal. If the legislature failed to consider their measure, the business group threatened to take it to the voters as a ballot initiative. MTF wrote the first draft of the tax limitation proposal, but Muehlmann and AIM had problems with its language and decided to write their own proposal. MTF's proposal, Muehlmann recalls, had so many holes you could "drive a truck through it."[121] AIM's draft, penned by Muehlmann and an outside lawyer, included an overall tax cap suggested in High Tech's Social Contract and a local override provision. MTF, returning AIM's earlier slight, refused to support it. After the legislature failed to act on the AIM proposal, Foley and Muehlmann prepared to submit it to the Attorney General, the first step in the ballot initiative process. Like CLT, Muehlmann and Foley decided to submit their measure as both a statute and a constitutional amendment. But a problem quickly arose: Who would go out and collect the necessary signatures?

Foley and Muehlmann approached CLT and its new Executive Director, Greg Hyatt. An informal agreement was brokered: CLT would drop its constitutional amendment and AIM/High Tech would drop its statutory initiative, and then AIM/High Tech and CLT would simultaneously collect signatures for the remaining two petitions. The constitutional amendment offered by AIM/High Tech differed only slightly from CLT's statutory petition. AIM/High Tech's constitutional amendment, if approved by two successive Con-Cons, would not be placed before the voters until 1982. Broader than CLT's initiative, it called for three different limits on taxes: an overall state and local tax limit tied to a ratio personal income and previous state and local revenues; a limit on state and local taxes based on an average tax rate on personal income in all the other states; and a 2.5 percent limit on property taxes. It did not have the narrower provisions concerning school board autonomy, the auto excise tax, binding arbitration for public employees, or tax breaks for renters.[122] Officially, AIM never endorsed CLT's measure, but it promised that its members would help to collect signatures for both petitions.[123] As it turned out, though, only a handful of employees working for the member firms of High Tech and AIM collected signatures; CLT "collected the lion's share" of signatures for both initiatives.[124]

CLT struggled to gather enough signatures for each of the measures during the fall petition campaign. During the drive, AIM and High Tech were little help, financially or organizationally. Neither AIM nor High Tech contributed the financial resources they had promised for the campaign, though CLT did receive some large contributions from AIM and High Tech executives who happened to individually belong to CLT. Michael Valerio, the Papa Gino's pizza chain magnate, provided CLT cheap office space when they were "really tight on money."[125]

Organizationally, CLT was in dire straits. Feder, who had run a couple of petition drives, had departed for Washington a few weeks before CLT received its petitions from the Secretary of the Commonwealth. Before leaving, he gave Anderson and Faulkner a set of instructions on how to run a petition drive.[126] Hyatt, appointed by the board as Feder's replacement, had no experience running an initiative campaign. The young lawyer focused primarily on fundraising activities with Savitz and did some public speaking, although he also helped to collect signatures when the group was still short of the required number. The bulk of the petition drive, though, was left to Anderson and Faulkner, neither of whom had ever run a petition drive. The two ended up doing it, according to Faulkner, "from the seat of our pants."[127] Faulkner, whose position was funded by the National Taxpayers Union throughout the campaign, was nominally in charge of the petition drive. Anderson, when not in the office answering the phones, dealing with volunteers, and typing memos, was in the field with Faulkner collecting thousands of signatures. "We were in shambles," Anderson recalled.[128]

That fall, CLT needed to collect 58,868 valid signatures for each of the proposed ballot questions. To do so, it turned to various local taxpayers groups and their members, as well as to its own members.[129] Volunteers from some of the groups that CLT reached out to collected signatures, as did some members of CLT, but it was the paid staffers—Anderson, Faulkner, and Hyatt—who gathered the bulk of the signatures.[130] On December 5, 1979, CLT turned in its petitions for the two measures, each with only slightly more than the minimum number of signatures required by law. The Secretary of the Commonwealth certified 60,529 signatures for the statutory initiative, only 1,661 more signatures than required, and certified only 59,227 for the constitutional amendment, barely topping the minimum.[131] Yet before the two measures were sent to the legislature to be voted on, the Massachusetts Teachers Association (MTA) challenged both measures with the Ballot Law Commission for not having enough valid signatures. The Ballot Law Commission invalidated the AIM/High Tech constitutional amendment, but upheld CLT's statutory initiative. Both sides appealed the unfavorable decisions made by the Superior Court . On April 28, Judge George Keady found both initiatives to have a sufficient number of signatures to qualify.[132]

The leaders at CLT knew they were very fortunate to collect enough signatures for the two measures. A memo drafted by Don Cassidy, CLT's Chairman of the Board of Directors, after the submission of the signatures in December, listed twenty-eight "things that hurt" the petition drive and twenty-five "things that helped." Among those factors cited by Cassidy that negatively affected the campaign were:

- Nonparticipation of EFK [Edward F. King] and his faithful;
- Lack of money, which prevented hiring better/more support staff and which forced diversion of efforts;
- A lot of promises that were broken, and we didn't figure it out until it was too late;
- Inability to attract committed, dedicated help of large members of taxpayer group members (we failed to discard the false assumption that loyalties are transmittable and transferable; should have learned that from 1977);
- Lack of signature-gathering help from many companies that could have done it; promised but did not deliver; or delayed;
- Slowness/shallowness of some endorsers to act (MAR [Massachusetts Association of Realtors], MHTC are examples);
- We dumped our own amendment petitions and therefore dumped on the egos of 9 tax group leaders who had signed it.

Of the 25 positive aspects of the petition drive, Cassidy cited:

- Money from corporate sources freed our time to petition;
- Some, but not much, signature work by AIM companies;
- Modest auto dealer activity, although not up to promises;
- Damn hard work on final sweep to find/salvage signatures on Dec. 3–5;
- Dedicated signature gathering by office staff;
- Excellent, quick working relationship/understanding between D. Cassidy and G. Hyatt. No problem of ego conflict as sometimes existed w/ D. Feder;
- Excise tax and rent deduction added attractiveness.

Cassidy noted with great relief and understatement at the end of the memo, "We were really lucky to be one percent over and not one percent short!"[133]

The legislature was required to vote on CLT's statutory measure by May 7. The General Court did not greet CLT's measure with much fanfare. On May 6, 1980, the House of Representatives voted against CLT's statutory initiative by a vote of 146 to five. Don Cassidy and others at CLT were not surprised. "We expected the Legislature to vote against us; we expect a weak alternative to appear on the ballot with Prop. 2 1/2," Cassidy asserted at a press conference. "The legislature in California put Proposition 8 [the legislature's alternative property tax measure] on the ballot with Prop. 13 and fooled no one."[134] According to the labyrinth-like initiative process, CLT was required to collect an additional 9,811 signatures by June 18 in order to have Prop. 2 1/2 placed before the voters on the November ballot. CLT managed to do so, collecting nearly 24,000 signatures in a matter of weeks.[135] However, CLT's ship was not financially sound, and Greg Hyatt, the Executive Director, was in the midst of leaving CLT for a better paying job. One influential member of the Board of Directors remarked how CLT's "rag-tag army" was "in a serious financial condition," and that during the signature campaign the previous fall, "it became evident that CLT's financial position [was] unstable and . . . the life expectancy of [the] organization could be considered limited."[136]

After a brief recess, the joint legislature reconvened in Constitutional Convention to consider, among other items, the AIM/High Tech constitutional amendment. According to some accounts, Foley and Muehlmann made an arrangement with the Democratic leadership to get the required fifty votes (twenty-five percent) in order to advance their measure to the next stage of the constitutional amendment initiative process. In return, if the legislature supported their constitutional amendment, or "an acceptable alternative," AIM/High Tech would not financially support CLT's statutory Prop. 2 1/2 campaign in the fall.[137] The Democratic leadership, though, began to vacillate. In an effort to hold off the amendment for more deliberation, the legislature adjourned before it took a vote, a clear violation of the state Constitution. Warren Brookes was seething. He wrote in his column, "The 60,000 registered voters who signed this amendment petition, and the sponsoring organizations behind it, CLT, AIM, and HiTech, all worked at this long and tedious process under the assumption that the Legislature would be forced to deal with it."[138] Governor King, sensing the public outcry, forced a legislative recall for a second Con-Con in mid-September.

Before the legislature reconvened, Representative Gerald M. Cohen (D-Andover), the Chairman of Taxation Committee, was able to hash out an agreement for an amended version of the AIM/High Tech constitutional amendment. In a series of intricate maneuvers, the joint legislature killed the AIM/High Tech measure, but approved a substitute measure, dubbed the Cohen Amendment, by an impressive vote of 172 to nine.[139] The Cohen Amendment would limit increases in state and local taxes to the annual percentage increase in total personal income, estimated to be about ten percent. Anderson, who by that time was ensconced as CLT's new Executive Director, viewed the altered Cohen Amendment as "something entirely different" than the original amendment, and refused to back it.[140] Muehlmann and AIM championed the modified amendment, and decided to honor, at least publicly, their earlier agreement with the legislative leadership not to back CLT's measure.[141] Foley and the High Tech Council, in contrast, reluctantly supported the Cohen amendment publicly, but were mulling over the possibility of financially backing CLT's fall campaign for 2 1/2. Prior to the vote on the Cohen amendment, Anderson was able to sell Foley and the High Tech Council on how imperative the passage of Proposition 2 1/2 was for real tax reform, and that the Cohen Amendment was not "what they were supposed to get."[142] Anderson remembers:

> By late September of 1980, it became clear to the High Tech Council—and I of course did nothing to disavow them of the notion—that CLT couldn't make it without them, that the other side was already running TV ads . . . and we had enough money for a couple of radio ads, that's all we had.

Anderson succeeded in convincing Foley and the High Tech Council to financially back CLT's measure. On September 8, the High Tech Council's Board of Directors approved a motion to "commence planning" to support Prop. 2 1/2.[143] CLT finally had a full partner for the final two months of the campaign.[144]

## The Ascent of Barbara Anderson

The financial and organizational support provided by the High Tech Council in September and October 1980, turned out to be critical for the success of Prop. 2 1/2. Less than a month before High Tech privately announced it would sponsor the measure, Anderson was frantically sending out press releases, begging for free media exposure. "Since we will not have the funding for a paid media campaign," she pleaded, "we will have to count on your sense of fairness in giving us air time to express our point of view." At the time, Anderson informed the media that CLT did "not have

Big Money from Big Business."[145] A month later, that all had changed. The pact with Foley and the member firms of High Tech, according to Anderson, gave CLT instant "credibility that we wouldn't have just as a grassroots organization when the number one growth industry would support it."[146] Rather than relying on the financial and organizational support of its members, CLT tapped the business community as it headed into the final stages of the campaign.

The relationship between CLT and the High Tech Council, which at times had been bumpy, began to gel in July 1980.[147] On July 1, Anderson took control of CLT, or more accurately, she was begged by the Board of Directors to become Executive Director after several other members of the organization declined the post. With self-deprecating humor, Anderson fondly recalls "clawing my way to the top in a two person organization, taking the job that nobody else in his right mind would take." She had just gone through a second divorce, was still working as a lifeguard, and "now needed another job" to support herself and her son.[148] Anderson and Foley quickly became "soulmates in this cause."[149] Foley thought the previous two executive directors of the organization, Greg Hyatt, and before him, Don Feder, did not advance the issue of tax limitation with the same deftness as Anderson. Unlike her predecessors, she was able to successfully tap not only the widespread malaise among Massachusetts homeowners, but also sell CLT's solution to the business community. Anderson proved to be an adept tactician during the final months of the campaign, mimicking as best she could the moves of the inimitable Howard Jarvis. As Foley recalls, "CLT was lucky to have Anderson take responsibility to get the ball over the goal line."[150]

Anderson was a quick study on the job. Thrust into the spotlight, she drew from every imaginable source to get up to speed on the legal intricacies of the measure. Immediately after assuming her post, she sent a letter to each member of CLT's Board of Directors asking him or her for a section-by-section analysis of the measure. Only Don Cassidy and one other Board member responded, but the two did not agree in their interpretations of the measure.[151] In August, Anderson poured over her marked-up copy of the Legislative Research Council's Summary Analysis of Prop. 2 1/2.[152] A month later, she knew the issues and CLT's policy positions better, but she was still not self-assured in her ability to articulate them in public. Fortunately for her, Walter Robinson of the *Boston Globe* began a series of articles on the various provisions of Question 2, as Proposition 2 1/2 was labeled on the ballot, in late September. Anderson remembers how Robinson set up an interview with Anderson at the CLT office:

> Walter Robinson came in to interview me and I remember sitting down
> because I couldn't stand up I was so scared, because I knew one misstate-
> ment and it was all over, and I didn't have the slightest idea what all this stuff
> was . . . . I knew that in general that property taxes were too high and we
> should cut them . . . . I was just horrified.[153]

After the interview, Robinson started doing his own independent analysis
of the measure, which Anderson thought was "brilliant." Anderson vividly
remembers how during her interviews with Robinson:

> He would ask me questions and I'd ask him questions back, "Yeah, what do
> you think?" He did all this analysis of everything, and I'd get the *Globe* first
> thing in the morning, memorize it all . . . and then going in and doing my
> interview with the Associated Press, and [I would say], "Well, of course as
> you all know," and hoping nobody would know . . . that I had *no* idea, but
> everyone was gone. Feder had left the state, and [Hyatt] never really knew, he
> was working on the strategy not the specifics.

By the time October rolled around and the campaign was in full swing,
Anderson felt confident that she "actually knew what was in this petition."[154]

## Financing 2 1/2: Citizens, Small Businesses, and the Auto Dealers

On the fundraising front, CLT's efforts started out slowly but gradually
improved during the fall. Contributions to CLT in the final stages of the
campaign came primarily from three sources: citizens, various small businesses, and the automobile dealers. Between July 2, 1980 and election day,
November 4, 1980, CLT brought in $152,936. Of the total contributions
which poured into CLT's coffers, only fifty-four percent came from individuals. Businesses, including an disproportionate number of automobile
dealers (twelve percent), contributed $70,351 to CLT in less than four
months.

The importance of business contributions to CLT, especially money
from the automobile dealers, had a pronounced effect on CLT's ability to
wage a viable campaign. CLT filed seven separate Campaign Finance
Reports between July 2 and election day. Under the first filing, which covered contributions made between July 2 and August 22, CLT netted only
$22,711. Of the contributions, over half of the checks (fifty-one percent)

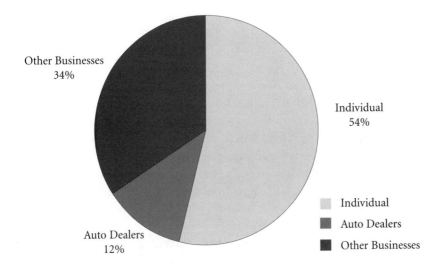

*Figure 5.4* Total Campaign Contributions to Citizens for Limited Taxation, July 2–November 4, 1980

came from corporate donors, although only three percent came from auto dealers. This would change quickly.

In August, CLT launched a mass mailing to the members of Massachusetts State Automobile Dealers Association (MSADA). Highlighting the 62 percent cut in the auto excise tax, CLT looked again to the state's auto dealers for support. Soon after the letter was sent out, money started pouring in from MSADA members. Although the next reporting period was only two weeks long, CLT raised $14,571 between August 23 and September 5. Businesses accounted for three-quarters of the contributions made to CLT. The auto dealers gave CLT $5,840 during these two weeks, nearly forty percent of the total contributions. Other businesses contributed another $5,050 (thirty-five percent) of the total. On September 15, CLT filed its third Campaign Finance Report. Over the previous ten days, contributors gave CLT $8,247, of which thirty-five percent came from businesses. Auto dealers accounted for twenty-one percent of the total. Between September 16 and October 1, businesses continued to show their support for Prop. 2 1/2. Of the $22,169 raised by CLT, forty-seven percent came from business, although the share from automobile dealers dropped to twelve percent of the total.

With the campaign for the tax limitation measure entering its final month, CLT pushed its fundraising efforts into high gear. Between October 2 and October 15, CLT brought in $30,276, an average of $2,163 per day. While the contributions from the automobile business slackened, down to eight percent of the total amount, business still accounted for forty-seven percent of the contributions made to CLT. Between October 16 and the first day of November, Anderson and her group amassed another $48,924 in contributions. Over those crucial seventeen days, with the measure rising in the polls, citizens began to contribute a majority share of the money coming into CLT headquarters. In that period, sixty-four percent of the contributions made to CLT came from citizens; small and medium-sized businesses accounted for the balance, with the auto dealers contributing nine percent of the total.

It should be noted that only a small percentage of the contributions made to CLT were plowed into the campaign for Question 2. Of the

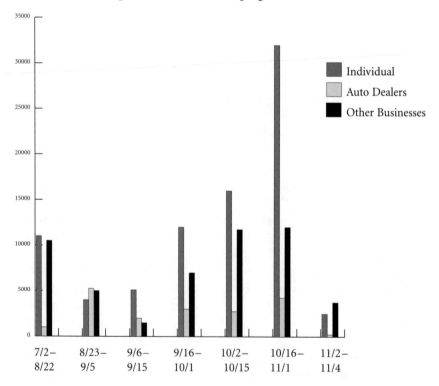

*Figure 5.5*  Campaign Contributions to Citizens for Limited Taxation by funding period, July 2–November 4, 1980

$152,936 CLT raised between July and election day, the organization paid its finance chairman and chief fundraiser, Elliot Savitz, a hefty sum for his work soliciting contributions. Over the four month period, CLT paid Savitz $79,054, or fifty-two percent of the organization's total contributions.[155] Rent, before moving into subsidized office space provided by Papa Gino's patron Michael Valerio, cost CLT $4,000, and reimbursements for staff expenses another $3,800. In addition, CLT paid its small staff a total of $13,481 (nine percent of its gross) in salaries over the same period. The staff, of course, was working hard getting the pro-2 1/2 message out to citizens by way of the free media (talk radio and news interviews), arguing with opponents at pre-arranged debates and public forums, and speaking to various civic groups and clubs. But not including other expenses, such as office supplies and phone bills, two-thirds of the contributions made to CLT were spent just on the organization's fixed overhead costs.

## The Parallel Campaign: High Tech and the New York City Consultants

Although CLT raised a substantial sum of money during the fall campaign, it had little left to spend on a paid media campaign due to Savitz's cut for his fundraising activities. As a result, the important paid advertising campaign for Proposition 2 1/2 was left to Howard Foley and the High Tech Council. In September, Foley took the issue of 2 1/2 directly to his members and convinced the technology executives "if they didn't do it, it wouldn't happen."[156] He linked CLT's measure to High Tech's Social Contract. He convinced them that property tax reduction was just as an important issue as an overall tax cap. He made dozens of phone calls and personally met with the executives to solicit contributions from them. Anderson was duly impressed. It was "very unusual" for "a bunch of high tech cowboys" to back "a people tax cut as opposed to doing just a business tax cut."[157]

With AIM out of the picture, and CLT spending too much on its overhead, High Tech assumed full responsibility for providing the financial resources to promote the measure to the public. In order to deflect attention away from the concentrated fundraising effort of the high tech industry and to comply with campaign finance laws, Foley set up a populist-sounding front organization, Concerned Citizens for Lower Taxes (CCLT). Over the span of one month, October 1 through October 31, Foley raised

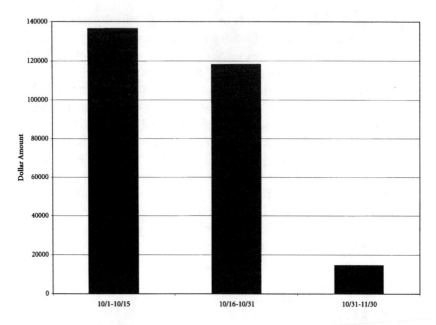

*Figure 5.6*  Campaign Contributions to Massachusetts High Tech Council (Concerned Citizens for Lower Taxes) by funding period, October 1–November 30, 1980

$254,650, more than enough to launch a parallel campaign championing Prop. 2 1/2. By election day, CCLT had raised a total of $269,085 from seventy-two contributors, an average of $3,737 per contribution.[158] Despite its name, only a few citizens actually gave to CCLT. Five individuals contributed money to CCLT during the month of October, giving a total of $4,050. Nearly all of this amount was given by four lawyers from the Boston firm Coopers & Lybrand, who made contributions of $1,000 each.[159] Of the seventy-two total contributions to CCLT, only seven were made by citizens (including the lawyers), for a total of $4,085. The balance came from the cluster of high tech industries belonging to Foley's group. Of the contributors, Data General provided $16,000; Foxboro Company gave $14,500; GenRad, Teradyne, Prime Computer, Computervision, and Millipore each parted with $12,000; and New England Nuclear and Wang gave $8,000 and $6,000 respectively.[160] Foley came up big. It was "one of the most impressive displays of fundraising I had ever seen anywhere," Anderson recollects.[161]

Just as he began soliciting the high technology executives for contributions, Foley hired a respected New York City consulting firm, Dresner, Morris & Tortorello to help run High Tech's campaign. In mid-September,

Dick Dresner, Dick Morris and Barry Kaplovitz left for Boston to meet with Foley and Anderson to talk strategy.[162] The Madison Avenue consultants had worked in Massachusetts previously. In 1978, they ran Edward J. King's successful campaign for Governor. At the time of the meeting, DM&T gave Foley a memo outlining its strategy for High Tech's campaign.[163] On September 18, they would have a "pre-field" briefing, which would be followed a few days later by a "field survey" of Massachusetts voters. On September 30, DM&T promised to deliver its survey data and presented an "oral briefing" complete with "strategy recommendations." The following day, High Tech would form its grassroots-sounding campaign committee, Concerned Citizens for Lower Taxes, and sign a contract with its "media creator," New Sounds, also of New York City. During the month of October, DM&T would make four separate television and radio "media buys" to saturate the airwaves across the state.[164] While Anderson and others at CLT were out stumping for the measure, High Tech would run an impassioned sound-bite campaign on radio and TV.

Despite the infusion of cash from High Tech's members, and the expertise of DM&T, public opinion polls still showed that Prop. 2 1/2 faced an uphill battle going into the election. According to DM&T's own field survey poll done in late September, only slightly more than one-third of Bay Staters favored the measure.[165] DM&T's poll registered lower support than some other polls conducted, but at the time public opinion was not all that favorable for the measure. The survey research done by DM&T, though, disclosed how Anderson and Foley could increase public support for 2 1/2.

On October 11, CLT sent a "confidential" memo to its "Spokesmen for Question Two." The memo detailed what DM&T thought was the "best approach" to sell Prop. 2 1/2 to the public. Drawing on DM&T's survey research, it stressed several "key themes." First, it warned, "The voters are not particularly impressed by the fact that 2 1/2 is supported by CLT, High Tech, or the auto dealers. . . . Therefore, it is advisable to begin your presentations by pointing out that Prop 2 1/2 is on the Nov. 4 ballot because '*100,000 of your friends and neighbors wanted it there.*'" Second, it recommended that the backers "stress the particular provisions of Prop 2 1/2." Third, the memo suggested emphasizing "that contrary to what the Stop 2 1/2 folks are saying, *2 1/2 actually increases local control.* . . . It is important not to be perceived as a slap at local government." Fourth, the "spokesmen" were instructed in the memo to "*Send Them a Message,*" "Them" being the state legislature. Finally, and most prominently, the survey research directed the proponents to downplay the conservative side of the measure: "*Don't sell 2 1/2 as a conservative, limited government concept.* Research indicates it just won't wash that way in liberal Mass. Sell it instead as a liberal compassionate measure." The memo concluded with advice on how the advocates of 2 1/2 should conduct themselves when presenting the issue: "Unless you are in a debate and are directly attacked, don't be belligerent. The paid media advertising will do all the rough stuff we need to do. We should be perceived as moderate, sober, reasonable, and statesmanlike."[166] Anderson's troops, dealing with the realities of a liberal Massachusetts electorate and with the polling data to inform its strategy, intentionally deviated from the bombastic style employed by Jarvis two years earlier.

DM&T took care of the media blitz, running a barrage of TV and radio ads during the final two weeks of the campaign. Dick Morris and New Sounds media guru Tony Schwartz designed what turned out to be a very effective TV ad, known as the "Alka Seltzer spot." A series of bar graphs showed a countless number of Massachusetts taxes going up and up, with voices in the background groaning louder with every hike. After the final "oooh," there was an audible "plop, plop." Following a brief pause, the voices responded with a collective "ahhh," as an image of Proposition 2 1/2 burned into the screen.[167] The opposition never had a chance.

## The Opposition Flounders

Opponents of the measure were not adequately prepared for the late media onslaught expertly waged by DM&T. Although a coalition of organizations raised an impressive $535,779 in its effort to defeat the measure, it failed to convince the public that Proposition 2 1/2 would be disastrous public policy.[168] Twenty-five groups, including the likes of the powerful Massachusetts Teachers Association , the AFL-CIO, the Massachusetts Association of Firefighters, the Massachusetts Municipal Association, the non-partisan League of Women Voters, and other good-government organizations came together as an umbrella group to form the "Vote No on Question 2 Committee." Calling Prop. 2 1/2 a "tax deform" measure, the coalition congregated in Boston in mid-October to draft a strategy to oppose the measure.[169] By then it was already too late. DM&T was already in high gear with its pro-2 1/2 campaign.

Part of the reason the anti-2 1/2 message failed to make an impact with the voters was the fact that opponents of the measure were really running two separate campaigns.[170] The opposition, which was led chiefly by the MTA, simultaneously supported its own tax limitation measure it had placed on the November ballot, known as Question 3. Instead of con-

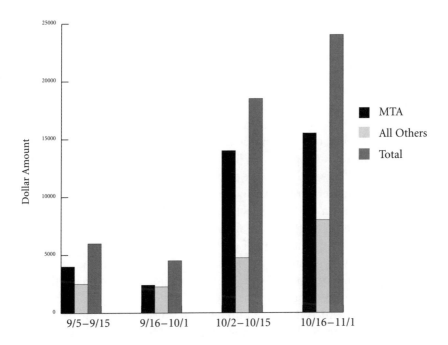

*Figure 5.7* Campaign Contributions to Vote No on Question 2 Committee, by funding period, September 5–November 30, 1980

fronting 2 1/2 directly, the MTA decided in May 1979, that it would offer voters an alternative tax reduction measure.[171] The MTA's proposal would change the tax code by requiring the state to increase its share of the cost of local education.[172]

But during the final weeks before the election, the MTA's strategy clearly backfired. The MTA's push for Question 3 as an alternative to Prop. 2 1/2 detracted from a head-on effort to defeat Question 2. The business-oriented Massachusetts Taxpayers Foundation (MTF), which opposed Proposition 2 1/2 as being "too extreme," also came out against the MTA's measure. Dick Manley, President of MTF, called Question 3, "a smokescreen" designed exclusively "to knock off Question 2."[173] At the same time, Manley told a reporter, "I don't blame anyone for voting for Proposition 2 1/2 because this is all the Massachusetts Legislature has left, a very frustrated public."[174] Anderson and others at CLT, not surprisingly, rejected the MTA's measure even more strongly: "Question 3 is the teacher's pet . . . meant to confuse voters."[175] While polls showed that voters were not confused by the two competing measures, they also showed that voters were not biting on the alternative measure put forth by the teachers.

The Vote No on Question 2 Committee was bolstered somewhat a week before the election when the *Boston Globe* ran an editorial which was strongly against Prop. 2 1/2. The editors of the influential paper opined, "We think it is a gamble with the welfare of many of Massachusetts' 351 cities and town that is simply not worth the risk. We recommend a 'no' vote on Question 2."[176] Proponents of the measure, the *Globe* claimed, were "pushing 2 1/2 on the basis of the 'bomb theory'" but had not "advanced alternative tax schemes and, in fact, have been in the forefront of opposition to more equitable taxing schemes in the past." According to the editors, CLT only offered, "the very lame hope that tens of millions of dollars of 'waste' can be found somewhere in state government and returned to the localities, through nothing in the law compels state action."[177]

By the time the *Globe* editorial came out, public opinion was already beginning to shift in support of CLT's measure. A couple of important events, which were completely independent of CLT or High Tech, hurt the opposition's chances. In early October, the coalition failed to secure the key endorsement of an important politician, the popular Mayor of Boston, Kevin White. While White had publicly announced that, "The best thing that could happen for the state is for 2 1/2 to die," he equivocated by declaring that property taxes were excessive, and "as real as the injustice of sitting in the back of the bus."[178] His palliative comments during the campaign only hurt the opposition's chances to defeat Question 2. The director of the "Vote No" coalition, Michael Ventresca, said of the White administration, "We'd love to have them work with us."[179] But White never ended up throwing his political weight or sizeable city resources behind the opposition.

In addition, Chelsea Mayor Joel Pressman, who laid claim to governing the state's poorest city, also backed Prop. 2 1/2. Pressman, while concerned about the possibility that his city might lose seventy-six percent of its revenue from property taxes if the measure passed, saw no other option but to support the measure. "I realize it's risky," Pressman told a reporter a week before the election:

> I quite frankly would interpret the vote [if favorable] to mean that people do not so much want Proposition 2 1/2. I personally would interpret the vote to mean that they wanted property tax reform, that they did it out of frustration.[180]

Pressman understood all too well the voter frustration over property taxes and the inclination of the voters, despite the possible dire consequences, to support the measure.

In addition, similar to what transpired in California days before the June 6 election, the Vote No coalition suffered a major blow when the Department of Revenue announced the largest increase in property taxes in three years. As in California, the sudden shock felt by homeowners as they read their letters with their new property tax statements, pushed some to become supporters of Proposition 2 1/2. George Crossman, a fifty-six-year-old retired city worker, summed up the feelings of many homeowners when he said, "I'm voting for Proposition 2 1/2 because the politicians get too much money to steal now. It's about time the taxpayers got a break. The city's service stinks. The streets are very dirty. It looks like Tobacco Road."[181] With retired city workers like Crossman supporting the measure, Anderson and Prop. 2 1/2 were almost assured of a big victory on election day.

## Conclusion

The broadly accepted interpretation of Proposition 2 1/2—that the property tax limitation measure constituted a grassroots, populist uprising fueled by angry citizens—endures today. Like Howard Jarvis and his California followers, Massachusetts voters were "Mad as Hell" and were prepared to fight, or at least vote for property tax reduction. However, this interpretation of Proposition 2 1/2 severely misrepresents the history of the campaign. It falsely builds upon the similarly flawed interpretations of Prop. 13 that tax limitation initiatives are inherently populist undertakings. It wrongly equates a "yes" vote with grassroots participation in the initiative process.

The understanding of Prop. 2 1/2 as a populist movement obfuscates the less-than-populist process that led to the favorable vote by a majority of citizens for the ballot measure. While the Vote No on 2 Committee did have the imposing organizational and financial backing of organized labor and good government groups, the proponents of the measure had the solid financial backing of the state's high tech industry and small businesses, including the automobile dealers. While Citizens for Tax Limitation did operate out of a small room above a pizza parlor, its staff was primarily bankrolled by an array of business interests. While the advocates of the measure were narrowly outspent by their opponents, in no way can it be said of Proposition 2 1/2, as a *Boston Herald American* headline declared following the election, "It's one election that money could not buy."[182] As in California, the contributions in favor of Proposition 2 1/2 came from vested special interests, and not from the taxpayers at-large.

# SIX

# A SOLO CRUSADE

*Douglas Bruce and Colorado's Taxpayers Bill of Rights*

"We've ended the tyranny of unlimited taxation, and
they don't like it."

⁓

—*Douglas Bruce*[1]

⁓

"Actually, I started this initiative so I could meet
women."

—*Douglas Bruce*[2]

## Introduction: Tax Crusading in the 1990s

On November 3, 1992, Colorado voters approved a statewide ballot measure designed to severely restrict the taxing and spending powers of all
state and local governmental entities. Listed on the ballot as Amendment 1,
the measure passed with relative ease, garnering 53.6 percent of the vote.
Among its other provisions, the initiative required that a public vote be
taken on any new or increased state or local taxes or government debt. It
also limited future government spending to a set formula based on population growth and the consumer price index. If the total annual revenue of a
given governmental unit exceeded its total annual spending, under this
amendment, the governmental unit would have to refund the difference to
taxpayers. Hailed by its author, Douglas Bruce, as "the single most important political event in Colorado since statehood,"[3] the complex, 1,703 word
initiative was marketed as a way to curb "runaway taxes" and downsize the
state's "bureaucratic Big Brother."[4]

Polling precinct officials were kept busy on election day. Turnout of registered voters equaled eighty percent, the highest level in the state since 1984. The spirited turnout, combined with the numerous ballot questions on which citizens were asked to vote, led to slow-moving lines as well as good conversation at the polling stations. Even though it was a presidential election year, and in Colorado Ross Perot was running a strong independent campaign for the White House, many voters were more engrossed by the ballot questions than by the races for political office. While the rest of the country (including Republican-leaning Colorado) was busy turning George Bush out of office and electing Bill Clinton as the nation's new President, Coloradans were also making legislation and amending their state constitution. In addition to pulling the levers for the candidates running for political office, voters were trying to decipher the ballot title summaries of ten citizen initiatives and three referenda submitted to the electorate by the General Assembly. Of the twenty-four states using the initiative process in 1992, Colorado's ten citizen-initiated measures were second only to California's twelve ballot measures.

As in Massachusetts in 1980, the races for political office in Colorado, including the presidential race and a U.S. Senate contest, took a back seat to the ballot questions in election-year excitement. In particular, two controversial and hotly contested citizen-initiated ballot measures captured the eye of Coloradans: Amendment 1 and Amendment 2. While the tax and spending limitation measure received its fair share of media attention, it seemed to pale in comparison to the even more disputatious Amendment 2. Leading up to election day, the preponderance of local press coverage of the ballot questions focused on Amendment 2, the punitive anti-gay rights measure. It was the first ballot measure of its kind in the nation explicitly aimed at restricting the civil rights of a certain class of citizens.

Perhaps more than coincidentally, both controversial ballot initiatives sprung from Colorado's wellhead of fundamentalism and conservativism, Colorado Springs. Amendment 2 was placed on the ballot by Colorado for Family Values, an evangelical group established in 1991. Nurtured by fundamentalist Christian organization, Focus on the Family, and its $78 million annual budget, and supported by "big-name Christian leaders in Colorado, including Promise Keepers founder Bill McCartney and Focus on the Family president James Dobson," Colorado for Family Values was one of over fifty fundamentalist Christian organizations headquartered in the Springs.[5] The group claimed to be a "non-religious, single-issue organization" whose intent was to "educate the public on all the facts about the homosexual lifestyle," but it waged an intense, spiteful campaign against the alleged "special rights" that a handful of localities were granting gays and lesbians.[6] Despite the broad-based and well-financed coalition of activist groups that opposed the measure, Coloradans approved of Amendment 2 with 52.6 percent of the vote.

While the vote for Amendment 2 came as a shock to many Coloradans, it did not come without warning. The local press, along with the national press corps, covered the anti-gay rights measure with intense scrutiny. The issue, of course, merited the sharp media coverage. However, the close coverage of Amendment 2 by the press detracted media play from Amendment 1. Prior to the election, the state's two major daily newspapers, the *Denver Post* and the *Rocky Mountain News*, nonchalantly portrayed Amendment 1 as just the latest in a tiresome line of tax limitation ballot measures championed by an iconoclastic and unrelenting tax crusader. Opponents of the measure proclaimed that Amendment 1 would cripple state and local governments, but the public, it seemed, was busy concentrating on the other ballot measures. As the votes for the initiatives were being tallied, many people were startled not only by the affirmative vote for Amendment 2, but by the success of Amendment 1.

The tax and spending limitation measure was the brainchild of a portly lawyer who ran his initiative campaign out of the basement office of his Colorado Springs home. Douglas Bruce, a self-described "short-haired, middle-aged bachelor with a paunch living in the suburbs with a puppy,"[7] conceived and wrote the measure himself. He coordinated the petition drive for signatures and conducted his own fundraising. In addition, he engineered the election campaign by himself, hiring a public relations firm to produce ads and carry out the media buys. Peripherally, Bruce was aided by a handful of members of the skeleton organization he had founded four years earlier, the "Taxpayers Bill of Rights" Committee (TABOR).[8] Unlike Howard Jarvis and Barbara Anderson, Bruce did not rely on the business community or fellow property owners for his financial or organizational support. Nor did he hire a political consulting firm to raise money for his measure. Instead, the prosperous landlord, real estate investor, and nonpracticing attorney willfully, although somewhat reluctantly, shelled out thousands of dollars of his own money when his campaign was running short on cash. The passage of Amendment 1 by the voters was directly attributable to Bruce's yeoman-like effort and single-mindedness.

It took several years, but Bruce gradually mastered the process of direct democracy with uncanny deftness. During the late fall of 1991, Bruce and his less-than-intimate band of voluntary and paid supporters successfully gathered enough signatures to qualify the measure for the ballot. Acting as his own legal counsel, Bruce withstood a stiff legal challenge by opponents of the initiative regarding the validity of some of the petitioned signatures.[9] The following fall, Bruce was outspent by a three-to-one margin by his opposition and had to confront a volley of negative TV and radio ads run by the adversarial "No On #1 Committee." Nevertheless, Amendment 1 prevailed in a convincing fashion on November 3, tallying 812,308 favorable votes against only 700,906 negative ones.

On election day, Bruce, a perennial gadfly, took the victory to heart. Targeting government "tax parasites" with his pet solution,[10] the fervent and irreverent author of the tax-limitation measure was understandably jubilant. The measure, he claimed, would usher into the state a new political era. "It is a new day in Colorado," Bruce heralded. "We shall be the freest state in America. We have proven beyond a doubt who is in charge in Colorado—we the people."[11] Confounding the business community, good government groups, the Colorado Municipal League, and government officials who were unilaterally opposed to the measure, a solid majority of Coloradans embraced Amendment 1. The press, while wary of the possible effects of the measure, viewed Bruce as the leader of a burgeoning conservative populist movement in Colorado.[12] Effectively weaving together the same populist-sounding rhetorical fibers used by Jarvis and Anderson, Bruce converted the negative images advanced by his adversaries into a positive picture of less government and more individual freedom. Roaring at a press conference following the election, Bruce, ever the populist, declared, "This is a chance for the alienated, disenfranchised voter who thinks that his position doesn't count anymore to regain some control in many, many different ways."[13] While those ways were not made explicit during the campaign, the tax crusader's strident message struck a cord with a majority of Coloradans.

## Taxes, Government, and the Public Mood in Colorado

An appreciation of the prevalent anti-tax and government limitation public mood in Colorado is necessary to understand and explain Douglas Bruce's ability to become an effective tax crusader. In the early 1990s, the public mood among Coloradans towards taxes and government could be best described as a rolling boil. Yet, it was quite a different atmosphere than what had existed in California and Massachusetts prior to their tax revolts. The pervasive tax and government limitation animosity in Colorado long preceded Douglas Bruce's arrival to Colorado in the mid-1980s. Colorado had always had a strong libertarian political undercurrent and the sentiment was never limited to just property taxes. Unlike the citizens of California and Massachusetts, Coloradans were not interested in merely sending their state and local government officials "a message" to reduce their taxes; many wanted to actually downsize government and cut public services at the state and local levels. In this sense, the public mood in Colorado was much more antagonistic towards taxes and government than in either of the other two states.

While heavily dependent on local taxes, Colorado's tax system—unlike Massachusetts's—was not overly dependent on local property taxes. The original state constitution of 1876 limited property taxes to a rate of six mills on the assessed valuation, with a majority override of a given locality necessary to increase the rate.[14] In addition, the legislature made sure to periodically reevaluate the state's system of taxes. In 1959, a Governor's Tax Study Group issued a detailed report which was very critical of Colorado's existing tax structure. The commission stated that over several decades Colorado's tax structure "grew up like Topsy," with "little evidence that any unified or consistent policy guided its formation."[15] Taxes on the state level were found to be "highly complex and sharply regressive," and the local tax structure, based almost exclusively on the property tax, had "lost its capacity to meet increasing costs."[16] The Tax Study Group recommended implementing, among other things, "new standards for assessing property, new provisions regarding the use of the sales tax and its administration . . . revision of the income tax structure, extension of the severance tax to additional minerals . . . and [an] increas[e] [in] the efficiency of state government."[17]

Over next two decades, the legislature substantially revised the state's tax code in order to make it more balanced. By the mid-1980s, income taxes (individual and corporate) accounted for forty-eight percent of state sources of general revenue, with sales taxes and all other taxes making up twenty-seven and twenty-six percent respectively.[18] However, in terms of combined state and local revenues, Colorado still had a heavy dependence on local taxes. Local governments nationwide accounted for a large percentage of the total revenue raised each year by both state and local government. Only New Hampshire relied more on its local governments for generating revenue. In 1986, Colorado raised less than half (48.3 percent) of its total revenue from state sources.[19] Not surprisingly, property taxes accounted for the largest source of Colorado's combined state and local revenues. In 1988, thirty-six percent of Colorado's total state and local receipts were derived from property taxes, with the general sales tax accounting for twenty-six percent, and income taxes amounting to twenty-four percent.

Property taxes in Colorado, as a result of the local tax burden on total state and local revenues, were considerably higher than in other states. In 1986, property taxes ranked fifth on a per capita basis.[20] Local governments also relied more heavily on the local sales tax. During the mid-1980s, Colorado ranked third in the nation in terms of municipal dependence on the sales tax.[21] In 1986, Coloradans paid an average of $768 in local taxes, including property and local sales taxes.[22] Municipalities raised approximately seventy percent of their revenue from the property tax, with another twenty-five percent from the sales tax and five percent from miscellaneous fees.[23] Unlike California, Colorado homeowners did not experience the problem of rapid inflation causing higher property values, and hence higher property taxes. Property assessments were actually decreasing in the late 1980s. Between 1987 and 1988, for example, assessed valuations of Colorado property declined by 4.8 percent.[24] In addition, a 1982 amendment to the state constitution equalized property tax assessments, so there were not huge disparities in property tax assessments across the state. The amendment required that residential property be assessed so that it would account for only forty-five percent of the total statewide property tax base.[25] On average, between 1985 and 1990, property taxes increased at a rate of 5.2 percent annually, with the 1990 levy amounting to only 2.5 percent more than the previous year.[26]

By the late 1980s, when Douglas Bruce came upon the scene, Colorado's taxes, compared with other states, were not exceptionally high. While Colorado's combined state and local taxes rose 44.6 percent between 1983 and 1988, the rest of the nation averaged a per capita tax rate increase of 45.7 percent.[27] Contrasted with other states, Colorado's overall tax burden was relatively low. Between 1970 and 1985, Colorado's ratio of taxes to income was equal or below the national average.[28] In 1986, Colorado ranked sixteenth in the nation in terms of combined state and local taxes per capita.[29] The state's three percent sales tax was one of the lowest in the country, the state's corporate income tax rates were among the lowest, and personal income taxes were slightly above average. Only local property taxes and local sales taxes in Colorado fell above the national average.[30] "On balance," Thomas Cronin and Robert Loevy noted in 1993, "Colorado taxes, state and local combined, are at the national mean."[31] As one longtime observer of Colorado politics observed, "This isn't a tax-happy state. If anything, it's too tax-timid for its own fiscal health. The legislature started slashing taxes in 1977, when there was a big budget surplus, and didn't stop even after the economy started to go sour in 1982."[32]

Instead of trying to understand the public mood in Colorado with respect to taxes by focusing on specific numbers, it is more helpful to appreciate the political culture of the state. Embedded in the psyche of Colorado is an intense and deep-seated skepticism towards government and taxes. In the 1940s, journalist John Gunther remarked poignantly that Colorado "is conservative politically, economically, financially . . . I do not mean reactionary. Just conservative, with the kind of conservativeness that does not budge an inch for anybody or anything unless pinched or pushed."[33] Historically, the outlook of Coloradans towards their government has been closely tied to the state's economic fortunes. With its heavy economic dependence on natural resources, Colorado has gone through several turbulent boom-and-bust cycles over the years. In turn, Coloradans have tended to lash out at the government during times of economic hardship.[34]

This libertarian attitude sets the political culture of Colorado apart from Massachusetts and to a lesser extent California.[35] As such, the tax revolt of the 1990s was not a result of inflation and skyrocketing property taxes or the overdependency on one tax. Rather, the widespread negative public mood in the state towards taxes and government was simmering for years. The negative attitudes towards government and taxes can be traced directly to the Great Depression. Writing during the depression in 1936, Don Sowers, a professor at the University of Colorado at Boulder, commented, "The overall tax limitation movement [in Colorado] is of comparatively recent development, and may be said to be an outgrowth of the depression period."[36] According to Sowers, "The depression presented an opportunity for the distressed alarm of heavy tax burdens to place restrictions on tax levies in the state constitution."[37] In the early 1990s, following another harsh recessionary period, arguments for less government intervention and more economic freedom resurfaced. Calls for tax cuts and smaller government once again started to fill the political arena. So, unlike Massachusetts and California, the primary reason for the attack on government in Colorado seemed not to be due to property taxes rising too fast, but that the economy was still sluggish following the state's latest recession.

In the early 1990s, Colorado's political culture was similar to what Gunther had described over four decades earlier. Citizens of the Centennial State could still be characterized by their rugged individualism, frontier ethos, and skepticism towards government. The state's hallmarks were still limited government, economic freedom, and a boom and bust economy. As two students of Colorado state politics summarized in the early 1990s, "Colorado is a pro-business, pro-work, antigovernment, and antitax state."[38] The anti-tax and government limitation attitude in Colorado was not a fleeting reflection of the national mood that permeated the U.S. during the 1980s. Coloradans did not blindly follow the lead of Californians after they passed Proposition 13 in 1978. Property tax reduction was never a fad in Colorado. In many ways the approval of Amendment 1 in 1992 demonstrated how Colorado's anti-tax and government limitation attitude was rooted much deeper than in either California or Massachusetts.

Polling data from the early 1990s revealed the widespread anti-tax mood in Colorado prior to the vote on Amendment 1. In the fall of 1990, a statewide poll found that sixty-nine percent of Colorado residents thought the state government was "doing only a fair or poor job of 'keeping state taxes down.'"[39] Another fifty-seven percent of those surveyed "agreed with the statement that 'taxes in Colorado are too high, and the state legislature has got to do something about cutting the state's tax burden.'"[40] The lingering effects of the state's severe economic downturn during the 1980s convinced many citizens that the state government needed to curtail its taxes and spending. Despite the numbers to the contrary, the perception among Coloradans was that their state and local governments in the early 1990s were appropriating too much money in taxes.

The overarching sentiment toward government of Coloradans was even more tempestuous. In contrast to the residents of California and Massachusetts prior to their "tax revolts," Coloradans were on the whole more suspicious of their government. A surprising number of Coloradans in the early 1990s were displeased with how their state government generally functioned. In a 1990 statewide survey, less than forty percent of Coloradans polled believed their state government was run "efficiently and effectively." More than half of those polled added that "their state government was wasteful and inefficient."[41] Most Coloradans also believed that special interests had "undue influence and that state officials do not decide in the best interests of the people."[42] In spite of Colorado's reputation for a "squeaking clean" state government, Coloradans in the early 1990s expressed deep-seated skepticism toward their public officials and institutions.[43] They perceived state government as being hostile toward the interests of ordinary people. Of those polled in the 1990 survey, over fifty percent believed that they could trust the state government "almost never" or only "some of the time."[44] Sixty percent of those polled believed that state government was "unduly influence by big campaign contributions."[45] Over three-fifths of those surveyed believed that "the state does what is right only some of the time, or 'almost never.' "[46] "On balance," the authors of the survey concluded, "Coloradans are skeptical, if not hostile, to state government."[47]

The widespread negative attitude of Coloradans in the early 1990s toward their government and state and local taxes was indeed striking. Yet, apparently the enmity of Coloradans did not run that deep. Surveys indicated harsh views of Coloradans towards the taxation powers of the state, but when the surveys probed deeper, people were not very inclined to alter the tax system. Political pollster Floyd Ciruli noted that, "While Colorado public opinion is in favor of tax limitation, its views are not strongly held."[48] Still, many Coloradans, if given the chance, would choose to lower their taxes and curtail government spending. Douglas Bruce offered them that chance.

## Waging A War of Attrition

During the fall of 1992, Bruce realized his ballot initiative faced an uphill battle. The 1992 election was not the first time residents of Colorado were given the opportunity to vote directly on an anti-tax/government-limitation initiative. In 1988 and 1990 Bruce placed similar measures on the ballot which were voted down by his fellow citizens. Prior to Bruce's involvement, Coloradans had cast their votes six times between 1966 and 1986 on a variety of anti-tax popular initiatives. Each time, voters soundly defeated the proposed measure.[49] Coloradans, it seemed, did not have a great penchant to reduce the taxation powers of the state. Thus, for many residents of the state, it came as somewhat of a shock when Amendment 1 won the approval of a majority of the state's voters. No one was more surprised than Douglas Bruce.

The story behind Bruce's involvement with initiatives limiting the taxing and spending powers of state and local government dates back to 1986. As Californians were once again ratcheting in government by requiring a majority vote by citizens on local tax increases, Coloradans were voting down another tax limitation initiative.[50] On November 4, 1986, Coloradans rejected Amendment 4 by 243,500 votes—sixty-two to thirty-eight percent—a sizable twenty-four percent margin.[51] Amendment 4 was the first popular initiative placed on the Colorado ballot in nearly a decade that called for a restriction on taxes and government spending. The measure would have diminished the taxing authority of state and local governments by requiring voter approval for any new tax or increase in taxes, although it excluded increases in licenses, fees, fines and permits from a plebiscite.

Conceived by John and Diane Cox, farmers from the western slope town of Palisade, the initiative began literally at the grassroots level. Concerned with rising property taxes, increased government spending, and the falling property value of their western slope farm, the Coxes started a petition drive by contacting "their friends" and fellow farmers.[52] Soon after, they established the Association for Colorado Taxpayers to support their effort. During the fall of 1985, the Coxes and their supporters collected over 80,000 signatures to place the initiative on the statewide ballot. Amendment 4 stipulated that state and local elected officials could not impose any new, or increase any existing taxes without the majority of voters approving such a measure during a general election in an even-numbered year.[53] The measure received most of its popular support in Colorado west of the continental divide, but was aided along the more densely populated front range by several conservative people and groups. The Coxes were helped by the organizational support of the Colorado Union of Taxpayers, the financial support of Denver businessman and official spokesman of the initiative, Jake Jabs, the backing of Ruth Prendergast, the Colorado Director of the National Conservative Political Action Committee, and the out-of-state endorsement by Paul Gann, Jarvis's erstwhile Proposition 13 sidekick.[54]

The Coxes and their allies had a leg up on their detractors rolling into election season. In early fall, the measure still faced no formal opposition, as the public opinion polls reflected. In mid-September, surveys indicated that nearly sixty percent of likely voters favored the measure. By early October, the margin increased to sixty-three percent backing the measure and only twenty-seven percent opposing it. But the margin of support quickly started to narrow during October. On October 20, a poll found support and opposition for the measure was nearly deadlocked, with forty-five percent in favor and forty-four percent opposed; by October 29, support hovered around thirty-six percent. As support for the measure dwindled, the general public was beginning to register serious doubts about the proposed amendment.[55]

*Figure 6.1*   Mike Keefe (*Denver Post*) editorial cartoon on Amendment 4

The steep decline in favorable public opinion was fairly predictable. This was, after all, the first tax limitation measure to be placed on the ballot since the late 1970s. As election day neared, the natural constituencies opposing the measure began to mobilize their troops. In September, an alliance of over fifty business, education, and government interests organized a political committee, Citizens for Representative Government, to oppose Amendment 4. Among the outspoken opponents of the measure was the three-term Democratic Governor of Colorado, Dick Lamm.[56] By late October, Citizens for Representative Government had raised $274,910 to oppose the measure, whereas the Association of Colorado Taxpayers had amassed only $24,986.[57] The non-partisan, citizen-supported Colorado Public Expenditure Council came out against the measure as well. Calling the proposed amendment, "an impractical solution to the frustration of taxpayers," the non-profit research agency argued that the state had plenty of statutory limits on state and local spending, which were "a far better solution than placing constitutional handcuffs on those we elect to represent us."[58] By late October, Citizens for Representative Government, out-spending and out-advertising the supporters of the initiative by a twelve-to-one margin, was able to gradually sway public opinion against the measure.[59]

Bruce became involved with the campaign for Amendment 4 almost immediately upon his arrival in Colorado. Although a resident of Colorado for less than a year, Bruce served as the El Paso County spokesman for Amendment 4. He claims to have put in "about forty hours" campaigning for the measure between August and November, 1986.[60] A California transplant, Bruce was quite familiar with, but not active in Howard Jarvis and Paul Gann's various tax-limitation efforts. He voted for Prop. 13 in 1978, but did not meet Jarvis until some time after the election.[61] In contrast to the successful 1978 Proposition 13, Bruce thought the Coxes' initiative was "not well written," and the Association for Colorado Taxpayers had, "no organization, no campaign." Instead, Bruce was attracted to Amendment 4 because it was a "statement of principle."[62]

After the defeat of Amendment 4, a group of people who had been involved in promoting the measure called a meeting to critically assess what went wrong. Bruce was the only attorney in the group, but he was new to the state and was seen as an outsider. After the meeting, Bruce drew up a draft of a tax and government limitation ballot measure. Other members of the group thought it was too long; they wanted a more simple version. The tax limitation group then split into two factions. The faction opposed to Bruce's measure – what Bruce labeled the "kick 'em in the balls school"—was dominated by residents of Freemont County who wanted a measure similar to California's Prop. 13, which would include commercial properties in a property tax cut.[63] The other faction, led by Bruce, wanted a broad tax relief measure "that would work." Both factions collected signatures in an effort to get their measures on the ballot: "We did, they didn't," Bruce recalled later.[64]

Characterizing the failed Amendment 4 as, "just a tap on the shoulder" of government officials bent on spending hard-earned tax dollars, Bruce described his 1988 initiative as "a rap across the knuckles with a ruler."[65] At the press conference he called to launch his 1988 campaign, Bruce shunned the label "tax protestor." He claimed the image conjured up "tax evaders, people that live up in the Idaho Panhandle with a gun under their bed and meet around bonfires."[66] Rather, Bruce said his supporters were "ordinary citizens of all stripes, all walks of life, all income levels."[67]

Bruce's initiative, bolstered by his newly created political committee, the Taxpayers Bill of Rights (TABOR), ended up being one of four anti-tax measures proposed by various anti-tax groups that year. In addition to the measure proposed to the Secretary of State by the Freemont County group, John Cox and the Association for Colorado Taxpayers submitted another tax limitation measure.[68] Joseph Dodge, a mine operator and oil producer, formed a new group, Citizens That Love Colorado, and submitted a property tax limitation measure dubbed "Colorado's 13."[69] Bruce's initiative, however, was the only tax reduction measure to gather enough signatures to be placed on the November ballot. Over the summer, though, Citizens for Representative Government challenged the validity of some of the petitioned signatures. Secretary of State Natalie Meyer struck nearly a third—23,442—of Bruce's 65,340 petitioned names, leaving him 8,770 signatures short of the required number.[70] Bruce, who called Meyer's ruling "absurd," was "absolutely one hundred percent confident we are going to win in court."[71] Collecting nearly 18,000 additional signatures during a "cure period" to insure his measure, Bruce was proven correct when Denver District Judge John McMullen ruled that Secretary of State Meyer had wrongly removed valid signatures from TABOR's petitions, and that the initiative should be placed on the November 8 ballot.[72]

Amendment 6 was much more ambitious than its immediate predecessor, Amendment 4. Among other provisions, the measure would subject all new taxes and tax hikes, except in the case of emergency, to voter approval, cut state income taxes by ten percent (from five percent to four and one half percent), limit residential property taxes to one percent of the full market value, and tie state government spending to a ratio of inflation and population change.[73] Despite being more restrictive, Bruce claimed that his measure was "a moderate, comprehensive, responsible tax-and-spend limitation policy," and "not a radical major tax cut. It's not as devastating as they want to claim."[74] But in his breath, Bruce would revert to his militant declarations: "Taxes are out of control in Colorado . . . . We are leading a crusade for traditional American values—home ownership and the authority to decide how much government we are willing to pay for." Bruce continued, roaring that, "The government's power to take our money is a sword over our heads, and we must limit that power."[75] Others were not so convinced. Colorado State University political scientist, Wayne Peak, was quoted by the *New York Times* as saying, "This proposition has the superficial ring of good populist rhetoric . . . . Who's not for lowering taxes?"[76]

But during the fall campaign, Bruce summoned even more populist rhetoric. With a sharp tongue reminiscent of Jarvis's, Bruce claimed that his initiative was being unfairly maligned by establishment forces who he called "closet cowards." "They don't give a damn about anything or anybody that jeopardizes their unlimited access to our hard-earned money,"

Bruce wailed at a press conference at the state Capitol.[77] Later in the campaign he hollered, "People will lie in order to get our money, and the government wants our money."[78] No individual or group was immune from his scathing vituperation. "Young people," Bruce cried, "who never hurt anybody are paying the emotional price for the greed of the special interests and the lust for power of the politicians who want to keep their death grip on our wallets."[79] When questioned as to what would happen if his initiative suffered the same fate as Amendment 4 in 1986, Bruce commented, "If they buy this election, we will be back next time . . . with a two-by-four to hit them on the back of the head. . . . And like Dorothy, they will wake up in Kansas."[80]

Bruce was decidedly optimistic about the chances of his initiative, and with good reason. Just one month before the election, on October 1, 1988, an independent *Denver Post*-Channel 4 News (KCNC) poll revealed that the public favored the measure by a sixty-two to twenty-nine percent margin.[81] Subsequent tracking polls throughout October found people favoring the measure by over fifty percent.[82] It was not until October 31 that the *Denver Post*-Channel 4 poll registered a majority of voters in opposition to the measure.[83]

As in 1986, part of the explanation for the wide margin of support for Bruce's measure in October was the fact that opponents of Amendment 6 were slow to mobilize. Many groups opposed to Bruce's initiative expected that Judge McMullen would invalidate Bruce's measure. Citizens for Representative Government, the group that had formed two years earlier to oppose Amendment 4, had a paltry $3,000 in the bank in mid-October. But between September 4 and October 23, opponents of Amendment 6 raised $161,880, well on their way to reaching their goal of a quarter of a million dollars.[84] During that period, labor organizations contributed $31,000, with the Colorado Municipal Bond Dealers Association chipping in an additional $25,000. Contributions were sizeable. The average contribution was $1,217, and of the 133 contributions, only fifty-six were for $50 or less.[85] By election day, Citizens for Representative Government reaped an astounding $418,922 in contributions, nearly double its targeted goal.[86]

In addition to raising buckets of cash, several prominent organizations and individuals spoke out forcefully against the measure. The non-partisan Colorado Public Expenditure Council remarked that the "adoption of a far-reaching constitutional amendment, whose effects are unknown and subject to years of litigation, will not serve the best interests of Colorado as it works toward economic recovery."[87] For his part, Governor Roy

Romer "barnstormed the state" and gave as many as "nine speeches a day against the measure."[88] Calling the measure, "the most dangerous thing I've seen in thirty-five years,"[89] and "a terrorist amendment," Romer alleged Bruce's measure was "almost like if you wanted to put a bomb into the organized affairs of the state."[90] The president of the Colorado Association of Commerce and Industry (CACI), the state's most influential business association, called the measure, "a draconian disaster." A week before the election, U.S. West president Richard McCormick declared Amendment 6 "is bad business," as it "sends exactly the wrong signal at exactly the wrong time to businesses looking at Colorado."[91] Republican State Senator Ted Strickland, the Colorado Senate president, lambasted Bruce's measure as "a meat ax approach" to governance.[92] Strickland, who two years earlier had railed against the high level of taxes in his unsuccessful bid for Governor against Romer, said the measure spelled "the end of representative government."[93] Three former governors and arch-conservative U.S. Senator Bill Armstrong, denounced the measure.[94] Even tax-limitation proponent Joe Dodge, author of his own 1988 measure that failed to amass enough signatures to be placed on the ballot, called Bruce's Amendment 6 "a bad initiative."[95]

Despite altering the strategy of the 1986 initiative campaign, which had courted voters living in the western half of the state, Bruce was not able to generate much interest for his measure by focusing it at the more heavily populated front range.[96] The thirty-nine-year-old was having trouble raising money for his campaign. Less than a month before the election, on October 23, TABOR had raised only $11,930. In late October, Bruce received some much-needed financial relief from Jerry Brock of Lakewood, who gave $7,500 on October 28. But in the final days of the campaign, TABOR received contributions of only $35,049 from a total of seventy-five contributors. Desperate, Bruce pumped $50,000 of his own money into TABOR's empty war chest only days before the election.[97] Calling a press conference to announce his loan, Bruce said, "I'm doing it because I'm a patriot, because I care about democracy . . . . I'm putting my money where my mouth is."[98] Bruce's personal financial commitment to his measure, while honorable, was not nearly enough to hold off the advance of the better-heeled opposition. Contrary to his prediction that "On Nov. 8, the voice of the people will send a message that cannot be ignored—that government cannot push us around anymore, that it has no divine right to take our money without our permission," Colorado voters pummeled Bruce's first ballot initiative effort.[99] Falling woefully short of passage, Amendment 6 gained only thirty-eight percent of the popular vote.

A year later, in late 1989, Bruce was back in the news. Despite telling one reporter following his 1988 defeat that "he wouldn't try again," Bruce later recanted. According to the reporter, Bruce "blithely acknowledged that he'd lied" because he wanted "to put the media off his trail, allowing him time to regroup."[100] Less than a year after his 1988 defeat, Bruce and his small band of loyal supporters successfully gathered enough signatures to place his second anti-tax/government limitation measure on the November 6, 1990 ballot. On October 17, 1989, Bruce submitted 74,000 petition signatures, 23,000 more than the 50,668 valid signatures required by law.[101] At a press conference at the Secretary of State's Office, Bruce declared, "We are going to win in 1990. I say that unequivocally."[102]

According to Bruce, the new measure, designated on the ballot as Amendment 1, was "significantly rewritten to answer several criticisms of last year's Amendment 6."[103] Bruce's new measure called for a restrictive one percent residential property tax cap to be phased in over ten years, and voter approval for any new or increased taxes or fees that exceeded an index based on the rate of inflation and population growth. However, it allowed for some emergency tax increases and did not call for retroactive repeals of tax increases. Called by one political observer, a "toned-down and polished-up successor to Amendment 6," Amendment 1 was nevertheless an unwieldy measure consisting of 1,857 words.[104] "For sheer complexity," one journalist lamented, Amendment 1 "deserves a prize."[105] Not surprisingly, Bruce brushed aside criticisms, referring instead to his initiative as a "moderate, responsible curb on the tax-and-spend politics of the recent past."[106] "We are not anti-tax," Bruce declared euphemistically, "we are pro-democracy."[107]

As was the case two years earlier, Bruce's measure faced an array of interests opposing his measure. Foremost in opposition was the Colorado legislature. During the spring of 1989, the legislature considered placing its own version of a tax limitation referendum, which was backed by business groups, on the 1990 ballot in order to defuse Bruce's efforts. In addition, business groups, in an attempt to preempt what they perceived as Bruce's more radical anti-tax/government limitation measure, led a brief campaign to get their own version of tax limitation on the ballot. However, the two business umbrella groups leading the effort—the National Federation of Independent Business and CACI—failed to gather enough signatures to place their alternative measure on the November ballot.

Still, foes of Bruce's amendment began to unite earlier than they did in 1988, with Governor Romer, himself running for re-election, spearheading the opposition.[108] Bruce expected as much, saying that "this will be the hot issue of the year," whereas "the governor's race is going to put you to sleep."[109] Calling themselves Common Sense Colorado, opponents of Bruce's measure once again gathered an impressive array of supporters from the ranks of business, labor, and government. Fearing the end of municipal bonds in Colorado, the bond dealers alone donated $43,000 against Amendment 1.[110] Yet, as Lyle Kyle, the retired director of the Colorado Public Expenditure Council, commented, "Many in the business community don't seem to be as exercised about it this time around."[111] While at first Common Sense Colorado raised less opposing Amendment 1 than Citizens for Representative Government did in 1988 against Amendment 6, the group still managed to collect $83,000 by mid-October.[112] By election day, though, the coalition had raised $443,787, $24,865 more than its predecessor had amassed to defeat Bruce's 1988 measure.[113]

Bruce knew his measure would face tough opposition. He accurately predicted that TABOR would "be outspent by the special interests, the politicians, and the bond dealers."[114] However, unlike in 1988, Bruce was able to round up some influential supporters of his own. Many people were attracted to his softer, less austere-sounding measure and agreed with Bruce that the opponents of his first effort, "basically bought and stole the election."[115] John Andrews, the Republican Party's nominee for governor, Vern Bickel, a wealthy Boulder businessman and Director of the Colorado Union of Taxpayers, prominent state Senators Terry Considine and Joe Winkler, and a handful of state Representatives all came out in support of Amendment 1.[116] Calling Bruce "a great Colorado patriot," Andrews appointed himself as the "chief political spokesman" for Amendment 1, although Bruce insisted that he was still in charge of the proposal.[117]

In October, largely because of the high profile endorsements Bruce was able to procure, Amendment 1 was up in the polls. Throughout the month, public opinion surveys commissioned by the *Denver Post* and TV station Channel 4 (KCNC) found the measure ahead in the polls. Although support for the measure had dropped from the high of 60 percent on October 2, 48 percent of these polled on October 31 still favored Amendment 1.[118] With growing confidence, Bruce announced, "We think the day of reckoning is coming."[119]

*Figure 6.2*   Doug Bruce delivering petitions to the Office of the Secretary of State. [A *Denver Post* photo]

Not only was Bruce's 1990 measure doing better than his 1988 effort in the battle over public opinion, his political organization, TABOR, was raising more money. Relying more heavily on mailing lists he purchased from the Colorado Republican Party and the El Paso County Republicans to solicit contributions, Bruce greatly increased not only the dollar amount, but also the number of contributions to TABOR.[120] Over the first six months of 1990, more than 1,000 people gave money to Bruce's outfit. Between January and September 1990, TABOR collected over $45,000 in support of Amendment 1.[121] By mid-October, Bruce and his TABOR Committee received additional money from over 700 people, and had collected a total of $114,477, over nine times as much money as in 1988 at that time.[122] TABOR ended up raising $179,352 for Amendment 1 in 1990, including two separate $15,000 contributions made by Bruce and Vern Bickel in late October.[123]

Although TABOR was substantially outspent by the opposition, the ballot measure was too close to call on election night. On November 6, 1990, Bruce's statewide initiative lost by the thinnest of margins, 51.1 to 48.9 percent, only 21,600 votes. His proposed amendment to the state constitution won a majority of votes in seventeen of the state's sixty-three counties, whereas in 1988, Bruce's measure posted a majority of votes in only six counties.[124] Once again Bruce claimed that the political establishment "outspent and outscared us."[125] But surprisingly, Bruce assigned some of the blame for the measure's defeat to the voters themselves. Bruce maintained disapprovingly that the voters "did not fight back, but they timidly and gullibly surrendered to this blackmail."[126] After the election, still reluctant to admit defeat, Bruce reflected that it did not seem as though in the future citizens of Colorado were "going to enact anything close to Amendment 1."[127] His tax and government limitation measures evidently failed to capture the public mood in Colorado. Two short years later, however, Bruce would prove himself wrong.

## The Push for a Revamped Amendment 1

Bruce may not have successfully tapped the public mood in 1990, but his initiative was certainly a step in the right direction. "Many taxpayers out there," Bruce noted in the fall of 1990, "are just frustrated enough—particularly at the federal government—they're just wanting to strike out against something."[128] The Republican leadership of the Colorado legislature, visibly shaken by the near victory of Bruce's 1990 measure, also felt the frustrations of Colorado taxpayers. Many in the state capitol sensed the impending triumph of a popular tax revolt led by Bruce. Before the legislature began its 1991 session, legislative leaders placed on the legislative calendar a tax limitation measure that would incorporate "about sixty-five percent of Amendment 1's provisions."[129] The elected leadership, though, made it quite clear they would not "be bullied into Doug Bruce's calendar."[130]

While the legislature again slowly deliberated its own measure under the golden dome of the state house, Bruce was busy foisting his anti-tax efforts on his hometown, Colorado Springs. After being shutout in his first two statewide efforts, Bruce and his supporters collected enough signatures in Colorado Springs to place two tax limitation measures on the city's April 2, 1991 ballot. With almost no organized opposition, both of Bruce's measures passed easily. Amending the city's charter, the initiatives required that a public vote be held on any proposed tax increases, limited the property tax rate to seven mills, and lowered the city's sales tax."[131] His "campaign rekindled," Bruce indicated that "we have our eye on" other Colorado municipalities, including Arvada, Lakewood, Grand Junction and Pueblo.[132] He warned, "This is really guerrilla warfare . . . . You go around and you grab a city here and one there, and pretty soon you are ready to take the capital."[133]

In truth, Bruce had no intention of giving up his statewide tax reform effort. Immediately after his triumph in Colorado Springs, he curtly reminded state legislators that, "the clock is ticking." He politely told the legislators that, "If they think they can stall and the issue will go away, they're mistaken."[134] He threatened to place another initiative on the 1992 ballot if the state legislature did not pass what he considered to be a satisfactory tax and government limitation bill by the end of the legislative session. When both houses failed to muster two-thirds majorities to place an acceptable referendum on the 1992 ballot, Bruce made good on his threat.

During the fall of 1991, Bruce and his supporters collected just enough signatures to land his third statewide attempt on the November 1992 ballot. Concerned that he would not secure the minimum 50,279 valid signatures necessary to place his constitutional amendment on the ballot, Bruce started paying individuals to circulate petitions.[135] On November 16, Bruce submitted 71,120 petitioned signatures to the Office of Secretary of State. Momentum seemed to be in Bruce's favor. An independent poll in early

November 1991 on the question of tax limits found voters favoring Bruce's amendment sixty-four to thrity-one percent, with the rest undecided.[136]

Once again, though, Bruce's petitioned signatures were found wanting by the Office of the Secretary of State. Secretary of State Meyer, Bruce's seasoned nemesis, ruled on December 6 not to certify the initiative after she disqualified thousands of signatures. Meyer threw out more than a third of the signatures, leaving Bruce's measure 2,224 signatures short of the required number.[137] The Secretary ruled that most of the contested signatures did not belong to registered voters. Furious, Bruce called a press conference to castigate Meyer: "The woman is a crook. She is corrupt. She is viciously anti-petition and anti-democratic . . . . She's not going to get away with this."[138] Bruce declared he was going to refuse to collect additional signatures during the fifteen day "cure period" as allowed by the constitution. Instead, he vowed to challenge the voided names, "signature-by-signature."[139] As an administrative hearing was being set to test the legality of the Secretary's removal of the petitioned signatures, Bruce publicly confronted Meyer, calling her "Meyer the Liar."[140] A few days before the hearing was to go forward, though, Meyer acquiesced, reversing her earlier decision not to certify the measure for the ballot. With the measure approved, Bruce claimed he was "vindicated," and recommended Meyer "go on a long ocean cruise to regain her mental and moral balance."[141]

With the petition victory under his belt, Bruce regained his momentum. His campaign was bolstered when a competing tax limitation measure failed to make it on the November ballot as many of Bruce's opponents had hoped. During the spring, the Republican leadership of the legislature, again dawdling, failed to place a watered-down version of a tax-limitation referendum on the ballot. Although the CACI lobbied hard, the House of Representatives was unable to muster the super-majority needed to offer the voters a ballot measure to compete with Bruce's initiative.[142] Following the legislative defeat, CACI attempted to place its own alternative tax-limitation proposal on the ballot—which it called a "moderate alternative" to Bruce's measure—but the group failed to collect enough valid signatures.[143] Bruce's initiative, again dubbed Amendment 1 by the Office of the Secretary of State, was the sole tax and government limitation ballot measure that the voters would consider come November.

Bruce's 1992 version of tax and government reform partially resembled its 1990 namesake. On the whole, though, it was a much more complicated measure than any of its predecessors. The measure not only restricted the revenue-raising ability of state and local governments; it also limited the

---

TAX LIMITATIONS — VOTING

An amendment to the Colorado constitution to require voter approval for certain state and local government tax revenue increases and debt; to restrict property, income and other taxes; to limit the rate of increase in state and local government spending; to allow additional initiative and referendum elections; and to provide for the mailing of information to registered voters.

---

*Figure 6.3*   The Abbreviated Ballot Title of Amendment 1

spending ability of state and local governments. Specifically, Amendment 1 called for a popular vote on any new taxes, tax hikes, or long-term government debt; required the state government to limit its annual spending to the rate of inflation plus population changes; constrained local governments to limit their annual spending to the rate of inflation plus changes in the property tax rate; and limited the annual growth of school district spending to the rate of inflation plus changes in student enrollment. Unlike his previous initiative, Bruce's 1992 measure did not require voter approval for fee increases.[144] In contrast to Proposition 13 and Proposition 2 1/2, the amendment did not place a ceiling on property tax increases or call for immediate property tax cuts. Rather, Bruce's measure concentrated on limiting future growth of state and local spending and taxation. David Keating of the National Taxpayers Union, one of the nation's oldest tax limitation organizations, praised the measure, calling it "the next wave of tax revolt," and "the most comprehensive tax and spending limitation in any state."[145]

The numerous enigmatic provisions of the labyrinth-like document made it difficult for critics to analyze; many claimed that the measure was "too lengthy and ambiguous."[146] The Denver Metro Convention and Visitors Bureau was one of the chief organizers of the coalition formed to oppose Amendment 1. It warned its members belonging to the tourist industry, "This is just the tip of the iceberg. Increased interest payments because of lower bond ratings, loss of economic development and jobs, elimination of services . . . [have] been the fallout of a similar bill in California."[147] John Lay, a spokesperson for the No On #1 Committee, said of Amendment 1, "I think it has kind of a devilish, counterproductive side to it;" even the proponents of the measure, "don't necessarily know what it's going to do, they know good and well it's not going to be positive. They just want to be disruptive."[148] Throughout the fall, Amendment 1's "ponderous complexities" were frequently the subject of critical political commentary.[149] Although opponents remained dubious towards the measure, there was a sense this round that the amendment might pass. As opponent Pat Boyle, Vice President of CACI, stated, "Mr. Bruce is the avatar of a movement that has been growing over the past two election cycles. . . . Once you get forty-nine percent of the public to support a proposal—no matter how radical—the idea has become mainstream."[150]

Despite the ongoing and steady criticism from the usual suspects, Bruce was able to increase support for his latest proposal for three reasons. First, he convinced leaders as well as rank-and-file Republicans that his Amendment was sound fiscal policy. Bruce proudly bragged that his measure was, "explicitly endorsed by the Republican nominees for governor and lieutenant governor, and received the endorsement of seventy-one percent of the delegates to the Republican state convention."[151] Second, he reassured some of the business community that Amendment 1 would be good for the state's economy. In an op-ed piece, he noted that both the national Federation of Independent Businesses and the Colorado Farm Bureau endorsed the measure.[152] Third, Bruce consciously tried to distance himself from his measure. At forty-three, the non-practicing attorney played the innocent: "I'm no anarchist . . . . I'm not a threat. I just don't like government paternalism."[153] He objected to the notion that he pushed his initiatives purely for his own self-aggrandizement. "This is not an ego trip for me. I'm not on the ballot. But the fact that opponents keep attacking me suggests they don't have enough ammunition with which to attack the initiative."[154] Distancing himself from his measure seemed to lend credence to it, as it helped to draw in a broader array of supporters.

As a result of Bruce's new game plan, TABOR received more contributions than in either of his two previous campaigns. During the first six months of 1992, Bruce accepted 380 contributions of $25 or more, totaling $20,705. Nearly all of the money came from individuals, with an average donation of about $55 dollars. But between July 27 and September 5, TABOR netted only $3,746 from fifty-five people.[155] TABOR was hurting financially heading into the fall campaign.

In early September, TABOR bought a mailing list from the National Taxpayers Union in Iowa (to whom TABOR paid $5,849 for the list), and sent out a mass mailing to solicit contributions.[156] On the surface, the mailings seemed to work. In a little over a month, TABOR harvested over $120,000 in contributions. Over 350 people and small business contributed money for the measure. However, $94,930 of the $120,668 (seventy-nine percent) came from just two sources. Iowans for Tax Relief,

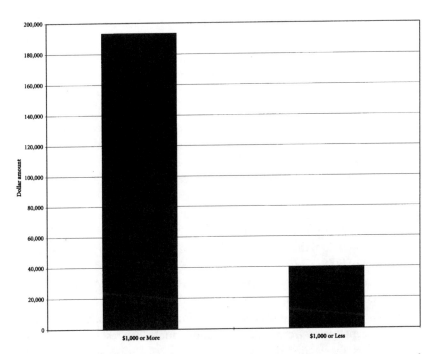

*Figure 6.4* Total Campaign Contributions to TABOR in 1992 in amounts greater and less than $1,000, September 6–November 3, 1992

headquartered in Muscatine, IA, the same little town in which the National Taxpayers Union was stationed, gave $30,000 in mid-September and early October to TABOR. Boulder businessman, Vern Bickel, wrote TABOR three checks in September and October for a total of $64,929.75.[157] Of the $233,144 that TABOR raised between September 6 and election day, eighty-three percent came from just five sources, including a check for $1,000 from the group Howard Jarvis founded after the passage of Proposition 13, American Tax Reduction Movement, and a $87,000 "loan" Bruce gave to his own campaign.[158]

With the influx of money, Bruce hired a Denver public relations and marketing firm, GW Marketing, to run the paid media side of his campaign. Greg Walerius, President and sole employee of the firm, had worked with Bruce on his two previous campaigns, but in a less formal capacity.[159] Bruce and Walerius teamed up to write a handful of campaign ads for the measure. The most effective ad they designed was a spot they called "Pinocchio." Armed with an inexpensive video camera, Walerius dressed up as the prevaricating marionette and solemnly cautioned viewers about all the cuts in public services that would happen if Amendment 1 passed. With each assertion, his nose grew longer. At the end of the thirty-second ad, Walerius discarded his mask with the ungainly proboscis, and stated in a deep voice, "They're lying. . . . None of it is true." Over the span of the fall campaign, TABOR ended up paying GW Marketing $170,661 to produce and advertise the low-cost spots over the airwaves.[160] As in previous campaigns, Bruce did not draw a salary and was not reimbursed for his work, although his long time treasurer, Clyde Harkins, did reimburse himself for food and travel.[161]

Organized opposition to Bruce's measure was again solid in 1992. As in past years, many elected officials were critical of Bruce's effort. The No On #1 Committee—spearheaded by the Greater Denver Chamber of Commerce, the Colorado Municipal League, the Colorado Municipal Bond Dealers Association, the Colorado Education Association and the American Federation of State, County and Municipal Employees—had little difficulty raising over half a million dollars to thwart Amendment 1. Although it had no money in its coffers in early September, the coalition was able to rake in $448,099 by October 18. Only a small fraction of the total collected, $14,664 (three percent), came from ninety-one individuals. The rest came from special interests. By election day, No on #1 had raised a total of $602,349. The bond dealers wrote checks to the No on #1 for $72,000, Colorado teachers gave $50,000, Colorado Ski Country USA anted up $30,000, the Colorado Association of School Executives gave $29,200, the Colorado Professional Fire Fighters chipped in $15,000, and the Colorado Realtors gave $7,500. In addition, the teachers and the Denver Art Museum and the Natural History Museum conducted separate polls for the opposition, totaling $46,700 in-kind contributions.[162] The coalition paid Stealey & Associates, a Denver consulting firm, $75,000 to direct the campaign, and it spent $463,623 on promotional materials, including a sum of $392,125 paid to the Englewood advertising firm, Karsh & Hagan, for television production and media buys. On advertising alone, No on #1 outspent Bruce's TABOR Committee by two-and-one-half times.[163]

While television and radio airwaves blared with thirty-second plugs for and against the measure, news coverage of the measure waned. The fray over tax and government limitations was not nearly as closely covered as in previous years. The attention given by the media was more diffuse. Fewer news stories, editorials, and op-ed pieces concerning the measure appeared in the state's major newspaper, the *Denver Post*.[164] The *Post*, unlike its coverage of Bruce's previous two measures, did not hire a firm to track public opinion about the measure. Independent presidential candidate Ross Perot was making a strong showing in Colorado. Most significantly, the other nine citizen initiatives on the November ballot, especially Amendment 2— the anti-gay rights amendment—seemed to divert the media away from Amendment 1. In 1992, a total of $6,863,051 was spent on ballot questions, more than twice as much as in 1990, nearly three times as much as in 1988, and seven times as much as in 1988.[165] As journalist John Racine perceptively noted:

> In past years, the amendment and its author . . . have been turned back with an aggressive, well-financed campaign waged by the state's bond dealers, business interests, government groups, and leading politicians . . . . This year, however, the diverse and complex mix of ballot issues may divert attention away from Mr. Bruce.[166]

Bruce too showed that he understood the significance of the relative lack of notice directed toward his measure when he stated, "The boring old tax limitation which usually loses isn't getting the attention it usually does."[167]

In addition to the media's focus on Amendment 2 and the three-way race for president, Governor Romer did not make Amendment 1 his principal concern. Romer, who again campaigned against Bruce's measure, attended to it with much less energy. His rather lackluster effort against Amendment 1 was partly due to the fact that he was lobbying hard against Amendment 2. But the Governor was also stumping on behalf of a statutory initiative (Amendment 6) that would increase the state sales tax by one percent to raise approximately $333 million annually for Colorado public schools, and against a school voucher amendment (Amendment 7). Bruce, realizing that Romer would not be able to focus his time against Amendment 1, commented sarcastically, "I'm happy the governor's going to be on the ballot . . . . He's basically just given me the election. I'm thinking about calling a press conference and appointing him my honorary chairman."[168]

Sounding more confident than in earlier attempts, Bruce predicted that, "I think this is the year we win. Taxes are a major issue in the national races. . . . They're playing my song."[169] An independent survey from September 30 showed voters favoring Bruce's constitutional amendment by a two-to-one margin. But in mid-October, a private poll carried out for the No On #1 Committee found support for Bruce's measure was dwindling, although a majority of potential voters still favored the measure. Bruce denounced the poll, saying "If anything, it makes me sleep better at night knowing they're so desperate they have to make things up."[170] This time, Bruce proved to be right about the public support for his measure. On November 3, 1992, Colorado voters passed Amendment 1 by nearly eight percentage points. According to political pollster, Floyd Ciruli, the fifty-four percent of Coloradans who voted for Amendment 1 wanted "to 'send a message' of disgust without much regard to the details."[171] On election day, Bruce quietly enjoyed sodas and snacks with his mother, Marjorie, before the election returns started. After the victory, though, and the obligatory election returns party, Bruce returned to his usual irascible self. "We have sent a message to the politicians; thou shall not steal," he proclaimed. "It is a new day in Colorado. We shall be the freest state in America. We have proven beyond a doubt who is in charge in Colorado—we the people."[172]

## Douglas Bruce: "Terrorist," "Patriot," or Populist Entrepreneur?

Bruce savored his role as a tax crusader, and more broadly as a populist entrepreneur. A property owner in Colorado since 1981, Bruce did not move to the Centennial State from California until 1986.[173] In California, Bruce worked as a prosecutor for the Los Angeles County District Attorney's Office until 1979, and then devoted full attention to his real estate investments. A bachelor—self-described as "single but looking"—Bruce claims he would have moved to Colorado in the early 1980s but had to first liquidate his properties in California.[174] Bruce was a resident of Colorado only a few months when he became attuned to the pervasive tax and government limitation mood in Colorado. Inspired by the success of California's tax-limiting Proposition 13—what he referred to as an inflammatory "hot rod" that stirred up government—Bruce was determined to transform the system of taxation of his adopted state.[175]

Because of his contentious ballot initiatives, the name "Douglas Bruce" rapidly became a household name in Colorado. A professional gadfly who, until the Oklahoma City Bombing in the spring of 1995, disseminated calling cards with the embossed sub-title "Terrorist" (he subsequently handed out cards with a illustration of the American flag and the word "Patriot" stamped beneath his name),[176] Bruce has sponsored at least one ballot initiative every biennial election since 1988. A Brucian initiative on the ballot has become as predictable as snow-capped Rockies in early November. But with his persistence and ever-rising notoriety for offering frivolous or self-serving ballot initiatives, Bruce has encountered an increasing number of detractors.

Public officials, from Democratic Governor Roy Romer to Republican stalwart Bill Armstrong, to conservative state Senator Ray Powers, have all denounced Bruce and his ballot-warrior tactics.[177] His antics even seem to have irritated a large chunk of the Colorado electorate. In a poll conducted in 1995, an astonishing seventy percent of Coloradans were familiar with Bruce's name. However, only sixteen percent of those polled gave him a positive rating, while a whopping forty-one percent viewed him in a negative light.[178]

Despite his low popularity rating, Bruce has managed to transform the way that the Colorado state and local governments must conduct their business. His 1992 ballot measure put a severe crimp in the way towns, cities, counties, special districts, school districts, and the state must raise and spend their tax dollars.[179] Governor Romer, a social liberal but a fiscal conservative, has accused Bruce of "throwing a bomb inside the internal workings of this society we call Colorado."[180] But Bruce had the help of a majority of Coloradans. As an anti-tax renegade, Bruce successfully tapped the tax and government limitation vein in Colorado. By securing a majority vote for his 1992 measure, in a single stroke he altered the political landscape of Colorado.

To advance his measure, Bruce did not try to mobilize the common people to act on their anti-tax/government limitation sentiment. Instead of relying on mass mobilization as a way to build support for his message, Bruce adopted a *faux* populist strategy. He never recruited people to join his organization to fight taxes and government. Furthermore, he never tried to incite the populace. Between 1988 and 1992, there were no mass demonstrations on behalf of Bruce's measures, or for that matter, any of the anti-tax/government limitation measures. The largest display of support for any of Bruce's proposals was in 1990, when "fifteen of his disciples showed up at the hearing" of a competing ballot measure, and "raised hell."[181] Instead of arousing the masses, Bruce would call up reporters to "ask for coverage and to unabashedly mooch free advertising—asking reporters to list telephone numbers in stories, hoping for contributions," and demanding not "to be referred to as a tax protester."[182] Instead of urging common people to act upon and mobilize their antipathy towards government and its taxing powers, Bruce did the leg work for them. Rather than relying on volunteers to collect petition signatures to place his measures on the ballot, Bruce in 1992 paid enterprising individuals to collect signatures. In terms of mobilizing popular support for his measures, all Bruce had to do was have people cast a "yes" vote for his initiative on election day.

Like Howard Jarvis and Barbara Anderson before him, Bruce eschewed mass-mobilization as the method to bring his message to the public. Rather, Bruce spread his message from the top-down. As a clever, able rhetorician, Bruce was a master of the sound-bite. Lacking the organizational resources to mobilize grassroots support, Bruce relied on the free media to broadcast his message. Like the "aspiring spokesmen of the 'plain people' in nineteenth-century America," Bruce understood that "the obstacles to the recruitment of a mass movement were many, varied, subtle, and in the aggregate, overwhelming."[183] Indeed, Bruce, who has remarked that "people are cheap" and "shallow," realized the importance of waging "superficial campaigns" in order to build support for his initiatives.[184] He designed a rambling tax limitation initiative and offered it to his fellow citizens as *the* solution to the Colorado's problematic tax system and intractable government. By doing so, Bruce was able to transform the ill-defined mass sentiment into a particular *faux* populist moment.

# SEVEN

# THE PROCESS OF DIRECT DEMOCRACY AND THE APPEAL OF *FAUX* POPULISM

Could any system be devised better adapted to the exaltation of cranks and the wearying of the electorate of their political duties than the giving of power . . . to the voters to submit all the fads and nostrums that their active but impractical minds can devise, to be voted on in frequent elections?
—*William Howard Taft* [1]

This new method of handling the basic law of the state is advocated in the name of democracy. In reality it is utterly and hopelessly undemocratic. While pretending to give greater rights to the voters, it deprives them of the opportunity effectively and intelligently to use their powers.
—*Editorial, New York Times* [2]

## Introduction: Initiative Fever

On June 6, 1978, Proposition 13 reignited the lost art of democracy by initiative in the American states. More than just altering the property tax landscape in California, Howard Jarvis's explosive ballot measure galvanized citizens across the nation. Prop. 13 spawned a new era of direct democracy. Elevating direct democracy to a new height, the Jarvis measure energized citizens to become involved in their state governments by participating in the initiative process.

Since the passage of the historic property tax limitation measure, the use of direct democracy has grown exponentially across the nation. *Wash-*

*ington Post* columnist David Broder has observed that, "Ballot measures are as copious in California as convertibles. They pop up in primaries and in general elections like Shasta daisies."[3] The flowering of direct democracy, of course, is not confined to the fertile soil of California. Increasingly, citizens in the states that permit the citizen initiative are serving as election day lawmakers. Bypassing their state legislatures, citizens in these states now arrive at their polling precincts expecting to cast their votes on a staggering variety of ballot proposals.

In the early 1990s, political scientists anticipated that the use of direct democracy in the American states would only grow. Political scientist David Magleby, for example, predicted in 1994 that, "based on projections from the 1990 and 1992 elections, the 1990s will set new records for direct legislation activity."[4] Ballot warriors and their attendant campaign consultants have not disappointed. They have more than exceeded scholarly expectations of the number of initiatives proposed each year. In 1996 alone, voters in twenty-two states were asked to decide a total of ninety statewide initiatives, the most ballot questions proposed nationally by citizens in over eighty years.[5]

There is every indication that direct democracy will continue to expand in the coming years, and not only in the states that currently permit the citizen initiative.[6] For over a decade there has been a national drive to extend direct democracy to the twenty-six states that currently prohibit the citizen initiative. In many of these states, dedicated citizen groups have advocated the adoption of the procedure. Citizen coalitions in a half-dozen states, with the support of a national advocacy group, the National Referendum Movement, have actively petitioned their state governments to supersede Mississippi as the latest state to sanction the initiative process. While members of state legislatures have been understandably slow to champion direct democracy, a handful of governors, including Tom Ridge of Pennsylvania, Fob James of Alabama, George Bush of Texas, George Pataki of New York, and Mike Foster of Louisiana have enthusiastically endorsed the process.[7] As such, the number of states permitting the use of the initiative process is likely only to grow during the next millenium.

## The Purity of Direct Democracy

The principal argument for the expansion and the continued use of the citizen initiative rests squarely on the grassroots and populist aspects of direct democracy. Proponents of direct democracy, liberal and conservative alike, celebrate how the initiative process encourages popular rule and citizen participation. Direct democracy allows the people to decide important questions of public policy. As tax crusader Barbara Anderson reasons:

> Our basic premise is that the money belongs to us, and they have to justify needing more of it and account for what they already have before they expect to get more. And that premise is so much at the heart of the different philosophies of government that we're talking about. One is essentially that the state owns you and has entitlement to anything you produce unless you can prove otherwise. The other—ours—is that what's ours is ours unless they can justify taking it.[8]

Advertised as an uncorrupt alternative to representative democracy, the initiative process is venerated by most practitioners as a form of unadulterated democracy.

Citizens, too, tend to see the positive side of direct democracy. Most Americans take it as an article of faith that the direct participation by the people is somehow a purer form of democracy than representative democracy. After all, it is the people who are voting on the ballot measures, not the politicians. In 1996, for example, prior to the passage of Proposition 218, a tax limitation measure placed on the ballot by the Howard Jarvis Taxpayers Association, Californians could once again be heard sounding off against local property taxes. Willis Fowler, a retired resident of Rio Linda, vowed he would vote for, "[a]nything that keeps those knuckleheads from raising taxes."[9] Political scientist Jack Citrin, a veteran observer of the initiative process, argues that direct democracy "expresses a positive yearning for voice—for the chance to be heard and to participate."[10] As citizens have become increasingly frustrated and stymied by their elected officials, they have embraced the initiative process as a viable alternative to representative government. Preferred access to the halls and committee rooms of state capitol buildings is no longer a prerequisite for citizens to be able to alter state and local public policy. Theoretically, any citizen or interest group may propose a ballot measure. Hence, citizens understandably view the process of direct democracy as being radically democratic.

With respect to tax limitation measures, tax crusaders tend to peddle their ballot measures as the citizen initiative in its purest form. They promote their tax and government spending limitation efforts as broad-based tax revolts. Springing naturally from the people, they contend that their measures are quintessential populist uprisings. The tax crusader is merely directing a grassroots, people's army. With the small financial contributions from their members, they take up the good fight against the entrenched governmental and economic interests that thwart tax cuts. They see their pet solutions as being emblematic of what the Progressive reformers had in mind when they pushed for the initiative a century ago. They laud their tax limitation measures as examples of how direct democracy can help otherwise marginalized citizens and groups participate more fully in the making of public policy. Framing the practice of citizens voting directly on the taxing (and hence, spending) powers of the state as a question of justice, they rely heavily on populist-sounding pronouncements. "It's only fair," California tax crusader Joel Fox reasoned in 1996, that the taxpayers decide these fiscal questions directly. "[T]he money is coming out of their wallets."[11] As Fox and others bent on reining in government largess see it, the initiative process enables the little guy to take on Big Brother. It is democracy in action. "The initiative petition is pure, direct democracy," Anderson observed more than a decade after the passage of Proposition 2 1/2. "It's probably the wave of the future."[12]

The approbation of direct democracy by Anderson, Fox, and the other tax crusaders is largely grounded in their firm belief that the present system of representative government is fundamentally flawed. Anderson, for example, claims that the Massachusetts state legislature is generally unrepresentative of the interests of homeowners and small property owners. While the initiative process may not be perfect, she contends that it is surely better than the legislative process. Anderson reasons that:

> You have the ballot questions where the voters vote pro or con, and they may or may not have a lot of in depth understanding on it. Then you have the legislative process, where I guarantee that they [legislators] don't have an in-depth understanding of it. Plus they have the added confusion of having to appease their leadership and their party, and [they must] trade off their vote with the representative sitting next to them who will only vote on their issue if they vote on his. You throw all that together and the initiative petition process, no matter how compromised it is by money, or [voters'] attention span, or anything else, is better than what we have with representative democracy. . . . Better the people.[13]

Although he concurs with Anderson, Douglas Bruce is even more extreme in his criticisms of legislators and the system of representative government. Bruce asserts that, "The [legislative] system is fundamentally rotten to the core. The judges are bought off, the legislators are bought off."[14] The initiative process, for Bruce, is a way to bring government back to the people. Bruce, the former Los Angeles prosecutor, maintains that:

> If two heads are better than one, than one million are better than one hundred. And besides, it's our money, it's our future; we can change our minds. The greatest danger in society is government power.... They [legislators] say 'you've got this mob,' and they call me a 'rabble-rouser,' which is a revealing sneer at what they think of the citizens; they think of them as rabble. They're elitist, and they want to be able to control the system. And they think they know what they're talking about. I've forgotten more about tax law, and petition law, and criminal law...then they'll ever know.... They just want to have this handful of people to make the decisions.[15]

Democracy, for Bruce, can be found in numbers. More people participating in the making of public policy, and more options to select from, will result in more democratic decisions. Supplanting representative government with government by plebiscite is his ultimate goal.

While these claims made by the defenders of direct democracy can be debated *ad infinitum*, it is incontrovertible that the use of citizen initiative is here to stay. It is critical, then, that as citizens, we fully grasp how the initiative process works. It is not sufficient for us, if we strive to be responsible citizens, to accept at face value the claims that direct democracy is a purer form of governance than representative democracy. There is no logical reason why the initiative process should be immune from the same corroding forces that are criticized for debasing our system of representative democracy. Every facet of the political process is susceptible to corrosive elements; the corrosion that occurs in the initiative process is simply harder to detect.

By exposing the rather seamy underside of the politics of three tax limitation initiatives, we can begin to think more critically about the politics and process of direct democracy. What do the tax limitation measures tell us more generally about how ballot campaigns are run and who contributes organizational and financial resources to sustain them? What do they disclose about the role of the populist entrepreneur? And perhaps most importantly, what do they tell us about how democratic, representative, and participatory the initiative process really is? By shedding light on these and other questions, the three case studies can help us to begin to assess normatively the political implications of the initiative process.

## See How They Run: Campaign Resources and
## Populist Entrepreneurs

The three tax limitation measures explored in this book provide us with
some insight into how initiative campaigns are run and what kinds of individuals, groups, and businesses donate money and provide in-kind
resources to the campaigns. In both the signature collection and the election campaign phases of the initiative process, the tax crusaders drew heavily on the organizational and financial resources of interested economic
groups rather than average citizens. Contrary to the conventional wisdom,
they did not bank exclusively on the financial support of lower- and middle-class homeowners concerned about their rising property taxes.

Once the coating of populist rhetoric is scraped away from these ballot
initiatives, it is evident that all three populist entrepreneurs orchestrated
their campaigns from the top-down. They were not the product of a grassroots or dues-paying membership. Most certainly, the initiatives were not
populist movements. Instead, they can be better understood as *faux* populist
moments. As active participants in the initiative process, the "people" only
became involved in the process on election day, the *faux* populist moment.

During the early stages of his campaign for Prop. 13, Howard Jarvis
relied on the support of existing California homeowner and taxpayer
groups. Jarvis did not have to pay petitioners to collect signatures to place
his amendment on the ballot. Instead, he recruited housewives, including
his own wife, Estelle, and other members of the United Organizations of
Taxpayers, to stand outside of shopping malls to ask shoppers to endorse
his property tax reduction measure. But as the campaign drew to a close,
he began to draw more heavily on the financial and organizational support
of large real estate interests, particularly the Los Angeles Apartment Owners Association. In terms of drumming up public support for his measure,
Jarvis paid several professional consulting firms based in Los Angeles to
produce television and radio commercials and orchestrate the campaign.
To raise money for the massive media campaign (and to pay the consultants' sizable fees), Jarvis and the consultants targeted the members of the
LAAOA, as well as other large property owners in southern California. By
combining the early grassroots support of the UOT, his inflammatory
populist rhetoric, and the financial and organizational support of the
LAAOA, Jarvis helped to revolutionize the initiative process.

In Massachusetts, Barbara Anderson and her group Citizens for Limited
Taxation, were able to button-hole the business community for support of

their eclectic package of property tax cuts. Early on in the campaign, CLT secured a financial commitment from the state's automobile dealers as well as small business owners interested in across-the-board property tax cuts. Although CLT had a few thousand dues-paying members, Anderson and several other staffers on the CLT payroll collected the bulk of the signatures necessary to place the measure on the ballot. Once they narrowly qualified the measure for the 1980 ballot, Anderson once again turned to the business community, specifically the Massachusetts High Tech Council, to bankroll the fall campaign. With High Tech's experienced campaign consultants skillfully saturating the airwaves with pro-2 1/2 spots, Anderson was able to brush up on the substantive details of the measure and talk up a storm about all the grassroots support CLT was receiving. The dual punch of the silicon entrepreneurs and Anderson's homespun, populist appeal was enough to convince the public to support the property tax measure.

Unlike the other two tax crusaders profiled, Douglas Bruce was shunned by the business community during his three separate quests to halt increase in taxes and government spending in Colorado. Frightened by his draconian-sounding measures as well as his blustery personality and unpredictable antics, businesses actually lined up against Bruce's initiatives. Unable to cultivate a positive relationship with the business community, Bruce, somewhat surprisingly, did not attempt to mobilize average Coloradans to advance his cause. He did not build TABOR into a grassroots army of irate taxpayers. He did not sponsor any anti-tax rallies to garner support for his measures. He did not drive around the state in a Winnebago plastered with anti-tax campaign slogans to solicit support. Rather, Bruce orchestrated numerous press conferences outside the state Capitol and relied on the free media to get his anti-tax message out to the public. During the last few weeks of his 1992 campaign, Bruce relied on the savvy advertising strategy of a one-person marketing firm to produce some timely, but inexpensive, television ads. The shoe-string campaign was financed by a wealthy Boulder patron and Bruce's own personal loans to his political committee, TABOR. Although once again significantly outspent by the opposition, Bruce was able to tap into an anti-tax mood and coast to victory on election day.

While differing in terms of their campaign strategies and financial and organizational resources, the three tax crusaders successfully manipulated the initiative process to engineer the passage of their tax limitation measures. Using the process of direct democracy, these populist entrepreneurs—or "cranks," as President William Howard Taft once dubbed them—were able to avoid much of the leg-work that is usually involved in mobilizing popular support for a cause. Paying people either directly or indirectly to collect signatures and relying on mass mailing lists to solicit financial contributions, they were able to generate popular support for their ballot initiatives. The tax revolts in each state were similar to what sociologists like to call "checkbook quasi-movements," in which "individual identification [for a cause] may not extend beyond a bumper sticker."[16] The tax crusaders' populist-sounding manifestos on rising taxes and intrusive and unresponsive governmental power, combined with the financial contributions of a few vested benefactors, gave the campaigns immediate public credibility and presence. Although the measures were quite complicated fiscal policy statements, the media tended to focus on the tax crusaders' personalities. Reporters told the story of the underdog tax crusader protecting the people against an unresponsive government. With evocative television and radio ads flooding the airwaves, substantive disagreements over the issue of taxation were reduced to soundbites. Gearing up for the vote on election day, these populist entrepreneurs were able to deliver their messages to a quiescent public with only a shell of an organization; the "people" were conspicuously absent during the campaigns.

## An Adulterated Initiative Process?

Under the realm of direct democracy, tax limitation measures, more than other ballot measures it seems, *should* be populist, grassroots undertakings. They *should* flow from "the people." An incendiary issue, the question of taxes naturally resonates with most people because they are all, one way or another, taxpayers. Taxes—more so than questions concerning euthanasia, campaign finance reform, term limits, tort reform, or lactating mother bears—are part of the daily experience of most citizens. Theoretically, then, a wide array of taxpayers should participate, or at least be interested in, tax limitation ballot initiatives. The measures should be exceedingly democratic and participatory. They should be grassroots tax revolts. But how democratic and participatory are they?

The case studies speak for themselves. Far from embodying the spirit of the Populists who originally proposed democracy by initiative, few people actually participated in these tax revolts (other than casting a vote on election day). While the rank-and-file membership of Jarvis's United Organizations of Taxpayers was active in the collection of signatures for

Proposition 13, in Massachusetts, it was primarily the paid staff of Citizens for Limited Taxation who circulated Proposition 2 1/2 petitions. In Colorado, Bruce made no pretense of making TABOR a membership-based organization. It was a fund raising machine, pure and simple. For these tax crusaders, "the people," while helpful as a rhetorical device, were not necessary to advance their "populist" causes.

Perhaps even more telling, though, is what the ballot warriors themselves say about the initiative process and citizen participation. Anderson and Bruce, for example, readily agree that the initiative process is not a flawless vehicle for mass participation. They both acknowledge that there has been a big decline in citizen participation in ballot initiatives since the passage of Proposition 13. In particular, the two tax crusaders believe that citizen involvement during the early stages of the campaigns has tailed off dramatically. This drop in civic involvement especially concerns Anderson. She cites a failing education system as the major reason why citizen participation has fallen. As a result, she admits that the democratic process is compromised. Paraphrasing Thomas Jefferson, Anderson asserts that:

> The real thing is what Jefferson said, about how in order to have democracy you have to have a well-educated population, and we're losing around here rapidly. So, I fear also for the education system and what it's doing to the "dummying down" of America. I don't think you can have democracy once that happens, once the people are not intelligent and well-read as well as well-viewed. However, I also don't see how you can have representative democracy when that happens. . . . We have to start to have an educated populace again, because without it, we're doomed. Without it, you can not have a democracy, or a representative democracy, without an intelligent, educated population.[17]

Bruce also deplores the decline of an educated and political involved electorate. He claims that, "with the public school system, people are illiterate," and as a result, "they don't vote." He asks rhetorically, "What, do they [the public] watch forty hours a week of TV?" Because of what he perceives to be a decline in the civic participation, Bruce says that he has had to change his campaign strategy. When he ran his first citizen initiative in 1988, Bruce published and disseminated a detailed, one-page description of his proposal. No one read it. Now he relies heavily on "attention grabbing" radio and TV spots to get his message out, which he sees as "hypnotizing" the public.[18] Bruce readily admits that the initiative process does not encourage a substantive discussion of policy alternatives. With direct democracy,

the making of public policy, unlike the legislative process, is not an itera-
tive process, steeped in deliberative debate.

Somewhat ironically, Bruce, a self-proclaimed patriot and man of the
people, blames his fellow citizens for the lack of substantive debate in initiative campaigns. "A lot of people," Bruce complains, "are just so superficial."
Since people are "shallow," Bruce contends that he has had to run "superficial campaigns." In addition, Bruce complains that he has had an increasingly difficult time recruiting people to volunteer for his campaigns.
"Basically," Bruce says, "most people don't help." Instead, he says resentfully,
"people are cheap." "They sit there passively" during the petition drives and
the campaigns, Bruce grumbles. He claims that even the recruits he has paid
to collect signatures are not reliable. During his 1996 failed initiative
attempt to change the laws for the initiative process, for example, Bruce
avows that ninety percent of the people he hired "did nothing."[19]

Although difficult to measure, mass participation in the initiative
process does seem to have decreased since the passage of Proposition 13.
Simultaneously, and perhaps more troubling, there has been a growth in
the amount of corporate money and high-priced campaign consultants in
the initiative process. Beginning with Proposition 13, running citizen initiatives has become big business. In some sense, waging a profitable campaign has taken precedence over the substantive matter of the initiative.
Capitalizing on a populist-sounding message, populist entrepreneurs and
their campaign consultants have contributed to the shift away from deliberative discussion and mass participation in the initiative process. Even the
support for Proposition 13, the most dynamic of the three tax revolts, was
a far cry from the "democratic movement-building" that took place a century ago during populism's golden era.[20] Today, the *faux* populist moment
has replaced the populist movement. Populist entrepreneurs such as
Howard Jarvis, Barbara Anderson, and Douglas Bruce, are able to abbrevi-
ate the laborious process of "democratic movement-building" by tapping
directly into an equivocal popular sentiment and offering to the public
their ready-made political solutions via the ballot initiative. Enlightened,
participatory debate is replaced by an all-or-nothing media battle to cajole
people into voting for or against a single proposition.

## Conclusion: A Machiavellian Moment or Populist Facade?

While admitting that the initiative process may not be flawless, populist
entrepreneurs often point to outcomes when defending their ballot mea-

sures. They stress, after all, that it is the people who are deciding on election day whether an initiative passes or fails. It is the people who have the ultimate authority to accept or reject such measures. Tax crusaders in particular highlight the ends, if not always the means, of the initiative process when celebrating their tax-slashing measures. As Oregon tax crusader Bill Sizemore stated in 1996, "Which makes more sense—paying a politician to increase your taxes, or paying a petitioner to collect signatures to give you a chance to vote on lowering your taxes?"[21] Sizemore and others point to the fact that taxes have been cut in all the states that have passed Jarvisesque ballot measures. Indeed, property taxes were reduced substantially in California and Massachusetts after voters approved Proposition 13 and Proposition 2 1/2. In 1997, Colorado's state legislature was required as a result of Bruce's Amendment 1 to refund a $140 million budget surplus to the taxpayers.[22] There is a Machiavellian side to the arguments put forth by proponents of direct democracy. Pay no attention to the process: Ballot measures achieve desired outcomes.

The central question, though, arises as to whether or not tax crusaders and other proponents of the initiative process should be able to have it both ways. Should supporters of the initiative process be able to claim that the outcomes justify its use when they simultaneously defend the *process* of direct democracy on the grounds that it is superior to that of representative democracy? In other words, if the initiative process is no purer or representative or participatory than the legislative system, why should we assume that its outcomes are somehow more just? Citizens should be asking themselves this when they contemplate voting on ballot measures. If the process of direct democracy supposedly makes it a superior form of governance over representative democracy, then the process should be consist of more than just hollow paeans to "the people." Citizens should weary of the fact that the process of direct democracy is becoming more and more dominated by the same interest groups that the public generally bemoans for corrupting representative government. If indeed direct democracy is not procedurally purer than representative democracy, then sadly, all that distinguishes its politics from our more established system of representative democracy is its populist facade.

# NOTES

## Preface

1. Michael Pettier, "High Court Hearing Tax Limitation Arguments," *Port St. Lucie News* (Stuart, FL), December 2, 1996, B2.

2. David Broder, "Initiative Fever Still Grips California," *Denver Post*, August 15, 1997, 7B.

3. Bill Monroe, "Interview of Howard Jarvis on 'Meet the Press,'" vol. 78 (June 18), (Washington, DC: Kelly Press, Inc. 1978).

4. "Sound and Fury Over Taxes," *Time*, June 19, 1978, 13.

5. James Ring Adams, *Secrets of the Tax Revolt* (New York: Harcourt Brace Jovanovich, 1984), 345.

6. Jack Citrin, "Who's the Boss: Direct Democracy and Popular Control of Government," in Stephen Craig, ed., *Broken Contract? Changing Relationships Between Americans and Their Government* (Boulder: Westview Press, 1996), 268–93, 290.

7. Florida Department of State, Division of Elections, "Tax Cap Committee," *Campaign Treasurer's Report*, July 1993 to December 1996.

8. Diane Hirth, "Proposal May Make State Even More Of A Tax Haven," *Orlando Sentinel Tribune*, October 30, 1996, A1. In fact, in 1996, the average contribution made to Biddulph's Tax Cap Committee was $193.45. When accounting for the massive contributions made by sugar companies, the average contribution in 1996 was still over $70. Florida Department of State, Division of Elections, "Tax Cap Committee," *Campaign Treasurer's Report*, January 1996–December 1996.

## Chapter 1

1. Diane Hirth, "Proposal May Make State Even More of a Tax Haven," *Orlando Sentinel Tribune*, October 30, 1996, A1.

2. "Portland May Sue to Halt Tax Limit," *The Bulletin* (Bend, OR), December 1, 1996, B4.

3. E. E. Schattschneider, *The Semisovereign People* (New York: Harcourt Brace Jovanovich, 1960), 136.

4. Fred Brown, "What's Wrong With the Public?" *Denver Post*, November 2, 1994, 7B.

5. J. R. Moehringer, "Experts Fear Long Ballot Will Scare Away Voters," *Rocky Mountain News*, November 2, 1994, A4.

6. David Magleby, *Direct Legislation* (Baltimore: The Johns Hopkins University Press, 1984).

7. Thomas Cronin, *Direct Democracy* (Cambridge: Harvard University Press: 1989), 1.

8. *Constitution of South Dakota*, Art. 3, Sec. 1 (1898). Quoted in Joseph Zimmerman, *Participatory Democracy: Populism Revived* (New York: Praeger Publishers, 1986), 37. For a brief summary of Haire's role, see David Schmidt, *Citizen Lawmakers* (Philadelphia: Temple University Press, 1989), 267–68.

9. For discussions of the reform ideology of the Progressive Era and the use of the initiative, see Schmidt, *Citizen Lawmakers*, 14–20; Magleby, *Direct Legislation*, 20–23; and Cronin, *Direct Democracy*, 50–59.

10. Schmidt, *Citizen Lawmakers*, 21–23.

11. Ibid., 21–23; Magleby, *Direct Legislation*, 20–21.

12. There are two types of initiatives, the direct initiative and the indirect initiative. With the direct initiative, citizens may propose a measure (either constitutional or statutory), and once the measure is validated by the state, the measure is placed directly before the people for a vote. With the indirect initiative, citizens may propose a measure (either constitutional or statutory), and once the measure is validated by the state, the measure may be considered by the legislature before going to the people for a vote. Both types of initiatives are different from popular referendums. With popular referendums, citizens may request that an action taken by the legislature be put to a popular vote by the people. The principle distinction between initiatives and referendums is that the later originate from the legislature, not the people. See David Magleby, "Direct Legislation in the American States," in David Butler and Austin Ranney, *Referendums around the World* (Washington, DC: AEI Press, 1994), 218–257, 219–223; Cronin, *Direct Democracy*, 2.

13. Cronin, *Direct Democracy*, 4.

14. Elisabeth Gerber, "Legislative Response to the Threat of Popular Initiatives," *American Journal of Political Science*, vol. 40, no. 1 (February) 1996, 99–128; Gilbert Hahn and Stephen Morton, "Initiative and Referendum: Do They Encourage or Impair Better State Government?" *Florida State University Law Review*, vol. 5 (1977), 925–50.

15. Magleby, *Direct Legislation*, 96–98.

16. Jack Citrin, "Who's the Boss? Direct Democracy and Popular Control of Government," in Stephen Craig, ed., *Broken Contract? Changing Relationships Between Americans and Their Government* (Boulder: Westview Press, 1996), 268–93, 282.

17. While the aggregate number of statewide ballot measures increased following the passage of Proposition 13, a few states (Alaska, Idaho, Nevada, and Wyoming), because of their high signature thresholds for placing measures on the ballot, saw little growth in the initiative process. See Magleby, "Direct Legislation in the American States," 225–28.

18. Cronin, *Direct Democracy*, 3.

19. Magleby, *Direct Legislation*, 6.

20. Schmidt, *Citizen Lawmakers*, 144.

21. Citrin, "Who's the Boss?" 268.

22. B. Drummond Ayres, "Politics: The Initiatives," *New York Times*, November 4, 1996, B6; Elaine Stuart, "Voters Make Laws," *State Government News*, vol. 39, no. 11, December, 1996, 31.

23. Dan Morain, "Consultants Win in Fight Over State Initiatives," *Los Angeles Times*, November 3, 1996, A3.

24. Michael Marois, "Trends in the Region," *The Bond Buyer*, February 14, 1997, 30.

25. Michael Kazin, *The Populist Persuasion* (New York: Basic Books, 1995), 263.

26. Cronin, *Direct Democracy*, 110.

27. Betty Zisk, *Money, Media, and the Grass Roots: State Ballot Issues and the Electoral Process* (Newbury Park, CA: Sage, 1987); Daniel Lowenstein, "Campaign Spending and Ballot Propositions: Recent Experience, Public Choice Theory, and the First Amendment," *UCLA Law Review*, 86 (1982); John Shockley, "Corporate Spending in the Wake of the Bellotti Decision" (Paper presented at the annual meeting of the American Political Science Association, New York, September 1978), cited in Cronin, *Direct Democracy*, 106.

28. Eugene Lee, "The Initiative and Referendum: How California has Fared," *National Civic Review*, vol. 68, February, 1979, 69–84; Larry Berg, "The Initiative Process and Public Policy-Making in the States: 1904–1976" (Paper presented at the annual meeting of the American Political Science Association, New York City, August 1978, 54–55), cited in Magleby, *Direct Legislation*, 146–47.

29. John Shockley, "Testimony in House Committee on Government Operations," *IRS Administration of Tax Laws*, 1976, cited in Cronin, *Direct Democracy*, 110.

30. Lowenstein, "Campaign Spending and Ballot Propositions," 607–09.

31. David Magleby, "Campaign Spending in Ballot Proposition Elections" (Paper presented at the annual meeting of the American Political Science Association, Washington, DC, August, 1986), cited in Magleby, "Direct Legislation in the American States," 250.

32. David Magleby, *Direct Legislation*, 147.

33. Ibid., 147–49.

34. Betty Zisk, *Money, Media, and the Grass Roots: State Ballot Issues and the Electoral Process* (Newbury Park, CA: Sage, 1987), 90–137.

35. Ibid., 111.

36. David Schmidt, *Citizen Lawmakers*, 35.

37. Ibid., 36.

38. Cronin, *Direct Democracy*, 100, 116.

39. Magleby, "Direct Legislation in the American States," 250; Magleby, *Direct Legislation*, 148–49.

40. Ann Campbell, "The Citizen's Initiative and Entrepreneurial Politics: Direct Democracy in Colorado, 1966–1994" (Paper presented at the annual meeting of the Western Political Science Association, Tucson, AZ, March 1997).

41. According to Robert Yin, there are three reasons for conducting a "single-case" study. "[O]ne rationale for a single case is when it represents the critical case in testing a well-formulated theory (again, note the analogy to the critical experiment). The theory has specified a clear set of propositions as well as the circumstance within which the propositions are believed to be true. To confirm, challenge, or extend the theory, there may exist a single case, meeting all of the conditions for testing the theory. The single case can then be used to determine whether a theory's propositions are correct, or whether some alternative set of explanations might be more relevant." The other two reasons are the "extreme or unique case," and the "revelatory" case. For an authoritative account for using single-case studies, see Robert Yin, *Case Study Research: Design and Methods* (Newbury Park, CA: Sage Publications, 1989), 46–49.

42. Catherine Marshall and Gretchen Rossman, *Designing Qualitative Research* (Newbury Park, CA: Sage Publications, 1989), 46. Qualitative research also allows for the "use of close-up detailed observation of the natural world by the investigator," qualitative research attempts, "to avoid prior commitment to any theoretical model." J. Van Maanen, J. Dabbs, and R. Faulkner, *Varieties of Qualitative Research* (Beverly Hills, CA: Sage Publications, 1982), 16. See also Yin, *Case Study Research: Design and Methods*, 25.

43. Jack Citrin offers a five-fold typology of "so-called" "citizen" initiatives to categorize the different kinds of "sponsors and strategic purposes" behind each campaign. His typology includes what he labels "grassroots causes," "program protection," "partisan conflict," "self-promotion," and "corporate self-defense." Citrin, "Who's the Boss?" 282–84.

44. Alan Rosenthal, *The Decline of Representative Democracy: Process, Participation, and Power in State Legislatures* (Washington, DC: CQ Press, 1998), 4–5.

45. Jeanette Lona Furen, *Power in the People* (Far Hills, NJ: New Horizon Press, 1996), 178.

46. A recent study of ballot initiatives has found that "the initiative process in practice does not enhance the extent to which policies accord with public opinion." See Edward Lascher, et. al., "Gun Behind the Door? Ballot Initiatives, State Policies and Public Opinion," *Journal of Politics*, vol. 58, no. 3 (August) 1996, 760–75, 774.

47. Theodore Roosevelt, "Nationalism and Popular Rule," *The Outlook*, January 21, 1911. Reprinted in William Bennett Munro, ed., *The Initiative, Referendum, and Recall* (New York: D. Appleton and Co., 1912), 52–68, 65.

## Chapter 2

1. Marquis of Grandby, Speech in House of Commons, April 5, 1775. Cited in Charles Adams, *For Good and Evil: The Impact of Taxes on the Course of Civilization* (New York: Madison Books, 1993), 293.

2. "Sound and Fury over Taxes," *Time*, June 19, 1978, 12–21, 13.

3. Alvin Rabushka and Pauline Ryan, *The Tax Revolt* (Stanford: Hoover Institution, 1982), 201.

4. Susan Hansen, *The Politics of Taxation: Revenue without Representation* (NY: Praeger Publishers, 1983), 273.

5. Stephen Craig, "Change and the American Electorate," in Stephen Craig, ed., *Broken Contract: Changing Relationships Between Americans and Their Government* (Boulder: Westview, 1996), 1–20, 2–5.

6. Penelope Lemov, "The Tax Revolt That Wasn't," *Governing*, vol. 8, no. 4 (January), 1995, 25; Elaine Stuart, "Voters Make Laws," *State Government News* vol. 39, no. 11 (December) 1996, 31.

7. Fred Brown, "Possessing a License to Legislate," *Denver Post*, November 17, 1997, 1B.

8. Sheldon Pollack, *The Failure of U.S. Tax Policy* (University Park: Pennsylvania State University Press, 1996), 21.

9. John Brewer, *The Sinews of Power: War, Money, and the English State, 1688–1783* (New York: Knopf, 1989).

10. Sidney Ratner, *American Taxation* (New York: W.W. Norton, 1942), 13.

11. Adams, *For Good and Evil*, 293.

12. As Charles Adams points out:

Most people believe it [the Boston Tea Party] was a protest against British taxes on tea, but this is not true. American tea merchants had been boycotting British tea for five years. Smuggled Dutch tea was used throughout the colonies. In response, the British government decided to remove the duties on East Indies tea when it arrived in Britain so it could be sold in America at a price cheaper than smuggled Dutch tea. In addition, a monopoly on this cheap tea was given to loyal British merchants in the colonies. American tea smugglers would be put out of business. The Crown's plan was based on the assumption that American consumers would not boycott low-priced English tea but would purchase it rather than the higher-priced, smuggled Dutch product.

Adams, *For Good and Evil*, 302–03.

13. The maxim was likely a derivation of, "Taxation without representation is tyranny," which was attributed to James Otis in 1763. The following year Otis wrote, "No parts of His Majesty's dominions can be taxed without their consent." James Otis, *Rights of the British Colonies Asserted and Proved* (Boston: Edes and Gill, 1764), 64.

14. Roger Brown, *Redeeming the Republic* (Baltimore: The Johns Hopkins University Press, 1993), 34.

15. Robert Becker, *Revolution, Reform, and the Politics of American Taxation* (Baton Rouge: Louisiana State University Press, 1980), 5.

16. Ibid., 116.

17. Brown, *Redeeming the Republic*, 4.

18. Ibid., 110–12.

19. "Z," *Independent Chronicle* [Boston], July 20, 1786. Quoted in Brown, *Redeeming the Republic*, 113.

20. Ibid., 115–16.

21. George Washington stated at the time of the rebellion in western Massachusetts, "I am mortified beyond expression, when I view the clouds, that have spread over the brightest morn that ever dawned upon any country . . . . To be more exposed in the eyes of the world, and more contemptible than we already are, is hardly possible." George Washington, "Letter to Henry Lee," October 31, 1786, in Saul Padover, ed., *The Washington Papers* (New York: Grosset and Dunlap, 1955), 225–226. Thomas Jefferson, on the other hand, saw positive aspects of the turmoil in western Massachusetts. In a letter to James Madison in 1787, Jefferson wrote, "I hold it that a little rebellion now and then is a good thing, and as necessary in the political world as storms in the physical. . . . It is a medicine necessary for the sound health of government." Thomas Jefferson, "Letter to James Madison," January 30, 1787, in Merrill Peterson, ed., *The Portable Thomas Jefferson* (New York: The Viking Press, 1975), 415–18.

22. Trooper T. Thompson's Letter-Journal, March 22–April 4, 1787, April 3, 1787 entry, Morristown Collection, reel 55. Cited in Brown, *Redeeming the Republic*, 117.

23. Adams, *For Good and Evil*, 317.

24. Ibid., 316–320; Brown, *Redeeming the Republic*, 239–40.

25. "Sound and Fury over Taxes," *Time*, 21.

26. Justice Wendell T. Holmes. Quoted in Ratner, *American Taxation*, 17.

27. Robert Kuttner, *Revolt of the Haves* (New York: Simon and Schuster, 1980), 9.

28. David Magleby, "Direct Legislation in the American States," in David Butler and Austin Ranney, eds., *Referendums Around the World* (Washington, DC: AEI Press, 1994), 218–57, 239.

29. Eugene Lee, "California," in David Butler and Austin Ranney, eds., *Referendums: A Comparative Study of Practice and Theory* (Washington, DC: AEI Press, 1978), 87–122, 93–96.

30. Howard Jarvis, *I'm Mad as Hell* (New York: Times Books, 1979), 172.

31. "The Big Tax Revolt," *Newsweek*, June 19, 1978, 20–30, 20–21; "Sound and Fury Over Taxes," *Time*, 14–15.

32. Jack Citrin, "Who's the Boss? Direct Democracy and Popular Control," in Stephen Craig, ed., *Broken Contract: Changing Relationships Between Americans and Their Government* (Boulder: Westview, 1996), 268–93, 281.

33. "Sound and Fury Over Taxes," 21.

34. Jarvis, *I'm Mad as Hell*, 4.

35. "Sound and Fury over Taxes," 21; Tom Mathews, "Mr. Proposition 13," *Newsweek*, June 19, 1978, 25; "Taxpayer Revolt: Where It's Spreading Now," *US News and World Report*, June 26, 1978, 16–20; "California Earthquake," *The Nation*, June 17, 1978, 714–715; Peter Connolly, "The Voice of Raw Greed," *The Nation*, July 22, 1978, 77–78; "Me First," *The New Republic*, June 17, 1978, 5–6; "Election Roundup," *National Review*, June 23, 1978, 758; Arthur Blaustein, "Proposition 13=Catch 22: California's Rush for Fool's Gold," *Harper's Magazine*, November, 1978, 18–23; "Taxes Overboard," *Economist*, June 17, 1978, 11. In January 1979, *Time* selected Jarvis (along with Jimmy Carter, Pope John Paul II, and Reverend Jim Jones) as a runner-up for its prestigious "Man of the Year." *Time* praised Jarvis as "an unlikely prophet." "Four Who Also Shaped Events," *Time*, January 1, 1979, 40–41.

36. Magleby, "Direct Legislation in the American States," 239.

37. "The Big Tax Revolt," 25; "Sound and Fury Over Taxes," 21.

38. "The Big Tax Revolt," 27.

39. "The 'demagogue' proper," according to a leading translator and editor of Aristotle, Ernest Barker, has "no official position: he simply exercised, in a peculiar degree and with a permanent influence, the right of the private member of the assembly to take the initiative and propose a policy . . . . playing the part of an unofficial leader; and such a leader—having no official executive position—[the demagogue] could exercise initiative and determine policy without incurring political responsibility, since it was not his duty to execute the policy which he had induced the assembly to accept." As Aristotle himself commented, "The record of history attests the fact; and it may safely be said that most tyrants have begun their careers as demagogues, who won the popular confidence by calumniating the notables." For Aristotle, "Demagogues are always dividing the state into two, and waging war against the rich. Their proper policy is the very reverse: they should always profess to be speaking in defense of the rich." Ernest Barker, *The Politics of Aristotle* (New York: Oxford University Press, 1946), 169; 233–35.

40. Ed Busch, "Howard Jarvis," *Personality*, December, 1978, 13.

41. "Sound and Fury Over Taxes," 21.

42. As Jarvis was barnstorming the country in on his American Tax Reduction Movement in 1979, Gann was busy promoting Proposition 4—dubbed the "Spirit of 13"—a constitutional state spending limit ballot measure. In June 1980, Gann won the Republican bid for U.S. Senate, only to lose big in the November general election to incumbent Alan Cranston.

43. Mathews, "Mr. Proposition 13," 25.

44. "Sound and Fury Over Taxes," 13.

45. Robert Kuttner, *Revolt of the Halves* (New York: Simon and Schuster, 1980), 40.

46. Ibid., 36–37.

47. Rabushka and Ryan, *The Tax Revolt*, 186.

48. Ibid., 187.

49. Gary Grossman, "Prop 13 and Jarvis Won't Play in Boston," *Boston Herald American*, September 23, 1978.

50. Rabushka, "Tax and Spending Limits," in Peter Duignan and Alvin Rabushka, eds., *The United States in the 1980s* (Stanford: Hoover Institution Press, 1980), 93–97.

51. Rabushka and Ryan, *The Tax Revolt*, 187–88.

52. Roger Kemp, *Coping with Proposition 13* (Lexington, MA: DC Heath and Company, 1980), 7–9.

53. David Sears and Jack Citrin, *Tax Revolt* (Cambridge: Harvard University Press, 1982), 261–63.

54. *Newsweek*/Gallup, CBS/*New York Times*, and Harris each surveyed Americans about their views on taxes. Cited in Rabushka and Ryan, *The Tax Revolt*, 37.

55. Sears and Citrin, *Tax Revolt*, 34–36.

56. Ibid., 36–40; James Ring Adams, *Secrets of the Tax Revolt* (New York: Harcourt Brace Jovanovich, 1984), 169.

57. Ryan and Rabushka, *The Tax Revolt*, 193. David Schmidt, *Citizen Lawmakers* (Philadelphia: Temple University Press, 1989), 144.

58. Sears and Citrin, *Tax Revolt*, 41.

59. Sonja Hillgren, "General News," *UPI*, November 5, 1980. Voters in Missouri approved a measure limiting government spending and voters in Montana approved a measure easing an increase in the rate of income taxes.

60. Magleby, "Direct Legislation in the American States," 238.

61. Mathews, "Mr. Proposition 13," 25.

62. Colorado Department of State, "Report of Contributions and Expenditures," Tabor Committee, September 8 to October 20, 1996. Bruce loaned his TABOR committee a total of $154,000 in September and October, 1996, which TABOR then loaned to the Citizens for Petition Rights, the group officially sponsoring the November ballot measure, Amendment 13, also known as the Petition Rights Amendment.

63. Poll conducted by Floyd Ciruli and Associates. Cited in John Sanko, "Voters loosen Amendment 1 Restrictions," *Rocky Mountain News*, November 9, 1995, A5.

64. Several other tax crusaders deserve mention for their recent initiative efforts: Laird Maxwell and Ron Rankin in Idaho; Ed Jaksha in Nebraska; Jim Gibbons in Nevada; and Merrill Cook in Utah.

## Chapter Three

1. Richard Hofstadter, *The Age of Reform* (New York: Vintage Books, 1955), 64.

2. Jack Citrin, "Who's the Boss? Direct Democracy and Popular Control of Government," in Stephen Craig, ed., *Broken Contract: Changing Relationships Between Americans and Their Government* (Boulder: Westview Press, 1996), 268–93, 268.

3. Steve Lipsher, "Ballot Drive a Job For Pros," *The Denver Post*, September 19, 1994 1A.

4. David Schmidt, *Citizen Lawmakers* (Philadelphia: Temple University Press, 1989), 145.

5. This is both an empirical and a normative question—are tax cuts good? Who is helped by the cut, who is hurt? What are the short and long term benefits and costs of the cuts? Is the public good bettered? Is the private sector bettered? While concerned with normative implications of the initiative process, this book does not deal with these important policy questions.

6. See, for example: Tom Wicker, "A 'New Revolution,'" *New York Times*, June 9, 1978; "Sound and Fury Over Taxes," *Time*, June 19, 1979; James Ring Adams, *Secrets of the Tax Revolt* (New York: Harcourt Brace Jovanovich, 1984); Don Wash, "Barbara Anderson's On the Money," *Cape Cod Times*, May 25, 1989; Michael Romano, "Ballot Issues Limit Power of Politicians," *Rocky Mountain News*, September 25, 1994, A4.

7. The term "populist moment" comes from the title of Lawrence Goodwyn's book, *The Populist Moment* (New York: University of Oxford Press, 1978), although my usage differs from his.

8. David Laycock. *Populism and Democratic Thought in the Canadian Prairies, 1910–1945* (Toronto: University of Toronto Press, 1990), 15.

9. Michael Kazin, *The Populist Persuasion: An American History* (New York: Basic Books, 1995), 5.

10. Goodwyn, *The Populist Moment*, xviii–xxi.

11. Lawrence Goodwyn, *Democratic Promise* (New York: University of Oxford Press,1976), xi; xv–xxiii.

12. George Tindall, ed., *A Populist Reader* (New York: Harper Torchbooks, 1966), xv–xvi.

13. Quoted in Margaret Canovan, *Populism* (New York: Harcourt Brace Jovanovich, 1981), 7.

14. Christopher Lasch, *The True and Only Heaven: Progress and its Critics* (New York: Norton, 1991), 217.

15. Hofstadter, *The Age of Reform,* 18.

16. Ibid., 4 (italics mine).

17. Canovan, *Populism,* 294.

18. Peter Wiles, "A Syndrome, Not a Doctrine: Some Elementary Theses on Populism," in Ghita Ionescu and Ernest Gellner, eds., *Populism* (London: Weidenfeld and Nicolson, 1969),166–79.

19. Kazin, *The Populist Persuasion,* 6.

20. Ibid., 295.

21. John Hicks, *The Populist Revolt: A History of the Farmers' Alliance and the People's Party* (Lincoln: University of Nebraska Press, 1961 [1931]); C. Vann Woodward, *Tom Watson: Agrarian Rebel* (New York: Macmillan Company, 1938).

22. Hicks, *The Populist Revolt,* 406.

23. See: Hofstadter, *The Age of Reform*; Richard Hofstadter, "The Pseudo-Conservative Revolt," in Daniel Bell, ed., *The New American Right* (New York: Criterion Books, 1955); Daniel Bell, "Interpretations of American Politics," in Bell, ed., *The New American Right.*; Seymour Martin Lipset, "The Sources of the 'Radical Right,'" in Bell, ed., *The New American Right.*

24. Hofstadter, *Age of Reform,* 5.

25. Paul Wilkinson, *Social Movement* (New York: Praeger Publishers, 1971), 87.

26. Kazin, *The Populist Persuasion,* 283.

27. Gene Clanton, *Populism: The Humane Preference in America, 1890–1900* (Boston: Twayne Publishers, 1991), 168.

28. Norman Pollack, ed., *The Populist Mind,* (New York: Bobbs-Merrill, 1967), xx.

29. Trevor Harrison, *Of Passionate Intensity: Right-Wing Populism and the Reform Party of Canada* (Toronto: University of Toronto Press, 1995), 5.

30. Wilkinson, *Social Movement,* 87–88.

31. Allen Hertzke, *Echoes of Discontent: Jesse Jackson, Pat Robertson, and the Resurgence of Populism* (Washington, DC: CQ Press, 1993), xiii.

32.Hofstadter, *The Age of Reform,* 64.

33. Ibid., 65.

34. Kazin, *The Populist Persuasion,* 5; 286. For his variation of "linguistically informed history," see Kazin's "A Note on Method," in *The Populist Persuasion,* 285–86.

35. Kazin, Letter to the Editor, "The Populist Tongue," *The Washington Post,* July 2, 1995, X14.

36. Kazin, *The Populist Persuasion,* 24–25. Kazin writes that "This symbosis [sic] was intrinsic to the political process. Without strong movements to arouse and mobilize grievances at the grassroots, elite reformers stood naked before their stand-pat adversaries. Yet, without the aid of insiders able to speak to a national

constituency and work the levers of government, movements withered away or became impotent, bitter shells."

37. Ibid., 36.

38. Lasch, *True and Only Heaven*, 217.

39. Harrison, *Of Passionate Intensity*, 257.

40. John Kingdon, *Agendas, Alternative, and Public Politics* (Boston: Little, Brown and Company, 1984), 153. Kingdon uses the term "national mood."

41. Ibid. The term populist entrepreneur is also similar to the term "moral entrepreneurs" used by Bernhard Giesen. See Klaus Eder, *The New Politics of Class* (Newbury Park, CA: Sage, 1993), 149.

42. The populist moment is akin to Kingdon's understanding of when public policies are adopted. For Kingdon, public policies become adopted when the "separate streams of problems, policies, and politics come together at certain critical times." A "policy window" opens—which allows for the adoption of a policy—when there are momentous developments in either the problem or political streams. When the two agenda-setting streams (the political and problem) become coupled with the independently flowing, alternative generating policy stream, policy can be decided upon and adopted. During this fleeting time of stream convergence, policy entrepreneurs, in the form of individuals or groups, are able to match their pet solutions to the pertinent problems, which in turn facilitates the decision making of important political actors. Kingdon, *Agendas, Alternative, and Public Politics*, 21; 173.

43. Stewart Burns, *Social Movements of the 1960s: Searching for Democracy* (Boston: Twayne Publishers, 1990), xii. Conceptually, the line between populism and social movements is a blurry one. This is largely due to the artificial disciplinary boundaries found in academia. The substantial literature on social movements—which, broadly speaking, concentrates on cultural, social, and political conflict and change—is potentially useful in explaining populist movements. The social movement literature can be divided into three camps: the process model; the resource mobilization model; and the new social movement model. According to Sidney Tarrow, social movements are *"collective challenges by people with common purposes and solidarity in sustained interaction with elites, opponents and authorities."* Sidney Tarrow, *Power in Movement: Social Movements, Collective Action and Politics* (Cambridge: Cambridge University Press, 1994), 3–4. Historians and political scientists tend to focus on populist movements, whereas sociologists tend to focus on social movements. Paul Wilkinson contends that populist movements can "become transmuted into more positive and assertive movements and their grassroots supporters may become committed to more ambitious and comprehensive ideologies." Wilkinson, *Social Movement*, 88.

44. Benjamin Ginsberg, "Money and Power: The New Political Economy of American Elections," in Thomas Ferguson and Joel Rogers, eds., *The Political Economy* (Armonk, NY: M. E. Sharpe, 1984).

45. Citrin, "Who's the Boss?" 282.

46. Ibid.

47. Daniel Smith and Robert Herrington, "The Process of Direct Democracy: The Case of Colorado's 1996 Parental Rights Amendment" (presented at the annual meeting of the American Political Science Association, August 1997).

48. For other notable examples of this practice, including a campaign consultant who launched a lottery initiative in California to "generate business for his signature-gathering firm," see David Magleby and Kelly Patterson, "Consultants and Direct Democracy" (presented at the annual meeting of the American Political Science Association, August 1997).

49. William Butcher and Arnold Forde signed a nineteen-year contract with Jarvis in 1979 to exclusively run his campaigns. According to sealed court documents made public, by "the mid-1980s Butcher and Forde were paying themselves $3 million to $5 million a year, while their firm was pulling in up to $12 million a year." Tracy Weber, "Making Politics Pay: Cashing in on Causes," *Los Angeles Times*, March 3, 1996, A1, and Tracy Weber, "Tax Group Guilty of Campaign Violation," *Los Angeles Times*, May 11, 1995, A3, both cited by Magleby and Patterson, "Consultants and Direct Democracy," 11. For more background on the campaign consulting practices of Butcher-Forde, see, Tracy Weber, "Suit Challenges Accounting on Political Funds," *Los Angeles Times*, November 22, 1994, A3; Tracy Weber, "Mystery Surrounds Suit Against O.C. Consultants," *Los Angeles Times*, November 20, 1994, A1; and Ronald Soble, "California Elections," *Los Angeles Times*, October 2, 1986, A3.

50. For some notable grassroots exceptions, see Harry Boyte and Frank Riessman, eds., *The New Populism* (Philadelphia: Temple University Press, 1986).

51. Personal interview with Barbara Anderson, Boston, May 7, 1997.

52. Phone interview with Douglas Bruce, June 24, 1996.


## Chapter 4

1. Howard Jarvis, "The American Tax Revolt," Distinguished Lecture Series, College of Business Administration, University of Cincinnati, November 1, 1979. California State Library, California Section, "Howard Jarvis Collection," Box 1671, Folder 5.

2. James Perry and James Hyatt, "Stopping the Bucks," *The Wall Street Journal*, June 6, 1978, A1.

3. Jack Citrin and Frank Levy, "From 13 to 4 and Beyond: The Political Meaning of the Ongoing Tax Revolt in California," in George Kaufman and Kenneth Rosen, eds., *The Property Tax Revolt* (Cambridge, MA: Balinger Publishing Co., 1981), 1–27; Eric Smith and Jack Citrin, "The Building of a Majority for Tax Limitation in California, 1968–1978." Research Report No. 1, State Data Program, University of California, Berkeley, 1979, 3–6; David Sears and Jack Citrin, *Tax Revolt: Some-*

*thing For Nothing in California*. (Cambridge, MA: Harvard University Press, 1982), 96–126.

4. James Pfiffner, "Inflexible Budgets, Fiscal Stress, and the Tax Revolt," in Albert Sbragia, ed., *The Municipal Money Chase: The Politics of Local Government Finance* (Boulder: Westview Press, 1983), 37–66, 51.

5. Sears and Citrin, *Tax Revolt*, 16.

6. Pfiffner, "Inflexible Budgets, Fiscal Stress, and the Tax Revolt," 49.

7. Robert Kuttner, *Revolt of the Haves* (New York: Simon and Schuster, 1980), 19. While his analysis of Prop. 13 probes the complexities of local tax assessments in California, the lack of political action by the Governor and state legislature, and the subsequent populist appeal of Jarvis, a political outsider, Kuttner's book nevertheless supports the conventional wisdom that Jarvis's measure was financed by "a long roster of unkowns, mailing in ten- and twenty-dollar checks" (page 70). Indeed, the only mention of the Los Angeles Apartment Owners Association in his book is on page 41, where he states that Jarvis, "took on a part-time paid job as the director of the Los Angeles Apartment Owners Association." Although he notes that Jarvis "worked for the landlords" (page 77), Kuttner does not examine the crucial financial and organizational contributions made by apartment owners to the campaign for Prop. 13.

8. Ibid., 79.

9. Ibid., 17.

10. Ibid., 77.

11. Ibid., 27–28.

12. James Ring Adams, *Secrets of the Tax Revolt* (New York: Harcourt Brace Jovanovich, 1984), 166.

13. Ibid., 3.

14. Ibid., 175–76.

15. Ibid., 175.

16. Ibid.

17. Terry Schwadron and Paul Richter, eds., *California and the American Tax Revolt* (Berkeley: University of California Press, 1984), 1.

18. Ibid., 70;187.

19. Ibid., 70.

20. Ibid., 1.

21. Thomas Edsall, *Chain Reaction* (New York: W. W. Norton & Co., 1991), 130.

22. Ibid., 131.

23. Kevin Phillips, *The Politics of Rich and Poor* (New York: HarperPerennial, 1990), 64.

24. Ibid., 64.

25. Anthony Lewis, *New York Times*, November 24, 1978.

26. Tom Wicker, "A 'New Revolution,'" *New York Times*, June 9, 1978, A27.

27. Carl Tucker, "Squeeze Play," *Saturday Review*, vol. 5, August 1978, 68.

28. Irving. Kristol, "The Meaning of Proposition 13," *Wall Street Journal*, June 28, 1978.

29. Charles Crawford, "Proposition 13: 'The Sky . . . Has Not Fallen.'" *Enterprise*, vol. 2, July 1978, 3–5.

30. Joseph Kraft, "And, Finally a Message of Populist Hedonism," *Los Angeles Times*, June 13, 1978.

31. William Baroody, "From the Publisher," *Public Opinion*, July/August 1978, 2.

32. Richard Musgrave, "The Tax Revolt." *Social Science Quarterly*, vol. 59, March 1979, 697–703; Martin Levin, "Department of Unintended Consequences," *Taxing & Spending*, vol. 2, April 1979, 12–15; Smith and Citrin, 1979; Alvin Rabushka and Pauline Ryan, *The Tax Revolt* (Stanford, CA: Hoover Institution, 1982); Citrin and Levy, 1981; Arthur O'Sullivan, et al., *Property Taxes and Tax Revolts* (Cambridge: Cambridge University Press, 1995).

33. Martin Levin, "Department of Unintended Consequences," *Taxing & Spending*, vol. 2 (April) 1979, 12–15.

34. Frank Levy and Paul Zamolo, "The Preconditions of Proposition 13," Working Paper, 1105–01, October 1978.

35. Ibid., 5.

36. Citrin and Levy, "From 13 to 4 and Beyond," 24.

37. Jack Citrin, "Introduction: The Legacy of Proposition 13," in Terry Schwadron, ed., *California and the American Tax Revolt* (Berkeley: University of California Press, 1984), 9.

38. William Oakland, "Proposition 13: Genesis and Consequences," in George Kaufman and Kenneth Rosen, eds., *The Property Tax Revolt* (Cambridge, MA: Balinger Publishing Co., 1981), 31–63.

39. Ibid., 36.

40. Ibid., 40.

41. Citrin and Levy, "From 13 to 4 and Beyond," 11.

42. Ibid., 11.

43. Sears and Citrin, *Tax Revolt*, 5.

44. Ibid., 110, 140.

45. Ibid., 140.

46. Ibid., 162.

47. William Fischel, "Did Serrano Cause Proposition 13?" *National Tax Journal*, December 1989, 465–74.

48. Richard Brody, "Who Voted for Proposition 13?" *Taxing & Spending*, vol. 2, February 1979, 26–28.

49. Ibid., 27.

50. Ibid., 28.

51. Mervin Field, "Sending a Message: Californians Strike Back," *Public Opinion*, July/August 1978, 3–7.

52. Citrin, "Introduction," 3.

53. O'Sullivan, et al., *Property Taxes and Tax Revolts*, 3.

54. Levy and Zamolo, "The Preconditions of Proposition 13," 2.

55. Smith and Citrin, "The Building of a Majority for Tax Limitation in California," 2.

56. Field, "Sending a Message: Californians Strike Back," 5.

57. Ibid.

58. Baroody, "From the Publisher," 2.

59. Field, "Sending a Message: Californians Strike Back," 5.

60. Jack Citrin, "Do People Want Something for Nothing?" *National Tax Journal*, vol. 32, no. 2, June 1979, 113–29.

61. Field, "Sending a Message: Californians Strike Back," 6.

62. Citrin, "Introduction;" Clarence Lo, *Small Property Versus Big Government* (Berkeley: University of California Press, 1990).

63. Citrin, "Introduction," 3.

64. Ibid.

65. Ibid.

66. Ibid.

67. Sears and Citrin, *Tax Revolt*, 26.

68. Smith and Citrin, "The Building of a Majority for Tax Limitation in California," 1.

69. Citrin, "Introduction," 52.

70. Lo, *Small Property*, xi, xiv.

71. Ibid., xv, 45.

72. Ibid., 43.

73. Ibid., 196.

74. Ibid., xiii.

75. Clarence Lo, "Mobilizing the Tax Revolt," in Richard Ratcliff, ed., *Research in Social Movement Conflicts and Change*, vol. 6 (Newbury Park, CA: Sage, 1984), 293–328, 301–06.

76. Lo, *Small Property*, 197.

77. Ibid., 158.

78. Lo, "Mobilizing the Tax Revolt," 310.

79. Lo, *Small Property*, 172.

80. Ibid., 142.

81. Ibid., 169.

82. Ibid., 2.

83. Ibid., 45.

84. Ibid.

85. Lo, "Mobilizing the Tax Revolt," 320–21.

86. Lo, *Small Property*, xi.

87. Bill Monroe, "Interview of Howard Jarvis on Meet the Press," vol. 78, June 18, (Washington, DC: Kelly Press, Inc, 1978).

184 ～ Notes to Chapter 4

88. Howard Jarvis, *I'm Mad As Hell* (New York: Times Books, 1979), 280.

89. Jerry Carroll, "The Return of Howard Jarvis," *New West*, May 5, 1980, 59–66, 64.

90. Jarvis, *I'm Mad As Hell*, 33–34; 41.

91. Ibid., 34, 41.

92. Ibid., 25.

93. Ed Busch, "Howard Jarvis," *Personality*, December 1978, 4–13, 4.

94. Dennis McDougal, "Jarvis, at 75, nurses a rebellion," *Long Beach Independent*, March 12, 1978.

95. Jarvis, *I'm Mad As Hell*, 32–40.

96. Ibid., 25.

97. Jarvis, *I'm Mad As Hell*, 3.

98. Jarvis, "The American Tax Revolt," 3; California Fair Political Practices Commission, "Committee Campaign Statement, United Organizations of Taxpayers," Sacramento, March 7, 1977.

99. According to Joel Fox, the President of the Howard Jarvis Taxpayers Association (the latest in the long line of successor organizations to the United Organizations of Taxpayers), the campaign consulting firm Butcher-Forde provided commercial loans "to help get the organization up and running." Joel Fox, "Letter to the Editor," *Los Angeles Times*, March 11, 1996, B4.

100. California Fair Political Practices Commission, "Committee Campaign Statement, United Organizations of Taxpayers," Sacramento, July 22, 1976; March 7, 1977.

101. Ibid.

102. Jarvis, *I'm Mad As Hell*, 23.

103. California Fair Political Practices Commission, "Committee Campaign Statement, United Organizations of Taxpayers," Sacramento, March 7, 1977.

104. Busch, "Howard Jarvis," 4–5.

105. Paul Gann, *Oral History Interview*, conducted in 1987 and 1988 by Gabrielle Morris, Regional Oral History Office, University of California Berkeley, California State Archives State Government Oral History Program, 1988, 18.

106. Paul Glenchur, "Interview: Paul Gann, 'Downhome' Crusader for the Taxpayer," *The Guide*, August 31, 1978, 4–5.

107. Gann, *Oral History Interview*, 11.

108. Busch, "Howard Jarvis," 5.

109. Jarvis, 1979, 50–51; California Fair Political Practices Commission, "Committee Campaign Statement, United Organizations of Taxpayers," Sacramento, December 30, 1977.

110. Gann, *Oral History Interview*, 36.

111. Ibid., 20.

112. Lo, *Small Property*, 171.

113. Ibid.

114. Jarvis, *I'm Mad As Hell*, 49–53.

115. Ibid., 48–49.

116. Jack Fox, "Jarvis Reveals Shrewd Mind and Ambitions," *Newark Star Ledger*, October 15, 1978.

117. Jarvis, *I'm Mad As Hell*, 52–53.

118. Ibid., 112.

119. Ibid., 23.

120. Ibid., 145.

121. Ibid., 142.

122. "Sound and Fury Over Taxes," *Time*, June 19, 1979, 12–21, 14.

123. Steven Lawrence, "Peter Behr," *Long Beach Independent*, February 13, 1978.

124. Ibid.

125. "Last Hope for Tax Relief: Brown Willing to Back Republican Bill," *Long Beach Independent*, February 1, 1978.

126. "Behr's Tax-Relief Bill Passes Assembly Test," *Long Beach Independent*, February 18, 1978.

127. "Taxpayers Rebel, Take the Initiative," *Los Angeles Times*, May 7, 1978; "Property Taxes and the Revolt," *Los Angeles Times*, May 9, 1978; "Grass Roots on Airwaves to push 13," *Los Angeles Times*, May 28, 1978.

128. Herman Turk, "Imageries of Social Control," *Urban Life*, vol. 8, October 1979, 335–58, 341–42.

129. Ibid., 343.

130. Not until after the June election did any journalist write critically of Jarvis. Syndicated columnist Jack Anderson wrote a scathing account of Jarvis and the questionable motives underlying the measure. Anderson asserted that Jarvis had been "active in right-wing, money raising scams," and was "a veteran political con man who has scored some noteworthy stings over the years." Anderson and his research assistants traced "Jarvis and two associates, William Morrison and Norton H. Nathan," to a shady operation in 1964. Jarvis and his associates purportedly "set up shop in Los Angeles as 'Businessmen for Goldwater,'" soliciting thousands of dollars for the Republican candidate's campaign for the presidency. Evidently Jarvis's committee was not approved or sanction by Goldwater's campaign organization or the Republican National Committee, and no money ever made it to Goldwater. Jarvis, according to Anderson, used the scheme again in 1976, when he chaired the "Friends for Hayakawa Committee," "which raised $57,454 ostensibly for the Senate campaign of California Senator Hayakawa." But according to the Hayakawa financial records, no money ever was contributed by Jarvis's group. Jack Anderson, "Jarvis a veteran of political stings," *Washington Post*, July 27, 1978.

131. Ann Salisbury, "After 15 Years on Sideline, Howard Jarvis Man of Hour," *San Francisco Herald Examiner*, June 7, 1978.

132. McDougal, "Jarvis, at 75, Nurses a Rebellion."

133. Jack Scheibman, "Jarvis, Behr in Heated Exchange," *Long Beach Independent*, May 13, 1978.

134. Bob Egelko, "Jarvis Skips Dues, Says Didn't Call Behr Senile," *Long Beach Independent*, February 28, 1978.

135. "Grass Roots on Airwaves to Push 13," *Long Beach Independent*.

136. "Sound and Fury Over Taxes," 13, 21.

137. Ronald Soble, "Prop. 13 Backers Lead Foes in Fund Raising," *Los Angeles Times*, May 31, 1978.

138. Jarvis, 1979, 25; Vlae Kershner, "Anti-Tax Crusade is Losing Steam," *San Francisco Chronicle*, June 3, 1978.

139. Bob Schmidt, "Jarvis Opponents Map Plans to Beat Initiative," *Long Beach Independent*, January 20, 1978.

140. California Fair Political Practices Commission, "Committee Campaign Statement, United Organizations of Taxpayers," Sacramento, December 30, 1977.

141. Lo, *Small Property*, 45.

142. Schmidt, "Jarvis Opponents Map Plans to Beat Initiative."

143. California Fair Political Practices Commission, "Committee Campaign Statement, United Organizations of Taxpayers," Sacramento, December 30, 1977.

144. Ibid.

145. California Fair Political Practices Commission, "Committee Campaign Statement, Yes on 13 Committee," Sacramento, April 23, 1978.

146. California Fair Political Practices Commission, "Committee Campaign Statement, Yes on 13 Committee," Sacramento, June 30, 1978; December 31, 1978.

147. Tom Furlong, "Jarvis's Mr. Inside Has Outsize Job," *Long Beach Independent*, May 19, 1978.

148. California Fair Political Practices Commission, "Committee Campaign Statement, Yes on 13 Committee," Sacramento, May 25, 1978; June 30, 1978.

149. California Fair Political Practices Commission, "Committee Campaign Statement, Yes on 13 Committee," Sacramento, June 30, 1978.

150. California Fair Political Practices Commission, "Committee Campaign Statement, Yes on 13 Committee," Sacramento, May 25, 1978.

151. California Franchise Tax Board, "Audit Report, Yes on 13 Committee." Sacramento, September 11, 1978.

152. Jarvis, *I'm Mad as Hell*, 143.

153. California Fair Political Practices Commission, "Committee Campaign Statement, Yes on 13 Committee," Sacramento, June 30, 1978.

154. According to Jarvis, Butcher-Forde was paid the standard industry commission of 15 percent by the television and radio stations for every ad it placed. Jarvis, *Mad as Hell*, 143–44.

155. California Fair Political Practices Commission, "Committee Campaign Statement, Yes on 13 Committee," Sacramento, April 23, 1978.

156. California Franchise Tax Board, "Audit Report, Yes on 13 Committee." Sacramento, February 5, 1980.

157. Jarvis, *Mad as Hell,* 144.

158. California Fair Political Practices Commission, "Committee Campaign Statement, United Organizations of Taxpayers," Sacramento, June 30, 1978; California Fair Political Practices Commission, "Campaign Contribution and Spending Report," Sacramento, September 28, 1978.

159. California Fair Political Practices Commission, "Committee Campaign Statement, Yes on 13 Committee," Sacramento, May 25, 1978; June 30, 1978.

160. California Fair Political Practices Commission, "Campaign Contribution and Spending Report." Sacramento, September 28, 1978. Carroll, "The Return of Howard Jarvis," 62.

161. California Fair Political Practices Commission, "Historical Overview of Receipts and Expenditures by Ballot Measure Committees." Sacramento, April, 1988. Of the total campaign contributions made to the numerous groups opposing Prop. 13, the Los Angeles No on 13 Committee raised $1,676,210, or 79 percent of the total. The No on 13 campaign was run by campaign consultants Winner/Wagner & Associates, one of the top political consulting firms in California. Charles Winner and Ethan Wagner managed the campaign from their Los Angeles and Sacramento offices respectively, but tried to create a statewide coalition of groups to oppose the measure. Over half of the money opposing the measure came in contributions of $1,000 or more. The big contributors were the American Federation of State, County and Municipal Employees (AFSCME), the California Teachers Association (CTA), the California State Employees Association (CSEA), and dozens of major corporations, including Ford, Rockwell International, Atlantic Richfield, Standard Oil, BankAmerica, Pacific Mutual Life Insurance, Pacific Gas and Electric, Pacific Telephone and Telegraph, and Pacific Lighting.

162. Kershner, "Anti-Tax Crusade is Losing Steam."

163. Jarvis, *I'm Mad as Hell,* 64.

164. Ibid. 67.

165. Adams, *Secrets of the Tax Revolt,* 164.

166. Jarvis, *I'm Mad as Hell,* 68.

167. Phil Tracy, "The Jarvis Revolt: Rallying 'Round An Old Man's Obsession," *New West,* May 22, 1978, 17. While Jarvis himself might not have profited by the property tax cut, apartment owners did. According to a Congressional Budget Office study, owners of rental, commercial, industrial, and agricultural properties received about 58 percent of the tax relief. See Pfiffner, "Inflexible Budgets, Fiscal Stress, and the Tax Revolt," 50.

168. Jarvis, *I'm Mad as Hell,* 69–70.

169. Ibid., 64–65.

170. California Fair Political Practices Commission, "Committee Campaign Statement, United Organizations of Taxpayers," Sacramento, June 22, 1976; March 7, 1977.

171. Ibid.

172. Lo, *Small Property*, 172.

173. "Campaign '78: The Jarvis Amendment," *Political Animal*, January 27, 1978.

174. Lo, *Small Property*, 172.

175. Jarvis, *I'm Mad as Hell*, 67.

176. Howard Jarvis, Form letter to Members of the Los Angeles Apartment Owners Association, April 3, 1978.

177. Ibid.

178. California Fair Political Practices Commission, "Historical Overview of Receipts and Expenditures by Ballot Measure Committees." Sacramento, April, 1988.

179. California Fair Political Practices Commission, "Campaign Contribution and Spending Report," Sacramento, September, 28, 1978, F–8, F–9.

180. Lo, *Small Property*, 173.

181. Jarvis, *I'm Mad as Hell*, 9.

182. Ibid., 129.

183. Michael Engle, "Proposition 13: Whose Tax Revolt?" (Paper presented at the annual meeting of the New England Political Science Association, April 1979), 13.

## Chapter 5

1. Rebecca LaVally and Russell Snyder, "Proposition 13 Paved Way for Tax Revolts Across U.S.," *Los Angeles Times*, February 14, 1988, A3.

2. Eugene L. Meyer, "California's Proposition 13 Spawned Brood of Antitax Laws," *Washington Post*, August 15, 1983, A23.

3. The electorate voted on five other questions that were on the statewide ballot, approving two of them.

4. Center for Studies in Policy and the Public Interest, "The University of Massachusetts Poll, No. 1" (Boston: University of Massachusetts-Boston), May 1980, 6–7.

5. "Statewide Vote on Referendums," *Boston Globe*, November 9, 1980, E20.

6. Massachusetts Executive Office of Communities and Development, "Technical Bulletin, Proposition 2 1/2: Estimated Impacts," June 1980, 1. The two-thirds override provision was later changed by the state legislature to a simple majority.

7. Barbara Anderson, "Feeling Guilty? Read This," *Taxachusetts* (newsletter) Boston: Citizens for Limited Taxation, August 1981.

8. Personal interview with Barbara Anderson, Boston, May 7, 1997.

9. James Ring Adams, *Secrets of the Tax Revolt* (New York: Harcourt Brace Jovanovich, 1984), 329.

10. Quoted in Jack Citrin, "Introduction: The Legacy of Proposition 13," in Terry Schwadron, ed., *California and the American Tax Revolt* (Berkeley: University of California Press, 1984), 7.

11. Don Wash, "Barbara Anderson's on the money," *Cape Cod Times*, May 25, 1989.

12. Adams, *Secrets of the Tax Revolt*, 328.

13. Personal interview with Barbara Anderson.

14. Phone interview with Howard Foley, May 15, 1997.

15. "The Hidden Referenda," *The Wall Street Journal*, October 29, 1980.

16. Ian Menzies, "Prop 2 1/2: It's Time to Forget All Those Doomsday Cries," *Boston Globe*, August

18. 1980.

17. Walter Robinson, "Prop. 2 1/2 fight: Pros v. Enthusiasts," *Boston Globe*, September 30, 1980, 13.

18. Ibid.

19. Ibid.

20. "Scare Fiction and Scary Facts," *Boston Herald American*, October 26, 1980, B10.

21. "Prop. 2 1/2 at the Wire," *Boston Herald American*, November 3, 1980, A10.

22. Greg O'Brien, "Prop 2 1/2 has the Pulling Power at the Polls," *Boston Herald American*, November 3, 1980, A6.

23. Michael Segal, "Proposition 2 1/2: It's One Election that Money Could Not Buy," *Boston Herald American*, November 6, 1980, A19.

24. Charles Kenney, "Prop 2 1/2 Going Directly to the Voter," *Boston Globe*, October 19, 1980, 82.

25. Charles Kenney, "In Mass., Prop 2 1/2 Shares the Spotlight," *Boston Globe*, November 4, 1980, 1.

26. Greg O'Brien, "Mass. OKs Prop 2 1/2 by 2–1," *Boston Herald American*, November 5, 1980, A1.

27. Personal interview with Anderson.

28. See Lawrence Susskind, *Proposition 2 1/2: Its Impact on Massachusetts* (Cambridge, MA: Oelgeschlager, Gunn & Hain, 1983); Alvin Rabushka and Pauline Ryan, *The Tax Revolt* (Stanford: Hoover Institution, 1982), 193–94; O'Sullivan, et. al, *Property Taxes and Tax Revolts* (Cambridge: Cambridge University Press, 1995), 95–97.

29. Rabushka and Ryan, *The Tax Revolt*, 193.

30. O'Sullivan, et. al., *Property Taxes and Tax Revolts*, 95.

31. Rabushka and Ryan, *The Tax Revolt*, 194–95. Prior to Prop. 2 1/2, Boston raised nearly 80 percent of its local revenues from property taxes. John Powers, "The Stress of the Cities," *Boston Globe*, May 11, 1981, Special Section, 3.

32. O'Sullivan, et al., *Property Taxes and Tax Revolts*, 95.

33. Citrin, "Introduction: The Legacy of Proposition 13," 51.

34. Adams, *Secrets of the Tax Revolt*, 308.

35. Ibid.

36. Statement made in October 1980 by Donald Feder, the former Executive Director of CLT (1978–1979), quoted in Charles Kenney, "Who Gave Us 2 1/2?" *Boston Globe*, October 31, 1980, 22.

37. Memo, Citizens for Limited Taxation, "PLANNED EXPENDITURES TO-WARD A SIX-MONTH 'GUERRILLA WAR' REQUIRING IMMEDIATE FUND-ING," n.d. (circa April 1980).

38. "Property Taxes: A Painful Tradition Nobody Has Been Willing to Change," *Boston Globe* (Special Section: *Crisis, The Squeeze on State and Local Spending*), May 11, 1981, 25.

39. Lawrence Collins, "Tax Data and 2 1/2, *Boston Globe*, November 2, 1980, A25. Adams, *Secrets of the Tax Revolt*, 313; Citrin, "Introduction: The Legacy of Proposition 13," 45.

40. Laurence Collins, "Petitions to Cut Bay State Taxes Filed for 1980 Ballot," *Boston Globe*, August 2, 1979, 18.

41. Massachusetts Taxpayers Foundation, Inc., "Municipal Financial Data," Boston: Massachusetts Taxpayers Foundation, Inc., 1980, 2.

42. Robinson and Collins, "Q&A on Proposition 2 1/2: President Richard Manley opposes 2 1/2," *Boston Globe*, October 19, 1980, 2.

43. Lawrence Collins, "Tax Data and 2 1/2," *Boston Globe*, November 2, 1980, 25.

44. "Property Taxes: A Painful Tradition Nobody Has Been Willing to Change," *Boston Globe* (Special Section: *Crisis, The Squeeze on State and Local Spending*), May 11, 1981, 25. According to the Massachusetts Legislative Research Council, between 1922 and 1980, 155 proposals for limitations on "state taxation and spending, local taxation and spending, or both, were introduced into the General Court." Legislative Research Council, "Report Relative to Limiting Taxation and Spending by State and Local Governments" (Boston: Commonwealth of Massachusetts, 1980), 18.

45. Legislative Research Council, "Report Relative to Limiting Taxation, " 18.

46. Ibid.; Adams, *Secrets of the Tax Revolt*, 123.

47. In 1968, voters defeated the graduated income tax measure by a vote of 543,772 to 1,290,303; in 1972, the measure lost 712,030 to 1,455,639; in 1976, a similar measure was crushed by the vote of 645,483 to 1,787,302. Robert Turner, "Don't put all the blame for high taxes on the Legislature," *Boston Globe*, October 23, 1980, 19.

48. Kuttner, *Revolt of the Haves*, 162–63.

49. Legislative Research Council, "Report Relative to Limiting Taxation,"18–19.

50. Lawrence Collins, "Tax Data and 2 1/2," *Boston Globe*, November 2 1980, 25; Massachusetts Taxpayers Foundation, Inc., "Municipal Financial Data," Boston: Massachusetts Taxpayers Foundation, 1980, 1.

51. Several polls were conducted after the election. See Paul Shiman, "Proposi-tion 2 1/2 and Massachusetts Schools," Washington, DC: U.S. Department of Edu-

cation, National Institute of Education, October 1983; Helen Ladd and Julie Wilson, "Why Voters Support Tax Limitations: Evidence from Massachusetts' Proposition 2 1/2," Cambridge, MA: John F. Kennedy School of Government, Harvard University, January 1982, Working Paper no. 76; Helen Ladd and Julie Wilson, "Proposition 2 1/2: Explaining the Vote," Cambridge, MA: John F. Kennedy School of Government, Harvard University, April 1981, Research Report R81–1.

52. Cited in Segal, "Proposition 2 1/2: It's One Election that Money Could Not Buy," A19.

53. Center for Studies in Policy and the Public Interest, "The University of Massachusetts Poll, No. 1," Boston: University of Massachusetts–Boston, May, 1980, 2–3.

54. Ibid., iii.

55. Ibid., 5.

56. "Prop 2 1/2 Alluring, Confusing, *Boston Globe*, October 13, 1986, 25.

57. "Tax-cutting Question is Given a Slight Edge" *Boston Globe*, November 2, 1980, 2. The poll was conducted by Research Analysis Corp. of Boston on public opinion toward Proposition 2 1/2. The poll had a 5 percent +/- margin of error. A separate private poll conducted about the same time found that voters favored a reduction in the auto excise tax by an impressive eight-to-one margin. Walter Robinson, "Proposition 2 1/2 Would Slash Auto Excise, Too," *Boston Globe*, October 14, 1980, 17.

58. As Sherry Tvedt Davis astutely notes, the "conventional explanation of this and other 'taxpayer revolts' is that voters want lower property taxes and smaller local government." Sherry Tvedt Davis, "A Brief History of Proposition 2 1/2," in Susskind, ed, *Proposition 2 1/2: Its Impact on Massachusetts* (Cambridge: MA: Oelgeschlager, Gunn & Hain, 1983), 3–10, 4.

59. Ibid.

60. Ibid.

61. Adams, *Secrets of the Tax Revolt*, 324.

62. Personal interview with Richard Manley, Boston, May 5, 1997.

63. Kenney, "Who Gave Us 2 1/2?" 21.

64. Personal interview with Anderson.

65. Kenney, "Who Gave Us 2 1/2?" 21.

66. Ibid.

67. Ibid.

68. Robert Turner, "Don't Put All the Blame for High Taxes on the Legislature," *Boston Globe*, October 23, 1980, 19.

69. Adams, *Secrets of the Tax Revolt*, 324.

70. Ibid, 317.

71. Anderson has always found the term "housewife" amusing. As she told a *Boston Globe* reporter in 1990, "My two ex-husbands would think it's pretty funny, too." As for her hair, she says she has it "colored to match my temper." Nathan

Cobb, "Some people put drama in their lives by going to horror movies. I work in Massachusetts politics," *Boston Globe*, (Magazine) January 14, 1990, 16.

72. Personal interview with Anderson.

73. Cobb, "Some people put drama in their lives by going to horror movies," 16.

74. Davis, "A Brief History of Proposition 2 1/2," 5.

75. Letter, Commonwealth of Massachusetts, Office of the Secretary of the Commonwealth, to Edward F. King, Director, Citizens for Limited Taxation, December 9, 1977. Form letter, Edward F. King, Director, CLT, to Republican State Committee Members, August 29, 1979. Form letter, Lee Nason, Libertarian Party of Massachusetts, to Libertarian party members, November 11, 1977.

76. Personal interview with Anderson.

77. Ibid.; Personal interview with Chip Faulkner, Boston, May 6 1997.

78. Mitchell Lynch, "Will Massachusetts Be the First State to Set Tax Limits?" *Wall Street Journal*, December 19, 1977.

79. Massachusetts uses the indirect initiative, and has a different process for statutory as opposed to constitutional amendment ballot initiatives. Citizens of the Bay State may propose both constitutional amendments and statutory initiatives, but unlike states with the direct initiative, such as California, the legislature is involved with each process. As a result, Massachusetts's initiative process is a much more elaborate and complicated process, which greatly increases the possibility for defeat of the measure along the way.

Citizens may circulate petitions for either statutes or constitutional amendments during the fall, after the measure is approved by the Attorney General. The number of votes needed equals three percent of the entire vote cast for governor in the last election (at the time, nearly 60,000 signatures). If enough certified signatures are gathered, the measure is automatically entered into the legislative session the following January. During the session, the legislature has until the first Wednesday of May to enact the measure. If this occurs, the initiative does not appear on the ballot for citizens to approve, as the legislature has already made the measure into a law. If the measure does not garner enough support in the legislature, the measure's sponsors are required to collect an additional .5 percent of the total vote for Governor in the preceding election (approximately 10,000 signatures in 1980), in order to place it on the ballot for the voters to consider. If this occurs, the legislature also has the option of offering an alternative ballot measure for the voters to consider on election day. If the additional signatures are collected, the electorate gets to vote on the measure at the following general election. With constitutional amendment ballot initiatives, after a group collects the required number of valid signatures, the legislature must vote on the measure in two successive Constitutional Conventions (a specially held joint session of the legislature), with one election in between them. If the legislature, in either of the two votes, fails to support the measure with less than a quarter of the vote, the measure does not appear on the ballot. With constitutional amendment initiatives, the legislature may, with the consent of the measure's sponsors, alter the language of the measure, and if a quarter of the members support it, place it on the ballot. For more information on these two processes, see Article XLVIII of the State Constitution.

80. Legislature Research Council, "Limiting Taxation and Spending by State and Local Governments," Boston: Commonwealth of Massachusetts, 1980, 14.

81. Personal interview with Anderson.

82. Anderson and CLT claimed that the changes made by the legislature would have "placed all state aid to local governments outside of the spending limit," and that "[a]dditional state aid above the current funding level would be excluded." Legislative Research Council, "Limiting Taxation and Spending,"1980, 13–15.

83. James Perry and James Hyatt, "Stopping the Bucks," *The Wall Street Journal*, June 6, 1978, 1.

84. Kenney, "Who Gave Us 2 1/2?" 21.

85. Davis, "A Brief History of Proposition 2 1/2," 5.

86. Chris Black, How Prop. 2 1/2 Became Law," *Boston Globe*, July 1, 1981, 41.

87. Donald Feder, "Statement of Donald Feder, executive director of Citizens for Limited Taxation," June 29, 1978.

88. Personal interview with Anderson.

89. Chris Black, "How Prop. 2 1/2 Became Law," *Boston Globe*, July 1, 1981, 41. Heinz Muehlmann, at the time the chief economist at AIM, analyzed CLT's ballot measure before they brought it to Bellotti, and said it "didn't add up," but Don Feder ignored his advice. Personal interview with Muehlmann.

90. Personal interview with Anderson.

91. Personal interview with Anderson.

92. Kuttner, 26.

93. Adams, *Secrets of the Tax Revolt*, 319.

94. Warren T. Brookes, "Property Taxes were the Key to Gov. Dukakis' Loss to King," *Boston Herald American*, September 28, 1978.

95. Ibid.

96. Nick King, "Jarvis Takes to Bay State Television to Give King's Candidacy a Boost," *Boston Globe*, November 3, 1978, 1.

97. Robert Dworak, *Taxpayers, Taxes, and Government Spending* (New York: Praeger, 1980), 95–96.

98. Citrin, "Introduction: The Legacy of Proposition 13," 45; Davis, "A Brief History of Proposition 2 1/2," 6; Adams, *Secrets of the Tax Revolt*, 320. CLT's Edward F. King urged the Governor to veto the four percent measure, calling it a "sham." "I would prefer no tax cap to the Legislature's 4 percent bill," King said. Lawrence Collins, "GOP King Backs Governor on Zero Cap," *Boston Globe*, April 25, 1979, 18.

99. Personal interview with Anderson.

100. Michael Conniff, "Jarvis Brings His Message to Newton," *Boston Herald American*, October 16, 1978, 26.

101. Personal interview with Anderson, May 6, 1997. According to Faulkner, CLT included the measure because many landlords in California refused to pass on their savings to their tenants. "We wanted to give the renters something." Walter Robinson, "Prop 2 1/2 would help some tenants," *Boston Globe*, October 15, 1980, 19.

102. Personal interview with Anderson.

103. Ibid.

104. According to a six-page CLT memo from mid-summer 1979, most probably written by Don Feder, MSADA's "board of directors has endorsed 2 1/2 and they're contributing $20,000. The MSADA has over 500 dealer-members. Arthur Bent (528–1111), head of their PAC will help us to involve dealers in the drive and to raise money from them." CLT Memo #2, "Preparing for the Petition Drive," n.d. (circa July 1979), 4. Elliot Savitz sent out a letter soliciting funds from the auto dealers, reading in part, "C.L.T. is basically a grass roots organization . . . . Our strength is our statewide association of members and dedicated volunteers who are capable of leading a petition drive . . . . However, this strength can only be harnessed by the support and muscle of the business community." Letter, to MSADA members, from Elliot Savitz, CLT finance chairman, n.d. (circa summer 1979).

105. UPI, "Tax Cut Plan Unveiled," *The South Middlesex News* December, 9, 1978, 2AY.

106. Comments made by Feder as quoted by Walter Robinson, "Tax-curb Backer Wants Services Cut," *Boston Globe*, May 10, 1979, 20.

107. Personal interview with Faulkner.

108. When Anderson eventually took over for CLT in 1980, reporters wanted to know if she wanted to cut public services along the same lines as Feder. Asked by a reporter, "Are you a Libertarian?" Anderson, not skipping a beat, replied, "No I'm an Aquarian, with Libra rising." Personal interview with Anderson.

109. Ibid. Feder evidently came within one vote of being fired. Kenney, "Who Gave Us 2 1/2?" 21.

110. Laurence Collins, "Petitions to Cut Bay State Taxes Filed for 1980 Ballot," *Boston Globe*, August 2, 1979, 18.

111. Anderson stated that until Elliot Savitz took over CLT's fundraising activities in 1979, "no one had cleaned up the list . . . . I doubt there were more than 2,000 people involved in 1979." Interview with Anderson.

112. Kenney, "Who Gave Us 2 1/2?" 21.

113. Personal interview with Anderson.

114. Personal interview with Muehlmann. In blatant understatement, Adams describes Jobs for Massachusetts as a "public-service organization." Adams, *Secrets of the Tax Revolt*, 317.

115. Personal interview with Muehlmann.

116. Ibid.

117. Lawrence Collins, "Tax Data and 2 1/2, *Boston Globe*, November 2, 1980, 25.

118. Phone interview with Foley.

119. Massachusetts High Technology Council, "A New Social Contract for Massachusetts" (Boston: Massachusetts High Tech Council, 1979[?]), 3. Quoted in Adams, *Secrets of the Tax Revolt*, 320.

120. Ibid., 319–20.

121. Personal interview with Muehlmann.

122. Legislative Research Council, "Limiting Taxation and Spending," 15.

123. AIM failed to collect the signatures it promised and left most of the money raising to Howard Foley and the High Tech firms. A CLT memo cited as a disadvantage of the petition drive, "Lack of co-ordination with AIM" and the "delay with AIM." CLT Memo, "OUTLINE ANALYSIS OF THE PETITION DRIVE," n.d. (circa Winter/Spring 1980).

124. Phone interview with Foley.

125. Personal interview with Anderson. The MTA urged a boycott of the Papa Gino's restaurant because of its efforts to assist the Prop. 2 1/2 campaign. According to the MTA, Papa Gino's "refused to allow petitions for the MTA's tax relief plan to be circulated in its restaurants in Massachusetts" in June, 1980. MTA, "MTA Urges Protests to Papa Gino's," *MTA Today*, June 16, 1980, 5.

126. CLT, "Memo #2," 4–5.

127. Personal interview with Faulkner.

128. Personal interview with Anderson.

129. Some of the groups included local taxpayers associations, Republican Party town committees, the National Federation of Independent Businesses, the Conservative Caucus, the American Conservative Union, the Massachusetts Libertarian Party, the Jaycees, MSADA, the National Taxpayers Union, and the Small Business Association of New England, and supporters of Edward F. King. CLT, "Memo #2."

130. In late November and early December, just before the petitions were due, CLT hired "temps" from The Shell Bureau, ostensibly to help collect signatures. Commonwealth of Massachusetts, Office of Campaign and Political Finance, "Summary of the Receipts, Expenditures, Disbursements and Liabilities," Citizens for Limited Taxation, August 22, 1980.

131. "Stop 2 1/2 Campaign Yields 110,000 Signatures," *MTA Today*, December 13, 1979, 1.

132. Commonwealth of Massachusetts, Superior Court No. 39898. Suffolk, ss. *William H. Herbert, Plaintiff v. State Ballot Law Commission*. The court, in finding for the State Ballot Law Commission which validated CLT's statutory petition, found that Gregory Hyatt "admitted that he had signed his wife's name as jurator ON one petition and his father's name as jurator on another petition," and also, "executed jurats in his own name on twenty-one petition pages containing a total of 117 certified signatures which the Commission found to be non-genuine (forged) signatures and which the Commission invalidated." According to AIM's Muehlmann, Hyatt "over promised signatures," but AIM provided Hyatt with legal

council who "outmaneuvered" the MTA's lawyers and "bailed out" Hyatt. Because of all the "brouhaha" AIM's legal council advised against getting involved with CLT or High Tech in the future. Interview with Muehlmann.

133. Don Cassidy, Draft Memo, "Analysis of Petition Drive, 1979," n.d.

134. Don Cassidy, "Legislature Votes no On Prop 2 1/2: CLT Prepares second Petition Drive," Press Release, May 6, 1980.

135. Barbara Anderson, CLT Executive Director, "Statement of Barbara Anderson, executive director," Press Release, July 2, 1980.

136. Form letter to CLT board members, from Ronald J. Graham, CLT board member, May 1, 1980. In the letter, Graham reminded the board that:

> We are currently dependent on contributions from a small group of generous tax-limitation advocates in the business sector and a larger group of small contributors in the grass-roots sector. We have learned from our Proposition 2 1/2 effort that we cannot depend on extensive assistance from business association because—as multi-issue organizations, it is not in their best interest to be tied too closely to a single interest organization over which they have little control. We have also learned that individual taxpayers are an emotional constituency that cannot be depended upon for financial support unless they are "hurting"— and this type of support would arrive too late to be of maximum value to CLT.

Graham submitted to his fellow board members:

> We looked to outside sources for assistance in generating additional funds; however, we now realize that these sources [High Tech and AIM] have diversified interests that limit their participation in CLT fund raising efforts. It is time for us to realize that our financial survival and program effectiveness is an internal responsibility . . . . Therefore, I believe that our Board of Directors should be expanded to include business and community leaders who are respected and influential in their own fields and who are philosophically in agreement with CLT's objectives . . . . [They] would be asked if they will allow their names to appear on CLT stationery in order to lend prestige and generate confidence in our organization.

137. Adams, *Secrets of the Tax Revolt*, 327. Anderson claims she did not "know what happened in the secret meetings with the legislature, whether the High Tech Council made a commitment to the legislative leadership or not." Personal interview with Anderson.

138. Warren Brookes, "How the Legislature Destroyed the Initiative Petition Process," *Boston Herald American*, July 11, 1980, A15. Brookes reasoned that, "Since it was the CLT who had to obtain more than two thirds of these signatures, the business community, specifically AIM and Hi-Tech, has an obligation to carry this forward."

139. Muehlmann remembers the amendment passing at 3AM. Personal interview with Muehlmann.

140. Personal interview with Anderson.

141. According to Anderson, "AIM came out against us, and were not going to support it . . . but he [Muehlmann] was going to find a way to help, which they did. They paid some of our bills or something." Personal interview with Anderson. Muehlmann remembers that publicly, CLT's measure wasn't endorsed by AIM, but its Board of Directors said push for them, "without an official declaration of support for 2 1/2." Personal interview with Muehlmann.

142. Personal interview with Anderson.

143. Massachusetts High Technology Council, "Minutes of Executive Committee of the Board of Directors Meeting," August 26; September 2; September 8; September 15; and September 30. Cited and quoted in Adams, *Secrets of the Tax Revolt*, 327–28.

144. Ray Stata, the Chairman of High Tech Council's Board of Directors, wrote in an Op Ed piece a day before election day in which he said:

The High Tech Council recognizes that Proposition 2 1/2 isn't perfect, but it's all we have. Some elements, such as the limitation to tax revenue growth, are ill conceived, and the council has vowed to work toward legislative revision of those sections. On the whole, however, Proposition 2/12 is the correct medicine for a chronic illness.

Ray Stata, "The Right Message," *Boston Globe* November 3, 1980, 15.

145. Anderson, Flier to Media, August 8, 1980.

146. Personal interview with Anderson.

147. Over the previous two years, the relationship between CLT and the wider business community was not tight. In an October 1980 interview, Feder recalled various differences between CLT and the business community over the years. Because "CLT was never run by their people. It wasn't organized or controlled by the country club set," Feder claims that it never received much financial support from business elites. Those in the business community, Feder says, "were very wary of us. They considered us extreme." Kenney, "Who Gave Us 2 1/2?" 21.

148. Personal interview with Anderson.

149. Phone interview with Foley.

150. Ibid.

151. Personal interview with Anderson.

152. Legislative Research Council, Legislative Research Bureau, "Two Tax and Spending Limitation Initiative Proposals on 1980 Massachusetts State Election Ballot," Boston: Commonwealth of Massachusetts, August 4, 1980.

153. Personal interview with Anderson.

154. Ibid.

155. Legislative Research Council, Legislative Research Bureau, "Two Tax and Spending Limitation Initiative Proposals."

156. Phone interview with Foley.

157. Personal interview with Anderson.

158. Commonwealth of Massachusetts, Office Of Campaign and Political Finance, Concerned Citizens for Lower Taxes, "Campaign Finance Report," October 1–October 15, 1980.

159. Commonwealth of Massachusetts, Office Of Campaign and Political Finance, Concerned Citizens for Lower Taxes, "Campaign Finance Report," October 1–October 15, 1980. Coopers & Lybrand provided the legal counsel for CLT and AIM after the MTA challenged the validity of the petition signatures in December, 1979. Personal interview with Muehlmann.

160. Ibid.

161. Personal interview with Anderson.

162. Personal interview with Anderson and phone interview with Foley. During the meeting, as Anderson recalls, "Dick Morris definitely made an impression." Phone interview with Richard Dresner, April 28, 1997.

163. Anderson and Foley both praised their working relationship with DM&T. Anderson remembers, "they didn't come in and try to run the campaign; we ran the campaign; Howard and I made all the decisions . . . they did all the production and the buys and gave some advice . . . they were great to work with." Personal interview with Anderson; Phone interview with Foley.

164. Memo, to Howard Foley, from Richard Dresner, Richard Morris and Barry Kaplovitz, regarding "Draft Campaign Plan," September 18, 1980. New Sounds was run by Tony Schwartz, the founder of political advertising. Produced ads almost exclusively for liberal and Democratic candidates, from John and Ted Kennedy to Bill Clinton. Schwartz conceived and produced what is most probably the most famous campaign spot in history, the 1964 "Daisy Spot" for the Johnson campaign. Personal interview with Tony Schwartz, New York City, April 18, 1997.

165. David Wilson, "A Vote for 2 1/2" *Boston Globe*, October 12, 1980, 31.

166. Confidential Memo, from The Office [CLT], to Spokesmen for Question Two, "The Best Approach on Behalf of Prop 2 1/2 in Light of Survey Research Conducted for the High Tech Council," October 11, 1980.

167. Personal interview with Anderson; Personal interview with Schwartz. Dick Morris is far from alone in calling the agoraphobic Schwartz, the man "who originated modern political advertising." Richard Morris, *Behind the Oval Office* (New York: Random House, 1997), 53.

168. Commonwealth of Massachusetts, Campaign Financing Report, "Vote No on Question 2 Committee," 1980. Thirteen other separate groups formed to oppose Prop. 2 1/2, but the Vote No committee accounted for 91 percent of the total amount raised in opposition to the measure. In addition to its own independent expenditures, the MTA funneled $363,040 to the Vote No coalition, accounting for nearly 70 percent of the total contributions.

169. UPI, "Prop. 2 1/2: Both Sides Step Up Their Crusades," *Boston Globe*, October 22, 1980, 26.

170. Ironically, the MTA's anti-2 1/2 strategy may have been complicated by the fact that on March 28, 1980, the teachers union entered into an agreement with their future adversaries, the High Tech Council, to retrain unemployed teachers in the high technology industry. With a $79,000 federal grant, the two organizations, beginning June 30, 1980, were to begin a twenty-six-week course to train teachers as entry-level programmers. The agreement was brokered by Howard Foley, President of High Tech, and William Hebert, the Executive Director-Treasurer of the MTA. MTA, "MTA/High Tech Council Plan for Retraining Teachers Gets a Big Reception," *MTA Today*, April 14, 1980.

171. MTA, "What we are fighting . . ." *MTA Today*, September 10, 1979, 8. In an effort to stymie CLT's initiative, the MTA claimed it was "forced to file an 'alternative' to Proposition 2 1/2 so that voters would have an option in November that would relieve local property taxes while preserving public services." During its petition drive, the MTA collected 110,000 signatures, twice as many as needed to secure a place on the November 1980 ballot. MTA, "Stop 2 /12 Campaign Yields 110,000 Signatures," *MTA Today*, December 13, 1979, 1.

172. Walter Robinson, "Question 3— Its Tax 'Limit' is the Issue, *Boston Globe*, October 29, 1980, 26.

173. Kenney, "Prop 2 1/2 Going Directly to the Voter," 82.

174. Robert Turner, "Don't Put All the Blame for High Taxes on the Legislature," *Boston Globe*, October 23, 1980, 19.

175. Walter Robinson, "Question 3— Its Tax 'Limit' is the Issue, *Boston Globe*, October 29, 1980, 26.

176. "Prop 2 1/2: Vote 'No,'" *Boston Globe*, October 27, 1980, 14.

177. Ibid.

178. Kirk Scharfenberg, "Steering Clear of 2 1/2 Fire," *Boston Globe*, October 11, 1980, 11.

179. Ibid; Peter Cowen, "In Boston, Official Opposition is Low-Key," *Boston Globe*, October 31, 21.

180. Walter Robinson, "Q&A: Pressman on Prop 2 1/2," *Boston Globe*, October 26, 1980, 2.

181. Richard Stewart, "Many in Hub Say Tax Bills Steer Them to Prop 2 1/2" *Boston Globe*, October 23, 1980, 34.

182. Segal, "Proposition 2 1/2: It's One Election That Money Could Not Buy," A19.

## Chapter 6

1. William Claiborne, "In Colorado, the Chips are Down—And Out," *Washington Post*, February 20, 1993, A4.

2. J. Sebastian Sinisi, "Proposal's Author Not Picture of a Firebrand," *The Denver Post*, October 30, 1988, 7B.

3. Jeffrey Roberts, "Tax Limit Hailed and Decried," *The Denver Post*, November 5, 1992, 1A.

4. Jeffrey Roberts, "Bruce: Taxpayers Must Seize Control," *The Denver Post*, October 14, 1992, 1A.

5. Steve Rabey, "Court Strikes Down Homosexual Rights Ban," *Christianity Today*, June 17, 1996, 68; George de Lama, "Colorado Springs Showdown: Gays Facing Fundamentalists," *Chicago Tribune*, April 27, 1993, 1; Tony Freemantle, "The 'Hate State' Label Dividing Colorado," *The Houston Chronicle*, January 17, 1993, A1; Sankar Sen, "Marketing and Minority Civil Rights: The Case of Amendment 2 and the Colorado Boycott," *Journal of Public Policy & Marketing* 15 (Fall 1996).

6. Tony Freemantle, "The 'Hate State' Label Dividing Colorado," *The Houston Chronicle*, January 17, 1993, A1. Colorado for Family Values' media campaign included "X-rated images from gay-pride parades" and warnings of homosexuals' influence on children. Michael Booth, "TV Blitz to Promote Amendment 2," *The Denver Post*, October 20, 1992, 1B.

7. Sinisi, "Proposal's Author Not Picture of a Firebrand," B7.

8. The name Tabor is one of the oldest and most revered in Colorado history. In the late 1800s, Horace A. W. Tabor, a silver mine operator, was one of the wealthiest men in Colorado. He built an opulent opera house in Leadville, CO, was the first mayor of Leadville, became Lieutenant Governor of Colorado, and had a brief stint as a U.S. Senator. His marriage to his second wife, the glamorous Elizabeth Bonduel McCourt Doe, known as Baby Doe, made waves in Leadville, CO, where the couple resided, but also in Washington, DC. But the Silver Panic of 1893 bankrupted him, and he died penniless in 1899. Percy Stanley Fritz, *Colorado: The Centennial State* (New York: Prentice-Hall, 1941), 304–06.

9. In late January 1992, the Office of the Secretary of State reversed its December 6, 1991 decision to block Bruce's proposal from appearing on the November 1992 ballot, as the office conceded it had erroneously disqualified thousands of valid signatures. John Racine, "Colorado," *The Bond Buyer*, February 4, 1992, 28.

10. Dana Milbank, "Ballot Warriors Challenge State, Local Governments," *Wall Street Journal*, May 20 1997, A20.

11. Jeffrey Roberts, "Tax-Limit Amendment Passes," *The Denver Post*, November 4, 1992, A1.

12. Michael Romano, "Bruce Proposal Going Down," *Rocky Mountain News*, November 9, 1994, A5; Michael Romano, "Ballot Issues Limit Power of Politicians," *Rocky Mountain News*, September 25, 1994, A4; Steve Lipsher, "Ballot Drive a Job for Pros," *The Denver Post*, September 19, 1994, A1; Steve Lipsher, "Grassroots Activists Target Bruce Election Reform Plan," *The Denver Post*, January 24, 1994, A1.

13. Roberts, "Tax Limit Hailed and Decried," 11A.

14. Fritz, *Colorado: The Centennial State*, 259.

15. E.T. Halaas, et al., *Financing Government in Colorado: Report of the Governor's Tax Study Group* (Denver: State of Colorado, 1959), quoted in Curtis Martin and Rudolph Gomez, *Colorado Government and Politics*, 4th edition, (Boulder, CO: Pruett Publishing Company, 1976), 68.

16. Ibid.

17. Ibid.

18. Robert Lorch, *Colorado's Government*, 3rd ed. (Boulder: Colorado Associated University Press, 1983), 224; Colorado Public Expenditure Council, "A Colorado Taxpayer Report," Vol. XXXVI, December 1990, 1.

19. John Straayer, *The Colorado General Assembly* (Boulder: University Press of Colorado, 1990), 282.

20. Dirk Johnson, "Taxpayer Revolt in Colorado Vote Raises Alarm About Lost Services," *New York Times*, November 15, 1992, A18.

21. Straayer, *The Colorado General Assembly*, 283.

22. Michelle Fulcher, "High Property Taxes Spark Debate, Ignite Colorado Tax Revolt," *The Denver Post*, October 31, 1988, 7B.

23. Colorado Public Expenditure Council, "A Colorado Taxpayer Report," Vol. XXXVI, December 1990, 1.

24. Colorado Public Expenditure Council, "A Colorado Taxpayer Report," Vol. XXXV, November, 1988, 1.

25. Colorado Public Expenditure Council, "A Colorado Taxpayer Report," Vol. XXXV, November, 1988, 1. In 1988, residential property was assessed at only 16 percent of actual value.

26. Colorado Public Expenditure Council, "A Colorado Taxpayer Report," Vol. XXXVI, May 1990, 4.

27. Fred Brown, "Amendment 1 Ads Play with Truth," *The Denver Post*, November 13, 1990, 5A. According to a study by the Legislative Council of the Colorado General Assembly, between 1982 and 1987, "the combined state and local tax burden jumped 57 percent," although personal income of Coloradans increased on 41 percent. "Taxes Climb Faster than Pay," *The Denver Post*, June 8, 1988, 1B.

28. In contrast, between 1955 and 1969 "Colorado's per capita state and local taxes as a percent of per capita income exceed the national average." Colorado Public Expenditure Council, "A Colorado Taxpayer Report," Vol. XXXIII, May 1987, 1–3.

29. Straayer, *The Colorado General Assembly*, 284.

30. Thomas Cronin and Robert Loevy, *Colorado Politics and Government: Governing the Centennial State* (Lincoln: University of Nebraska Press, 1993), 300.

31. Ibid.

32. Fred Brown, "Voting on Taxes," *The Denver Post*, October 28, 1992, 7B.

33. John Gunther, *Inside USA*. (New York: Harper and Brothers, 1947), 213. Quoted in Cronin and Loevy, *Colorado Politics and Government*, 18.

34. Carl Ubbelohde, et al., eds., *A Colorado History*, 3rd ed. (Boulder: Pruett Publishing Company, 1972), 329–48.

35. Political scientist Daniel Elazar has characterized aptly Colorado's political culture as a state with a "populist-cum-moralistic bent." Daniel Elazar, "Series Introduction," in Cronin and Loevy, *Colorado Politics and Government*, xxxi.

36. Don Sowers, *The Effect of Tax Limitation Upon State and Local Governments in Colorado* (Boulder: University of Colorado, 1936), 5.

37. Ibid., 7.

38. Cronin and Loevy, *Colorado Politics and Government*, 18.

39. Ibid., 116. All survey data is from the Colorado College – Colorado Citizens Poll, conducted by the polling firm Talmey-Drake, Denver, Colorado, September, 1990.

40. Ibid.

41. Ibid., 108–11.

42. Ibid., 111.

43. Alan Rosenthal, *The Third House: Lobbyists and Lobbying in the States* (Washington, DC: CQ Press, 1993), 103–04.

44. Cronin and Loevy, *Colorado Politics and Government*, 110–11.

45. Ibid., 110.

46. Ibid.

47. Ibid., 111.

48. Ibid., 300. As evidence, Cronin and Loevy cite how Coloradans, at both the state and local levels of government, have supported tax increases to pay for libraries, museums, public transportation, professional sports stadiums, and public schools.

49. Roberts, "Bruce: Taxpayers Must Seize Control," 18A. Prior to Bruce's first endeavor in 1988, Coloradans had defeated tax- and spending-limitation citizen initiatives in 1966, 1972 (two), 1976, 1978, and 1986. Jennifer Gavin, "Anti-Tax Crusader Bruce Strikes Again for 1992," *The Denver Post*, November 16, 1991, 20A.

50. California's Proposition 62, placed on the ballot by Howard Jarvis in 1986, passed by a margin of 58 to 42 percent. Jarvis died in August 1986, a little less than three months before to the election. The campaign for Prop. 62, which required a majority popular vote to be taken before any new taxes could be imposed by a local government, was run effectively by Jarvis' seasoned consulting firm Butcher-Forde Consulting. One Butcher-Forde direct mailing that asked supporters for contributions to the campaign stood out in particular. Targeting 325,000 California supporters of the measure, Butcher-Forde sent them a picture of the deceased Jarvis enclosed with a black border. It informed the potential contributors that Jarvis, "spent the last year of his life working to place Proposition 62 on the November ballot. And with your generous support, his work will not have been in vain." Ronald Soble, "California Elections," *Los Angeles Times*, October 2, 1986, A3.

51. Ann Schrader, "Coloradans Turn Down Amend. 4," *The Denver Post*, November 5, 1986, 1A.

52. Ann Schrader, "Harvesting Reform," *The Denver Post*, September 28, 1986, 10A.

53. Jeffrey Roberts and Robert Kowalski, "Proposal to Limit Taxes Takes Jump Toward Ballot," *The Denver Post*, August 2, 1986, 3C.

54. Ann Schrader, "Calif. Tax Activist Backs Amendment 4," *The Denver Post*, October 28, 1986, 3B. Keith Pope, "Groups Launch Tax-Limitation Drive," *United Press International*, June 10, 1986; "Tax-Limit Signatures Total 80,000," *The Denver Post*, August 1, 1986, 3B; Carl Miller, "Look Closely at Amendment 4," *The Denver Post*, October 5, 1986, 6F.

55. "*The Denver Post*/Center 4 Poll," *The Denver Post*, October 5, 1986, 14A; Carl Miller, "Wirth, Kramer Even; Amendment 4 Slips," *The Denver Post*, October 22, 1986, 4B; Ann Schrader, "Coloradans Turn Down Amend. 4," *The Denver Post*, November 5, 1986, 1A, 15A.

56. "Lamm Lashes Out at Amendment Four," *The Denver Post*, September 14, 1986, 7B.

57. Jeffrey Roberts, "Big Bucks Being Spent to Defeat Amendment 4," *The Denver Post*, October 25, 1986, 5A.

58. Colorado Public Expenditure Council, "A Colorado Taxpayer Report," Vol. XXXV, October 1988.

59. In late October 1986, opponents of Amendment 4, led by the Citizens for Representative Government, had raised $274,910; the Association of Colorado Taxpayers, the primary supporters of Amendment 4, had raised only $24,986. Jeffrey Roberts, "Big Bucks Being Spent to Defeat Amendment 4," *Denver Post* October 25, 1986, 5A. In the end, opponents of Amendment 4 outspent proponents of the measure by twelve times. Michelle Fulcher, "Business Raising $250,000 to Fight Tax-Limit Plan," *The Denver Post*, October 19, 1988, 11A.

60. Phone interview with Douglas Bruce, June 24, 1996.

61. Phone interview with Bruce. Although he was an apartment owner in Los Angeles during the late 1970s, according to Bruce as well as the campaign contribution records of the United Organizations of Taxpayers and the Yes on 13 Committee, Bruce did not make any financial contributions in support of Prop. 13.

62. Phone interview with Bruce.

63. Ibid.

64. Ibid.

65. Mary George, "New Tax-Control Ramrod Promises to Keep Trying," *The Denver Post*, July 27, 1988, 5B.

66. Jeffrey Roberts, "Campaign for Tax Limit Plan Kicks Off," *The Denver Post*, January 14, 1988, 4B.

67. Ibid.

68. Jeffrey Roberts, "Voted Down Last Year, Tax-Limitation Initiative Likely to be Resurrected for '88," *The Denver Post*, October 12, 1987, 3B.

69. Jeffrey Roberts, "Citizens Group Starts Drive to Limit Taxes," *The Denver Post*, March 8, 1988, 3B.

70. Michelle Fulcher, "Tax-Limit Ballot Issue Disallowed," *The Denver Post*, September 22, 1988, 1B, 5B.

71. Ibid.

72. Steve Garnaas, "New Tax-Limit Petitions Filed," *The Denver Post*, October 7, 1988, 1B; Howard Pankratz, "Taxpayers Bill of Rights Reprieved," *The Denver Post*, October 5, 1988, A1.

73. Roberts, "Campaign for Tax Limit Plan Kicks Off," 4B; Colorado Public Expenditure Council, "A Colorado Taxpayer Report," Vol. XXXV, October, 1988, 1–3.

74. Bruce Finley, "Tax-Limit Initiative Faces New Opposition," *The Denver Post*, July 22, 1988, 2B.

75. Charles J. Cannon, *United Press International*, July 26, 1988.

76. Johnson, "Taxpayer Revolt in Colorado Vote Raises Alarm About Lost Services," A18.

77. Charles J. Cannon, *United Press International*, July 26, 1988.

78. Carl Miller, "Foes of Tax Measure Surge Ahead in Poll," *The Denver Post*, October 31, 1988, 7A.

79. Michelle Fulcher, "Tax-Limit Author Says Foes Misleading Voters," *The Denver Post*, November 1, 1988, 1A.

80. Ibid.

81. Jeffrey Roberts, "Foes Vow Media Blitz to Defeat Tax Issue," *The Denver Post*, October 15, 1988, 1A.

82. "Voter Trends," *The Denver Post*, October 28, 1988, 1B.

83. Carl Miller, "Foes of Tax Measure Surge Ahead in Poll," *The Denver Post*, October 31, 1988, 1A.

84. Michelle Fulcher, "Business Raising $250,000 to Fight Tax-Limit Plan," *The Denver Post*, October 19, 1988, 1A; "Opponents of Tax-Limit Measure Raise $161,000," *The Denver Post*, October 29, 1988, 2B.

85. Ibid. Colorado Department of State, "Report of Contributions and Expenditures," Citizens for Representative Government, 1988.

86. Colorado Department of State, "Report of Contributions and Expenditures," *Colorado Campaign Reform Act Summary*, Denver: Office of the Secretary of State, 1988, 54.

87. Colorado Public Expenditure Council, "A Colorado Taxpayer Report," Vol. XXXV, October 1988, 4.

88. Michelle Fulcher and Jeffrey Roberts, "Tax Limits Lose; English Issue Wins," *The Denver Post*, November 9, 1988, 1A, 12A.

89. Dirk Johnson, "Coloradans to Vote on Drastic Tax Curb," *New York Times*, November 5, 1988, A6.

90. Michelle Fulcher, "Specter of Tax Limit Frightens State Leaders," *The Denver Post*, September 30, 1988, 3B.

91. Jeffrey Roberts, "U.S. West President Blasts Amendment 6," *The Denver Post*, October 28, 1988, 4B.

92. Jeffrey Roberts, "Foes of All Political Stripes Call Plan a Skunk," *The Denver Post*, October 5, 1988, 10A.

93. Johnson, "Coloradans to Vote on Drastic Tax Curb," A6.

94. Michelle Fulcher, "Ex-Governors Warn of 'Disaster' and 'Paralysis,'" *The Denver Post*, October 26, 1988, 9A; Henry Dubroff, "Businesses Unite Against Tax Limits," *The Denver Post*, October 31, 1988, 1A; Thomas Graf and Michelle Fulcher, "Armstrong Opposes Amendment 6," *The Denver Post*, November 2, 1988, 1A.

95. Roberts, "Foes Vow Media Blitz to Defeat Tax Issue," 15A.

96. Phone interview with Bruce. In 1986, over half (55 percent) of the state's residents lived in the five metro Denver counties. Nine contiguous counties along the Front Range accounted for 80 percent of the state's population. Colorado Public Expenditure Council, "A Colorado Taxpayer Report," vol. XXXIV, September 1987, 1–2.

97. Colorado Department of State, "Report of Contributions and Expenditures," TABOR Committee, September 4 to October 23; October 24 to December 3, 1988.

98. Jeffrey Roberts, "Tax-Limit Advocate Plows $50,000 into Campaign," *The Denver Post*, November 2, 1988, 1A. Bruce claims he spent $20,000 on a statewide mailing consisting of 4 pages of material. He quickly "learned that it took too long to read," and eventually reduced the background material in subsequent mailings to registered Republicans. Interview with Bruce, 1996.

99. Steve Garnaas, "New Tax-Limit Petitions Filed," *The Denver Post*, October 7, 1988: 1B.

100. Caroline Schomp, "Douglas Bruce Just Won't Give Up," *The Denver Post*, December 13, 1991, 15B.

101. Fred Brown, "Bruce Files New Tax-Limit Petition," *The Denver Post*, October 18, 1989, 1B.

102. Ibid.

103. Jeffrey Roberts, "Colorado Tax-Curb Plan Wins '90 Ballot Spot," *The Denver Post*, December 9, 1989, 1B.

104. Fred Brown, "The Grace of a Simple Idea," *The Denver Post*, October 3, 1990, B7; Fred Brown, "Hearing Turns Nasty a la Bruce," *The Denver Post*, April 21, 1990, 3B.

105. James Lyons, "Tax-Cutting Frustration," *Forbes*, November 12, 1990, 164.

106. Douglas Bruce, "TABOR II Offers Coloradans a Chance to Limit Taxes," *The Denver Post*, June 9, 1990, 7B.

107. Fred Brown, "Bruce Files New Tax-Limit Petition," *The Denver Post*, October 18, 1989, 1B.

108. Jennifer Gavin, "Amendment 1 Foes Unite," *The Denver Post*, Sept. 1, 1990, 3B. Governor Romer stated at the time, "I'm really pleased with what I did with Amendment 6 (in 1988). The amendment before I got into it was leading 60–40.

We flat defeated it. It's one of the best things I've done for Colorado." Brad Smith, "Gov. Romer Seeks Re-Election," *United Press International,* April 2, 1990.

109. Roberts, "Colorado Tax-Curb Plan Wins '90 Ballot Spot," 1B.

110. John Racine, "Sweeping Antitax Proposal in Colorado Rattles Government and Bond Industry," *The Bond Buyer,* October 11, 1990, 1.

111. Jennifer Gavin, "Tax-Limit Plan Gains Strength," *The Denver Post,* October 10, 1990, A1.

112. Ibid.; Colorado Department of State, "Report of Contributions and Expenditures," 1990.

113. Colorado Department of State, "Contributions and Expenditures," *Colorado Campaign Reform Act Summary,* Denver: Colorado Department of State, 1990.

114. Racine, "Sweeping Antitax Proposal in Colorado Rattles Government and Bond Industry," 1.

115. Keith White, "Group Says Tax Revolt Alive, Well Out West," *Gannett News Service,* August 24, 1990.

116. Jennifer Gavin, "Support Growing, Tax-Lid Author Says," *The Denver Post,* June 28, 1990, 2B; Vern Bickel, "Colorado's Amendment 1 is Just Common Sense," *The Denver Post,* October 27, 1990, B7.

117. Jennifer Gavin, "Andrews Joins Bruce in Tax War," *The Denver Post,* October 17, 1990, 3B; Bruce 1996.

118. Fred Brown, "Amendment 1 Remains Out in Front," *The Denver Post,* November 1, 1990, 18A.

119. White, "Group Says Tax Revolt Alive, Well Out West."

120. Colorado Department of State, "Report of Contributions and Expenditures," TABOR, January 1 to July 31, 1990.

121. Colorado Department of State, "Report of Contributions and Expenditures," TABOR, July 30 to September 9; Gavin, "Tax-Limit Plan Gains Strength," 8A.

122. Colorado Department of State, "Report of Contributions and Expenditures," TABOR, September 9 to October 21, 1990.

123. Colorado Department of State, "Report of Contributions and Expenditures," 1990; Fred Brown, "Bruce Preaches the Gospel on Friendlier Turf," *The Denver Post,* December 12, 1990, 11B.

124. Fred Brown, "El Paso Led Failed Anti-Tax Charge," *The Denver Post,* November 11, 1990, 14A; Colorado Department of State, "Report of Contributions and Expenditures," TABOR, 1990.

125. Michelle Fulcher, "Tax-Limit Proposal Loses," *The Denver Post,* November 7, 1990, 1A.

126. Michelle Fulcher, "Gambling, Cap on Terms Get Nod From Voters," *The Denver Post,* November 7, 1990, A1.

127. Fred Brown, "Bruce Preaches the Gospel on Friendlier Turf," 11B.

128. Gavin, "Tax-Limit Plan Gains Strength," 8A.

129. Jennifer Gavin, "One Goal: To Head Off Tax Revolt," *The Denver Post*, January 6, 1991, 1C

130. Jennifer Gavin, "Bruce Threatens To File New Tax-Lid Plan," *The Denver Post*, April 10, 1991, 1B.

131. Jim Gibney, "Tax Foe Bruce is Back at It," *The Denver Post*, February 4, 1991, 2B; Jim Gibney, "Springs Caps Taxes, Limits Political Terms, *The Denver Post*, April 3, 8A. The Colorado Springs tax rollback measure passed 52 to 48 percent and the vote on taxes measure passed 61 to 39 percent. Fred Brown, "Tax-Limit Campaign Rekindled," *The Denver Post*, April 4, 1991, A1.

132. Brown, "Tax-Limit Campaign Rekindled," A1.

133. John Racine, "Tax Rollback Drive Scores Voter Victory in Colorado Springs; Two Amendments Win," *The Bond Buyer*, April 4, 1991, 4.

134. Ibid.

135. Colorado Department of State, "Report of Contributions and Expenditures," TABOR, July 15, 1992. In a letter dated November 30, 1991, TABOR Treasurer, Clyde Harkins, reported to the Office of the Secretary of State that it paid Jerry Franklin to collect signatures for the amendment. Letter, from Clyde Harkins, TABOR, to Natalie Meyer, Secretary of State, November 30, 1991.

136. Eric Anderson, "Voters Favor Plan to Limit Taxes by 2-to-1 ratio," *The Denver Post*, December 4, 1991, 1B.

137. Racine, "Colorado," 28; Eric Anderson, "Tax-Limitation Petitions Ruled Invalid," *The Denver Post*, December 7, 1991, A1.

138. Anderson, "Tax-Limitation Petitions Ruled Invalid," 1A.

139. Ibid., 13A.

140. Eric Anderson, "Tax Crusader Vows to Get Initiative on Ballot," *The Denver Post*, January 7, 1992, 2B.

141. Eric Anderson, "Bruce Tax Initiative to Make Ballot," *The Denver Post*, January 28, 1992, A6. A few months later, Bruce referred to Meyer as, "The Secretary of Sleaze." "Bruce Ready to Go to Court Over Election Reform Plan," *The Denver Post*, May 26, 1992, 4B.

142. Jennifer Gavin, "Alternative Tax-Limit Plan Fails," *The Denver Post*, March 20, 1992, 1B.

143. Eric Anderson, "Alternative Proposals in the Works," *The Denver Post*, December 24, 1991, 3B; Eric Anderson, "Bruce Blasts Rival Proposal," *The Denver Post*, May 21, 1992, 2B.

144. Roberts, "Bruce: Taxpayers Must Seize Control," 18A.

145. Jana Mazanec, "Colorado 'Tax Revolt' Hard to Interpret," *USA Today*, November 19, 1992, 8A.

146. Ibid. Indeed, after Amendment 1 passed, Bruce called various public officials to offer his assistance to interpret the document, "so that they understand the implications of the amendment and the interrelationship of the various sections, and they don't make any erroneous assumptions that are going to lead them down

the wrong road." Jeffrey Roberts, "Office-Holders, Bureaucrats Wringing Hands Over Impact of Amendment 1," *The Denver Post*, November 8, 1992, 8A.

147. Letter, from Denver Metro Convention and Visitors Bureau, to Members, September 1, 1992.

148. Ibid.

149. Bill Hornby, "Amendment 1 is Fighting a Paper Tiger," *The Denver Post*, October 15, 1992, B7; Betty Ann Dittemore, "Should We Vote on Tax Hikes?" *The Denver Post*, October 18, 1992, 1G; "Bruce's Big Lies," *The Denver Post*, October 22, 1992, 6B; Albert Yates, "Amendment 1 Could Devastate Higher Education in Colorado," *The Denver Post*, October 24, 1992, B7.

150. John Racine, "One Way or Another, Colorado May Get Tax, Spending Limits in 1992 Referendum," *The Bond Buyer*, November 15, 1991, 5; Eric Anderson, "Tax Crusader Tries to Save Petitions," *The Denver Post*, December 24, 1991, 1B.

151. Dan Cordtz, "Voter Initiatives Warn Politicians to Curb Spending," *Financial World*, October 30, 1990, 22.

152. Douglas Bruce, "Should We Vote on Tax Hikes? Yes, Let's Vote," *The Denver Post*, October 18, 1992, 1G; 5G.

153. Johnson, "Taxpayer Revolt in Colorado Vote Raises Alarm About Lost Services," A18.

154. Sinisi, "Proposal's Author Not Picture of a Firebrand," B7.

155. Colorado Department of State, "Report of Contributions and Expenditures," TABOR Committee, January 1 to July 26, 1992; July 27 to September 5, 1992.

156. Colorado Department of State, "Report of Contributions and Expenditures," TABOR, July 27 to September 5, 1992.

157. Colorado Department of State, "Report of Contributions and Expenditures," TABOR, September 6 to October 18, 1992. Bickel gave TABOR one more check on November 1 for $7,860, making his total contributions to TABOR in 1992, $72,789.75. Letter, Clyde Harkins, TABOR, to Natalie Meyer, Secretary of State, November 2, 1992. Bruce later reflected that the late contributions to the campaign made by Bickel "maybe helped." Phone interview with Bruce.

158. Total contributions to TABOR in 1992 exceeded $288,000. TABOR repaid Bruce $10,000 of his loan on October 11, 1992. Colorado Department of State, "Report of Contributions and Expenditures," TABOR, October 19 to November 28, 1992.

159. Personal interview with Greg Walerius, June 2, 1997.

160. Colorado Department of State, "Report of Contributions and Expenditures," September 6 to October 18; October 19 to November 28, 1992. According to Walerius, he only demanded a 5 percent broadcast commission (not the industry's standard 15 percent) for the commercials he placed on television for TABOR. Personal interview with Walerius.

161. Colorado Department of State, "Report of Contributions and Expenditures," September 6 to October 18; October 19 to November 28, 1992. An analysis

of TABOR's expenditures reveals some inconsistencies. Harkins reported identical expenditures made out to identical recipients on the same day for two different reporting periods. For the reporting period September 6 to October 18, 1992, Harkins reported payments of $435 to the U.S. Post Office for "postage" on September 2; $5,849.30 to the National Taxpayers Union for "printing; labeling & folding mailer" on September 4; and $671.40 to the Colorado Republican Party for "labels" on September 4. These are identical payments, recipients, and dates that Harkins reported earlier for the period covering July 27 to September 5. In addition, Harkins double-reported an expenditure on October 8 to Office Depot for $75.10 for a "Postage Meter" for the two reporting periods, September 6 to October 18, and October 19 to November 28.

162. Colorado Department of State, "Report of Contributions and Expenditures," "No on #1 Committee," September 6 to October 18; October 19 to November 28, 1992.

163. Ibid.; Colorado Department of State, *Colorado Campaign Reform Act Summary*, 1992, 36.

164. According to *The Denver Post* index, between October 14 and election day Amendment 1 was mentioned thirty-two times in 1990, whereas in 1992, it was mentioned only 17 times.

165. Colorado Department of State, *Colorado Campaign Reform Act Summary*, 1992, 75.

166. John Racine "From Bears to Bonds, Colorado Voters' Ballot Likely to Have it All," *The Bond Buyer*, August 3, 1992, 1.

167. Ibid.

168. Ibid.; John Racine, "Colo Lawmakers Pay Schools Bill; Governor Urges Sales Tax Rise for Future," *The Bond Buyer*, May 11, 1992, 2.

169. John Racine, "Colo Lawmakers Consider Measure to Steal Thunder of Citizen's Tax Drive," *The Bond Buyer*, March 4, 1992, 2.

170. Jeffrey Roberts, "Poll Shows Support Slipping for Tax-Limit Measure," *The Denver Post*, October 20, 4B.

171. Brian Weber, "State Voters Jump Off the Anger Wagon," *Rocky Mountain News*, November 9, 1994, 11A.

172. Jeffrey Roberts, "Tax-Limit Amendment Passes," *The Denver Post*, November 4, 1992, A1, 10A.

173. Phone interview with Bruce.

174. Ibid. According to reports in *Money* magazine and *US News & World Report* from 1983, Bruce was audited by the Internal Revenue Service in 1982 for claiming business deductions that he paid to "his girlfriend, Elissa Elliott," for managing his real estate investments. Bruce evidently "agreed to provide a home for Elliott and her son and to pay all their expenses, including a six-week trip to Europe" in exchange for her agreement "to run his household and take a major role in managing his extensive investment properties." A tax court disagreed with the

IRS ruling, and restored $2,730 of the original $9,000 deduction Bruce took. See: "Other Income?" *US News & World Report*, June 13, 1983, 87; Richard Eisenberg, "Tax Trends," *Money*, May, 1983, 214.

175. Sinisi, "Proposal's Author Not Picture of a Firebrand," B7.

176. Correspondence with Douglas Bruce. Al Knight, "Amendment 1 Changed the Landscape," *The Denver Post*, November 22, 1992, 1D.

177. Milbank, "Ballot Warriors Challenge State, Local Governments," A20.

178. Poll conducted by Floyd Ciruli and Associates. John Sanko, "Voters Loosen Amendment 1 Restrictions," *Rocky Mountain News*, November 9, 1995, A5. As pollster Ciruli commented to the reporter, "It's hard to get that low unless you actively work at it."

179. Since the passage of Amendment 1 in 1992, however, the fiscal impact of Amendment 1 has been mitigated somewhat. Using the local initiative process, citizens of local governments—from school boards, to counties, to special districts, to municipalities—have passed 169 out of the 186 "de-Brucing" measures that have been put to vote, thereby loosening the fiscal screws that Amendment 1 had noticeably tightened. John Sanko, "'De-Brucing' Measures Popular Throughout State, Voting Shows," *Rocky Mountain News*, November 17, 1995, A6.

180. Milbank, "Ballot Warriors Challenge State, Local Governments," A20.

181. Brown, "Hearing Turns Nasty a la Bruce," 3B.

182. Carl Hilliard, "Douglas Bruce: Reporter's Nightmare," *The Denver Post*, July 1, 1990, 2C.

183. Richard Hofstadter, *The Age of Reform* (New York: Vintage Books, 1955), 99.

184. Phone interview with Bruce.

## Chapter 7

1. William Howard Taft, *Popular Government: Its Essence, Its Permanence, and Its Perils* (New Haven: Yale University Press, 1913), 54.

2. "Anti-Democracy in California," *New York Times*, October 18, 1911. Quoted in California Commission on Campaign Financing, *Democracy by Initiative* (Los Angeles: Center for Responsive Government, 1992), 42.

3. David Broder, "Initiative Fever Still Grips California," *Denver Post*, August 15, 1997, 7B.

4. David Magleby, "Direct Legislation in the American States," in David Butler and Austin Ranney, *Referendums around the World* (Washington, DC: AEI Press, 1994), 218–57, 229.

5. David Schmidt, *Citizen Lawmakers* (Philadelphia: University of Temple Press, 1989) 21; B. Drummond Ayres, "Politics: The Initiatives," *New York Times*, November 4, 1996, B6; Michael B. Marois, "Trends in the Region: Initiatives: the People's Will or Sound-Bite Government?" *The Bond Buyer*, February 14, 1997, 30; Elaine

Stuart, "Voters Make Laws," *State Government News*, vol. 39 (December), 1996, 31–33, 31.

6. Charles Price, "Direct Democracy Works," *State Government News*, vol. 40 (June/July), 1997, 14–15; Jack Citrin, "Direct Democracy and Popular Control of Government," in Stephen Craig, ed., *Broken Contract? Changing Relationships Between Americans and Their Government* (Boulder: Westview Press, 1996), 268–93, 279; David Magleby, "Direct Legislation in the American States," in David Butler and Austin Ranney, eds., *Referendums around the World* (Washington, DC: AEI Press, 1994), 218–57, 218–19; Charles Price, "The Initiative: A Comparative State Analysis and Reassessment of a Western Phenomenon," *Western Political Quarterly*, vol. 28, 1975, 243–62.

7. Barbara Vincent, "Expanding the Process," *The Initiative Press & Seminars*, February, 1996, 6.

8. Nathan Cobb, "Some people put drama in their lives by going to horror movies. I work in Massachusetts politics," *Boston Globe*, (Magazine) January 14, 1990, 16.

9. Eric Young and Tony Bizjak, "Tax-restructuring Prop. 218 Leads Foes in Fund Raising," *Sacramento Bee*, October 11, 1996, B1.

10. Citrin, "Who's the Boss?" 290.

11. "Taxpayers Groups Urge Passage of Proposition 218," *Business Wire*, October 22, 1966.

12. Don Aucoin, "Asking Your Signature, Leaving Theirs," *Boston Globe*, October 2, 1993, B1.

13. Personal interview with Barbara Anderson, Boston, May 7, 1997.

14. Phone interview with Douglas Bruce, June 24, 1996.

15. Ibid. Bruce claims to "have a whole string of [ballot initiatives], but one of them would be legislative reform, and in part requiring them [legislators] to certify under penalty of perjury that they've read a bill before they can [vote] 'yes' for it."

16. Enrique Larana, Hank Johnston, and Joseph Gusfield, "Identities, Grievances, and New Social Movements," in Larana, Johnston, and Gusfield, eds., *New Social Movements* (Philadelphia: Temple University Press, 1994), 12.

17. Personal interview with Barbara Anderson.

18. Phone interview with Douglas Bruce.

19. Ibid. In 1996, Bruce helped to create a front organization to champion a petition rights amendment, known as Amendment 13.

20. Lawrence Goodwyn, *Democratic Promise: The Populist Moment in America* (New York: Oxford University Press, 1976), vii–xxiii.

21. Brad Cain, "Names Spell Cash for Most Petitions," *The Bulletin* (Bend, OR), June 3, 1996, B3.

22. Fred Brown, "Excess Revenue Will Be Refunded," *Denver Post*, August 6, 1997, 1B.

# RESOURCE GUIDE

If you want to learn more about the initiative process and current ballot measures in your state, or if you want to contact some of the existing state and national tax limitation organizations, this directory is a good place to begin your inquiries.

## Five Questions to Ask Yourself Before Voting on a Ballot Measure

1) What changes will a ballot measure bring about if it passes?

    The wording of a ballot measure can be very complex, even in states that limit a measure to a single subject matter. The ballot title (the state's summary of the initiative) can be quite long and cumbersome; even the name of the initiative can be misleading. For example, post-election surveys found that many of the Californians who voted for the California Civil Rights Initiative (Proposition 209) in 1996, mistakenly thought they were voting to protect affirmative action programs, not to end them. Most of the states with the citizen initiative publish and distribute to all active voters ballot information booklets. Take the time to read through the full text of the ballot measure, deciphering the language as you go. Read carefully the "arguments for" and "arguments against" the measure, keeping in mind that they are usually written by partisan groups and individuals. Think about possible "unintended consequences" that might arise if the measure passes.

2) Who is behind the ballot measure?

This is often a tricky question to answer. At times, the names of the groups sponsoring or opposing an initiative can be misleading, intentionally so or otherwise. What special interests are behind or against the measure? Who has publicly endorsed or opposed the measure? Where is the preponderance of money supporting or opposing the measure coming from? Many groups campaigning for and against a measure are well-established and have proven track records. Many have extensive memberships and established programs that existed prior to the initiative campaign. Remember, though, that not all groups involved in an initiative campaign are equal participants, as many political committees are only tangential to the campaign they purportedly support or oppose. If you are interested in volunteering your time or giving money to a group, do some background research on the group to make sure it is a legitimate player in the initiative campaign. There are no state regulations that restrict how a registered political group may spend the monetary contributions it collects during a campaign.

3) Where is reliable information about a ballot available?

The world wide web (WWW) has quickly become the best place to obtain information about current and past ballot measures. The best place to find accurate information about ballot measures is your Office of Secretary of State. All of the states have home pages with links to their Secretary of State. Many of the states provide on-line documents detailing the initiative process, and most post voter guides with information on current and past ballot measures. A growing number of states post on their web sites the actual campaign contributions and expenditures of all political candidates and political organizations, including political committees that have organized to support or oppose citizen initiatives. If you do not have access to the internet, call or write your Secretary of State for this information. Also, be weary of the campaign materials (fliers, yard signs, radio, television, and newspaper ads, phone solicitations), public statements, and public opinion polls that are produced by groups either for or against a measure. Hyperbole and false claims are par for the course during ballot initiative campaigns, and populist-sounding rhetoric comes fast and cheap. Campaign rhetoric makes good news copy, but it tends not to tell the whole story.

4) When is it important to pay attention to an initiative campaign?

The campaign for ballot initiatives tends to begin much earlier than races for political office, as groups frequently begin circulating petitions for signatures more than a year before election day. A group's effort to place an initiative on the ballot can be quite revealing, as it usually demonstrates the organizational and financial resources the group is relying on for its support. During the actual election campaign, it is important to scrutinize the claims and counter-claims made by the groups in favor and against the measure. Initiative campaigns generally lack extensive deliberation; instead, soundbites and catchy slogans are the preferred tools of debate. In addition, unlike races for political office, there are no candidates and no party affiliations that are affiliated with ballot initiative campaigns. As such, citizens have fewer "cues" on which to draw to help them sort out the issue. It is exceedingly difficult to cast an informed vote on a ballot measure on election day without studying the issues before hand. It is important, therefore, to follow the developments and arguments for and against a ballot initiative closely and over time.

5) Why is the initiative on the ballot?

This is perhaps the most important question to ask during an initiative campaign. A group has gone through the arduous process of placing an initiative before the voters. Why? What is wrong with the *status quo*? What is the political or ideological agenda of the proponents? Why should citizens, rather than their elected officials, make the policy decision? It is incumbent upon the proponents of a measure to make a compelling argument that a change needs to be made, either statutory or constitutional, and that it should be done via the initiative rather than via the traditional legislative process.

## Information on the Initiative Process and Statewide Ballot Measures

For general information about the initiative process in a given state, contact your state's Secretary of State. In addition, several non-partisan organizations track current ballot initiatives, elections, and political organizations in the states. Many of them have their own web pages. Here are some of the better ones:

*Project Vote Smart*
129 NW 4th Street, Suite 204
Corvallis, OR 97330
Phone: 541-754-2746
Fax: 541-754-2747
http://www.vote-smart.org/state/

*Stateside Associates*
2300 Clarendon Boulevard, 4th Floor
Arlington, Virginia 22201-3367
Phone: 703-525-7466
Fax: 703-525-7057
http://www.stateside.com/

*The Council of State Governments*
P.O. Box 11910
Lexington, KY 40578-1910
Phone: 606-244-8000
Fax: 606-244-8001
http://www.csg.org/

*National Conference of State Legislatures*
1560 Broadway, Suite 700
Denver, Colorado 80202
Phone: 303-830-2200
Fax: 303-863-8003
http://www.ncsl.org/

*The Jefferson Project*
Stardot Consulting
Phone: 800-598-4005
Fax: 303-415-9811
http://www.voxpop.org:80/jefferson/

*Americans for the Environment*
1400 16th St., NW
Washington, DC 20036
Phone: 202-797-6665
http://www.ewg.org/pub/home/afe/homepage.htm

*The Center for Voting and Democracy*
P.O. Box 60037
Washington, D.C. 20039
Phone: 301-270-4616
Fax: 301-270-4133
http://www.igc.org/cvd/

*The Initiative Press and Seminars*
P.O. Box 1100
Carson City, NV 89702
Phone: 702-885-9978

## Tax-Related Organizations

In addition to the organizations profiled in this book, there are dozens of national and state organizations concerned with taxation issues. Some of them have sponsored ballot initiatives; others serve as national clearing-houses. A few of them have their own web sites. Here are some of the more prominent national organizations, as well as organizations in the states allowing the citizen initiative:

## National Tax-Related Organizations

*Tax Foundation*
1250 H Street, NW, Suite 750
Washington, DC 20005
Phone: 202-783-2760
http://www.taxfoundation.org/

*Americans for Tax Reform*
1320 18th St., NW, Suite 200
Washington, DC 20036
Phone: 202-785-0266
http://www.atr.org/

*National Taxpayers Union*
108 N. Alfred Street
Alexandria, VA 22314
Phone: 703-683-5700

Fax: 703-683-5722
http://www.ntu.org/

*Taxpayers for Common Sense*
651 Pennsylvania Ave., SE, 2nd Floor
Washington, DC 20003
Phone: 202-546-8500
Fax: 202-546-851
http://www.taxpayer.net/

*Citizens for Tax Justice*
1311 L Street, NW
Washington, DC 20005
http://www.ctj.org/

## State Tax-Related Organizations (in states allowing the initiative process)

ALASKA
*Alaskans for Tax Reform*
2509 Eide Street, Suite 4
Anchorage, AK 99503
Phone: 907-258-8888

ARIZONA
*The Lincoln Caucus*
P.O. Box 9854
Phoenix, AZ 85056
Phone: 602-248-0136

ARKANSAS
*Taxpayers Rights Committee*
Central Mall Plaza, Suite 516
5111 Rogers Ave.
Fort Smith, AR 72903
Phone: 501-452-3714

CALIFORNIA
*Howard Jarvis Taxpayers Association*
621 South Westmoreland, Suite 202
Los Angeles, CA 90005-3971
Phone: 213-384-9656

*Californians for Tax Reform*
250 1st St., Suite 330
Claremont, CA 91711
Phone: 909-621-6825

COLORADO
*Taxpayer's Bill of Rights Committee (TABOR)*
Box 26018
Colorado Springs, CO 80936
Phone: 719-550-0010

*Colorado Union of Taxpayers*
5550 Sunset Dr.
Littleton, CO 80123
Phone: 303-773-3399

FLORIDA
*Tax Cap Committee*
P.O. Box 193
New Smyrna Beach, FL 32169
Phone: 904-423-4744
Fax: 904-427-8004
Email: taxcap@aol.com

IDAHO
*Idahoans for Tax Reform*
1608 Bedford Dr.
Boise, ID 83705
Phone: 208-331-1996

ILLINOIS
*Tax Accountability*
59 E. Van Buren St., Suite 2517

Chicago, IL 60605
Phone: 312-427-5128

MAINE
*Tax Watch*
P.O. Box 10
Garland, ME 04939-0010
Phone: 207-924-3835

MASSACHUSETTS
*Citizens for Limited Taxation & Government*
18 Tremont Street #608
Boston, MA 02108-2301
Phone: 617-248-0022

MICHIGAN
*Michigan for Tax Reform*
1315 Westview, #10
East Lansing, MI 48823
Phone: 517-373-5228

MISSISSIPPI
*Concerned Taxpayers*
P.O. Box 700
Magee, MS 39111
Phone: 601-849-2210

MISSOURI
*Missourians for Tax Reform*
1 Metropolitan Square, Suite 2600
St. Louis, MO 63102
Phone: 314-621-5070

MONTANA
*Montanans for Tax Reform*
4525 Highway 12
Helena, MT 59601
Phone: 406-442-6682

NEBRASKA
*Nebraska Taxpayers Association, Inc.*
P.O. Box 34144
13406 Shirley
Omaha, NE 68144
Phone: 402-333-2912
http://www.phonet.com/~bsimon/nta-hp.html

NEVADA
*Coalition of Nevada Taxpayers*
P.O. Box 20312
Reno, NV 89515-0312
Phone: 702-786-9600

NORTH DAKOTA
*North Dakotans for Tax Reform*
P.O. Box 1473
Bismarck, ND 58502
Phone: 701-222-4860

OHIO
*Coalition of Taxpayers*
3289 Rochford Ridge Drive
Hilliard, OH 43221
Phone: 614-777-4071

*National Taxpayers Union of Ohio*
2029 Riverside Dr.
Columbus, OH 43221
Phone: 614-486-0315

OKLAHOMA
*Oklahoma for Tax Reform*
P.O. Box 700255
Oklahoma City, OK 73107
Phone: 405-947-2462

OREGON
*Oregon Taxpayers United*
16140 S.E. 82nd Dr.
Clackamas, OR 97015
Phone: 503-655-0600
Fax: 503-655-7414
http://www.otu.org/

SOUTH DAKOTA
*No More Taxes Coalition*
P.O. Box 638
Pierre, SD 57501

UTAH
*Utah Taxpayers Association*
1578 West 1700, Suite 105
Salt Lake City, UT 84104-3470
Phone: 801-972-8814

WASHINGTON
*Evergreen Freedom Foundation*
P.O. Box 552
Olympia, WA 98507
Phone: 360-956-3482

WYOMING
*Wyoming Citizens for Property Tax Reform*
P.O. Box 301
Dubois, WY 82513
Phone: 307-455-3758

# BIBLIOGRAPHY

## Archives and Manuscript Collections

California State Archives, Office of the Secretary of State. Sacramento.
California State Library. Sacramento.
    Paul Gann Archive, 1978–1986.
    Howard Jarvis Collection, 1970–1986.
Citizens for Limited Taxation. Boston.
Colorado Legislative Council. Denver.
Colorado State Archives, Office of the Secretary of State. Denver.
Institute of Governmental Studies, University of California. Berkeley.
Massachusetts State Archives, Office of the Secretary of State. Boston.
Massachusetts State Library. Boston.
Massachusetts Teachers Association. Boston.

## Interviews

Anderson, Barbara. Citizens for Limited Taxation. Boston. Personal Interview. May 7, 1997.
Biddulph, David. Tax Cap Committee. Phone Interview. July 21, 1997.
Bruce, Douglas. Taxpayers Bill of Rights. Phone Interview. June 24, 1996.
Dresner, Richard. Phone Interview. April 28, 1997.
Faulkner, Chip. Citizens for Limited Taxation. Boston. Personal Interview. May 6, 1997.
Flannigan, John. Massachusetts Teachers Association. Boston. Personal Interview. May 5, 1997.
Foley, Howard. Massachusetts High Tech Council. Phone Interview. May 15, 1997.
Fox, Joel. Howard Jarvis Taxpayers Association. Phone Interview. January 23, 1998.
Manley, Richard. Massachusetts Taxpayers Foundation. Boston. Personal Interview. May 5, 1997.
Muehlmann, Heinz. Boston. Personal Interview. May 6, 1997.
Robinson, Walter. *The Boston Globe*. Boston. Phone Interview. May 27, 1997.

Schwartz, Tony. New Sounds. New York. Personal Interview. April 18, 1997.
Walerius, Greg. GW Media. Denver. Personal Interview. June 2, 1997.


## Primary Documents

Anderson, Barbara. "Feeling Guilty? Read This." *Taxachusetts* (Newsletter). Citizens for Limited Taxation. Boston. August 1981.

Anderson, Barbara. Press Release, "Statement of Barbara Anderson, Executive Director." Citizens for Limited Taxation. Boston. July 2, 1980.

Anderson, Barbara. Flier to Media. Citizens for Limited Taxation. August 8, 1980.

California Commission on Campaign Financing. *Democracy by Initiative*. Los Angeles: Center for Responsive Government, 1992.

California Fair Political Practices Commission. "Campaign Contribution and Spending Report." Sacramento. September 28, 1978.

California Fair Political Practices Commission. "Committee Campaign Statement, United Organizations of Taxpayers." Sacramento. July 22, 1976; March 7, 1977; December 30, 1977; June 30, 1978.

California Fair Political Practices Commission. "Committee Campaign Statement, Yes on 13 Committee." Sacramento. April 23, 1978; May 25, 1978; June 30, 1978; December 31, 1978.

California Fair Political Practices Commission. "Historical Overview of Receipts and Expenditures By Ballot Measure Committees." Sacramento. April 1988.

California Franchise Tax Board. "Audit Report, Yes on 13 Committee." Sacramento. September 11, 1978; February 5, 1980.

Cassidy, Don. Press Release, "Legislature Votes No on Prop 2 1/2; CLT Prepares Second Petition Drive." Citizens for Limited Taxation. Boston. July 2, 1980.

Cassidy, Don. Draft Memo, "Analysis of Petition Drive, 1979." Citizens for Limited Taxation. Boston. No Date.

Center for Studies in Policy and the Public Interest. "The University of Massachusetts Poll, No. 1." Boston: University of Massachusetts. May 1980.

Citizens for Limited Taxation. Confidential Memo, "The Best Approach on Behalf of Prop 2 1/2 in Light of Survey Research Conducted for the High Tech Council." Boston. October 11, 1980.

Citizens for Limited Taxation. Memo, "Planned Expenditures toward a Six-month 'Guerrilla War' Requiring Immediate Funding." Boston. No Date.

Citizens for Limited Taxation. Memo, "Preparing for the Petition Drive." Boston. No Date.

Citizens for Limited Taxation. Memo, "Outline Analysis of the Petition Drive." Boston. No Date.

Colorado Department of State. "Report of Contributions and Expenditures." TABOR Committee. Denver. September 4 to October 23, 1988; October 24 to December 3, 1988; January 1 to July 31, 1990; July 30 to September 9, 1990; September 9 to October 21, 1990; January 1 to July 26, 1992; July 27 to September 5, 1992; September 6 to October 18, 1992; October 19 to November 28, 1992; September 8 to October 20, 1996.

Colorado Department of State. "Report of Contributions and Expenditures." Citizens for Representative Government. Denver. September 4 to October 23, 1988; October 24 to December 3, 1988.

Colorado Department of State. "Report of Contributions and Expenditures." No on #1 Committee. Denver. September 6 to October 18, 1992; October 19 to November 28, 1992.

Colorado Department of State. *Colorado Campaign Reform Act Summary.* Denver. 1988; 1990; 1992.

Colorado Public Expenditure Council. "A Colorado Taxpayer Report." Denver. December 1990; May 1990; November 1988; October 1988; September 1987; May 1987.

Commonwealth of Massachusetts. "Campaign Financing Report." Vote No on Question 2 Committee. Boston. 1980.

Commonwealth of Massachusetts. Legislative Research Council. "Report Relative to Limiting Taxation and Spending By State and Local Governments." Boston. 1980.

Commonwealth of Massachusetts. Legislative Research Council. "Two Tax and Spending Limitation Initiative Proposals on 1980 Massachusetts State Election Ballot." Boston. August 4, 1980.

Commonwealth of Massachusetts. Massachusetts Executive Office of Committees and Development. "Technical Bulletin, Proposition 2 1/2: Estimated Impacts." Boston. June 1980.

Commonwealth of Massachusetts. Office of Campaign and Political Finance. "Summary of the Receipts, Expenditures, Disbursements, and Liabilities." Citizens for Limited Taxation. Boston. August 22, 1980.

Commonwealth of Massachusetts. Office of Campaign and Political Finance. "Campaign Finance Report." Concerned Citizens for Lower Taxes. Boston. October 1 to October 15, 1980.

Commonwealth of Massachusetts, Office of the Secretary of the Commonwealth. Letter to Edward F. King, Citizens for Limited Taxation. Boston. December 9, 1977.

Commonwealth of Massachusetts. Superior Court. *William H. Herbert, Plaintiff V. State Ballot Law Commission.* No. 39898. Suffolk, MA, 1980.

Denver Metro Convention and Visitors Bureau. Letter to Members. Denver. September 1, 1992.

Feder, Donald. "Statement of Donald Feder, Executive Director of Citizens for Limited Taxation." Boston. June 29, 1978.

Florida Department of State, Division of Elections. "Campaign Treasurer's Report." Tax Cap Committee." July 1993 to December 1996.

Gann, Paul. *Oral History Interview.* Conducted 1987 and 1988 by Gabrielle Morris, Regional Oral History Office, University of California Berkeley. Sacramento: California State Archives State Government Oral History Program. 1988.

Graham, Ronald J. Board Member, Citizens for Limited Taxation. Form Letter to CLT Board Members. Boston. May 1, 1980.

Harkins, Clyde. Taxpayers Bill of Rights. Letter to Natalie Meyer, Secretary of State. Denver. November 30, 1991.

Harkins, Clyde. Taxpayers Bill of Rights. Letter to Natalie Meyer, Secretary of State. Denver. November 2, 1992.

Jarvis, Howard. "The American Tax Revolt." Distinguished Lecture Series, College of Business Administration, University of Cincinnati. November 1, 1979.

Jarvis, Howard. Form Letter to Members of the Los Angeles Apartment Owners Association. Los Angeles. April 3, 1978.

King, Edward F. Citizens for Limited Taxation. Form Letter to Republican State Committee Members. Boston. August 29, 1979.

Massachusetts High Technology Council. "A New Social Contract for Massachusetts." Boston. 1979.

Massachusetts Taxpayers Foundation. "Municipal Financial Data." Boston. 1980.

Massachusetts Teachers Association. "MTA/High Tech Council Plan for Retraining Teachers Gets A Big Reception." *MTA Today.* Boston. April 14, 1980.

Massachusetts Teachers Association. "MTA Urges Protests to Papa Gino's." *MTA Today.* Boston. June 16, 1980.

Massachusetts Teachers Association. "Stop 2 1/2 Campaign Yields 110,00 Signatures." *MTA Today.* Boston. December 13, 1979.

Monroe, Bill. "Interview of Howard Jarvis on 'Meet the Press,'" vol. 78 (June 18). Washington, DC: Kelly Press, Inc., 1978.

Nason, Lee. Libertarian Party of Massachusetts. Form Letter to Libertarian Party Members. Boston. November 11, 1977.

Savitz, Elliot. Finance Chairman, Citizens for Limited Taxation. Letter to Massachusetts State Automobile Dealers Association members. No Date.

## Books and Articles

Adams, Charles. *For Good and Evil: The Impact of Taxes on the Course of Civilization.* New York: Madison Books, 1993.

Adams, James Ring. *Secrets of the Tax Revolt.* New York: Harcourt, Brace, Jovanovich, 1984.

Allen, Gary. *Tax Target: Washington.* Seal Beach, Ca: '76 Press, 1978.

Baroody, William. "From the Publisher." *Public Opinion.* July/August 1978, 2.

Becker, Robert. *Revolution, Reform, and the Politics of American Taxation.* Baton Rouge: Louisiana State University Press, 1980.

Bell, Daniel. "Interpretations of American Politics. Daniel Bell, ed. *The New American Right.* New York: Criterion Books, 1955.

Berg, Larry. "The Initiative Process and Public Policy-Making in the States: 1904–1976." Paper Presented at the Annual Meeting of the American Political Science Association, New York City. August 1978.

Boyte, Harry, and Frank Riessman, eds. *The New Populism.* Philadelphia: Temple University Press, 1986.

Brewer, John. *The Sinews of Power: War, Money, and the English State, 1688–1783.* New York: Knopf, 1989.

Brody, Richard. "Who Voted for Proposition 13?" *Taxing & Spending.* 2 (February 1979): 26–28.

Brown, Roger. *Redeeming the Republic.* Baltimore: The John Hopkins University Press, 1993.

Burns, Stewart. *Social Movements of the 1960s: Searching for Democracy.* Boston: Twayne Publishers, 1990.

Butler, David, and Austin Ranney. *Referendums Around the World.* Washington, DC: AEI Press, 1994.

Campbell, Ann. "The Citizen's Initiative and Entrepreneurial Politics: Direct Democracy in Colorado, 1966–1994." Paper Presented at the Annual Meeting of the Western Political Science Association, Tucson, AZ. March 1997.

Canovan, Margret. *Populism.* New York: Harcourt Brace Jovanovich, 1981.

Citrin, Jack, and Frank Levy. "From 13 to 4 and Beyond: The Political Meaning of the Ongoing Tax Revolt in California." *The Property Tax Revolt.* George Kaufman and Kenneth Rosen, eds. Cambridge, MA: Balinger Publishing Co., 1981.

Citrin, Jack. "Introduction: The Legacy of Proposition 13." *California and the American Tax Revolt.* Terry Schwadron and Paul Richter, eds. Berkeley: University of California Press, 1984.

Citrin, Jack. "Who's the Boss? Direct Democracy and Popular Control of Government." *Broken Contract.* Stephen Craig, ed. Boulder: Westview Press, 1996.

Citrin, Jack. "Do People Want Something for Nothing?" *National Tax Journal* 32 (June 1979): 113–29.

Clanton, Gene. *Populism: The Humane Preference in America, 1890–1900.* Boston: Twayne Publishers, 1991.

Craig, Stephen. "Change and the American Electorate." *Broken Contract.* Stephen Craig, ed. Boulder: Westview Press, 1996.

Cronin, Thomas. *Direct Democracy.* Cambridge: Harvard University Press, 1989.

Cronin, Thomas, and Robert Loevy. *Colorado Politics and Government: Governing the Centennial State.* Lincoln: University of Nebraska Press, 1993.

Davis, Sherry Tvedt. "A Brief History of Proposition 2 1/2." *Proposition 2 1/2: Its Impact on Massachusetts.* Lawrence Susskind, ed. Cambridge, MA: Oelgeschlager, Gunn & Hain, 1983.

Dworak, Robert. *Taxpayers, Taxes, and Government Spending.* New York: Praeger Publishers, 1980.

Eder, Klaus. *The New Politics of Class.* Newbury Park, CA: Sage Publications, 1993.

Edsall, Thomas. *Chain Reaction.* New York: W.W. Norton & Co., 1991.

Engle, Michael. "Proposition 13: Whose Tax Revolt?" Paper Presented at the Annual Meeting of the New England Political Science Association, Boston, MA. April 1979.

Field, Mervin. "Sending A Message: Californians Strike Back." *Public Opinion.* (July/August 1978): 3–7.

Fischel, William. "Did Serrano Cause Proposition 13?" *National Tax Journal* (December 1989): 465–74.

Fritz, Percy Stanley. *Colorado: The Centennial State.* New York: Prentice-Hall, 1941.

Furen, Jeanette Lona. *Power in the People.* Far Hills, NJ: New Horizon Press, 1996.

Gerber, Elisabeth. "Legislative Response to the Threat of Popular Initiatives." *American Journal of Political Science* 40 (February 1996): 99–128.

Ginsberg, Benjamin. *Money and Power: The New Political Economy of American Elections. The Political Economy.* Thomas Ferguson and Joel Rogers, eds. Armonk, NY: M.E. Sharpe, 1984.

Goodwyn, Lawrence. *The Populist Movement.* New York: University of Oxford Press, 1978.

Goodwyn, Lawrence. *Democratic Promise.* New York: University of Oxford Press, 1976.

Hahn, Gilbert, and Stephen Morton. "Initiative and Referendum: Do they Encourage or Impair Better State Government?" *Florida State University Law Review* 5 (1997): 925–50

Hansen, Susan. *The Politics of Taxation: Revenue Without Representation.* New York: Praeger Publishers, 1983.

Harrison, Trevor. of *Passionate Intensity: Right-Wing Populism and the Reform Party of Canada.* Toronto: University of Toronto Press, 1995.

Hertzke, Allen. *Echoes of Discontent: Jesse Jackson, Pat Robertson, and the Resurgence of Populism.* Washington, DC: CQ Press, 1993.

Hicks, John. *The Populist Revolt: A History of the Farmers' Alliance and the People's Party.* Lincoln: University of Nebraska Press, 1961.

Hofstadter, Richard. "The Pseudo-Conservative Revolt." *The New American Right.* Daniel Bell, ed. New York: Criterion Books, 1955.

Hofstadter, Richard. *The Age of Reform.* New York: Vintage Books, 1955.

Jarvis, Howard. *I'm Mad As Hell.* New York: Time Books, 1979.

Kazin, Michael. *The Populist Persuasion: An American History.* New York: Basic Books, 1995.

Kemp, Roger. *Coping With Proposition 13.* Lexington, MA: D.C. Heath and Company, 1980.

Kingdon, John. *Agendas, Alternative, and Public Policies.* Boston: Little, Brown and Company, 1984.

Kuttner, Robert. *Revolt of the Haves.* New York: Simon and Schuster, 1979.

Ladd, Helen and Julie Wilson. "Proposition 2 1/2: Explaining the Vote." Research Report R81-1. Cambridge, MA: John F. Kennedy School of Government, Harvard University. April 1981.

Ladd, Helen and Julie Wilson. "Why Voters Support Tax Limitations: Evidence From Massachusetts' Proposition 2 1/2." Working Paper 76. Cambridge, MA: John F. Kennedy School of Government, Harvard University. January 1982.

Larana, Enrique, Hank Johnston, and Joseph Gusfield. "Identities, Grievances, and New Social Movements." *New Social Movements.* Enrique Larana, Hank Johnston, and Joseph Gusfield, eds. Philadelphia: Temple University Press, 1994.

Lasch, Cristopher. *The True and Only Heaven: Progress and Its Critics.* New York: Norton, 1991.

Lascher, Edward, et al. "Gun Behind the Door? Ballot Initiatives, State Policies and Public Opinion." *Journal of Politics* 58 (August 1996): 760–75.

Laycock, David. *Populism and Democratic Thought in the Canadian Prairies, 1910–1945.* Toronto: University of Toronto Press, 1990.

Lee, Eugene. "California." *Referendums: A Comparative Study of Practice and Theory.* David Butler and Austin Ranney, eds. Washington, DC: AEI Press, 1978.

Lee, Eugene. "The Initiative and Referendum: How California Has Fared." *National Civic Review* 68 (February 1979): 69–84.

Lemov, Penelope. "The Tax Revolt That Wasn't," *Governing* 8 (January 1995): 22–23.

Levin, Martin. "Department of Unintended Consequences." *Taxing & Spending* 2 (April 1979): 12–15.

Levy, Frank and Paul Zamolo. "The Preconditions of Proposition 13." Working Paper 1105–01. October 1978.

Lipset, Seymour Martin. "The Sources of the 'Radical Right.'" *The New American Right.* Daniel Bell, ed. New York: Criterion Books, 1955.

Lo, Clarence. "Mobilizing the Tax Revolt." *Research in Social Movement Conflicts and Change,* vol. 6. Richard Ratcliff, ed. Newbury Park, CA: Sage Publications, 1984.

Lo, Clarence. *Small Property, Big Government.* Berkeley: University of California Press, 1990.

Lorch, Robert. *Colorado's Government.* 3rd ed. Boulder: Colorado Associated University Press, 1983.

Lowenstien, Daniel. "Campaign Spending and Ballot Propositions: Recent Experience, Public Choice Theory, and the First Amendment." *UCLA Law Review* 86 (1982): 505–641.

Maanen, J. Van, et. al. *Varieties of Qualitative Research.* Beverly Hills, CA: Sage Publications, 1982.

Magleby, David. *Direct Legislation.* Baltimore: The John Hopkins University Press, 1984.

Magleby, David. "Direct Legislation in the American States." *Referendums Around the World.* David Butler and Austin Ranney, eds. Washington, DC: AEI Press, 1994.

Magleby, David and Kelly Patterson. "Consultants and Direct Democracy." Paper Presented at the Annual Meeting of the American Political Science Association, Washington, DC. August 1997.

Marshall, Catherine, and Gretchen Rossman. *Designing Qualitative Research.* Newbury Park, CA: Sage Publications, 1989.

Martin, Curtis, and Rudolph Gomez. *Colorado Government and Politics.* 4th ed. Boulder: Pruett Publishing Company, 1976.

Morris, Richard. *Behind the Oval Office.* New York: Random House, 1997.

Musgrave, Richard. "The Tax Revolt." *Social Science Quarterly* 59 (March 1979): 697–703.

Oakland, William. "Proposition 13: Genesis and Consequences." *The Property Tax Revolt.* George Kaufman and Kenneth Rosen, eds. Cambridge, MA: Balinger Publishing Co., 1981.

O'Sullivan, Arthur, et al. *Property Taxes and Tax Revolts.* Cambridge: Cambridge University Press, 1995.

Otis, James. *Rights of the British Colonies Asserted and Proved.* Boston: Edes and Gill, 1764.

Padover, Saul, ed. *The Washington Papers.* New York: Grossset and Dunlap, 1955.

Peterson, Merrill. *The Portable Thomas Jefferson.* New York: Viking Press, 1975.

Pfiffner, James. "Inflexible Budgets, Fiscal Stress, and the Tax Revolt." *The Municipal Money Chase: The Politics of Local Government Finance.* Alberta Sbragia, ed. Boulder: Westview Press, 1983.

Phillips, Kevin. *The Politics of Rich and Poor.* New York: Harper Perennial, 1990.

Pollack, Norman, ed. *The Populist Mind.* New York: Bobbs-Merrill, 1967.

Pollack, Sheldon. *The Failure of US Tax Policy.* University Park: Pennsylvania State University Press, 1996.

Price, Charles. "Direct Democracy Works." *State Government News* 40 (June/July 1997): 14–15.

Price, Charles. "The Initiative: A Comparative State Analysis and Reassessment of a Western Phenomenon." 28 *Western Political Quarterly* (June 1975): 243–62.

Rabushka, Alvin, and Pauline Ryan. *The Tax Revolt.* Stanford: Hoover Institution, 1982.

Rabushka, Alvin. "Tax Spending and Limits." *The United States in the 1980s.* Peter Duignan and Alvin Rubashka, eds. Stanford: Hoover Institution Press, 1980.

Ratner, Sidney. *American Taxation.* New York: W. W. Norton, 1942.

Roosevelt, Theodore. "Nationalism and Popular Rule." *The Initiative, Referendum, and Recall.* William Bennett Munro, ed. New York: Appleton and Co., 1912.

Rosenthal, Alan. *The Decline of Representative Democracy: Process, Participation, and Power in State Legislatures.* Washington, DC: CQ Press, 1998.

Rosenthal, Alan. *The Third House: Lobbyists and Lobbying in the States.* Washington, DC: CQ Press, 1993.

Schattschneider, E.E. *The Semisovereign People.* New York: Harcourt Brace Jovanovich, 1960.

Schmidt, David. *Citizen Lawmakers.* Philadelphia: Temple University Press, 1989.

Schwadron, Terry, and Paul Richter, eds. *California and the American Tax Revolt.* Berkeley: University of California Press, 1984.

Sears, David, and Jack Citrin. *Tax Revolt.* Cambridge: Harvard University Press, 1982.

Sen, Sankar. "Marketing and Minority Civil Rights: The Case of Amendment 2 and the Colorado Boycott." *Journal of Public Policy & Marketing* 15 (Fall 1996): 311–18.

Shiman, Paul. "Proposition 2 1/2 and Massachusetts Schools." Washington, DC: US Department of Education, National Institute of Education. October 1983.

Shockly, John. "Corporate Spending in the Wake of the Bellotti Decision." Paper Presented at the Annual Meeting of the American Political Science Association, New York City. September 1978.

Smith, Daniel A. and Robert Herrington. "The Process of Direct Democracy: The Case of Colorado's 1996 Parental Rights Amendment." Paper Presented at the Annual Meeting of the American Political Science Association, Washington, DC. August 1997.

Sowers, Don. *The Effect of Tax Limitation Upon State and Local Government in Colorado.* Boulder: University of Colorado, 1936.

Straayer, John. *The Colorado General Assembly.* Boulder: University Press of Colorado, 1990.

Susskind, Lawrence. *Proposition 2 1/2: Its Impact on Massachusetts.* Cambridge, MA: Oelgeschlager, Gunn & Hain, 1983.

Taft, William Howard. *Popular Government: Its Essence, Its Permanence, and Its Perils.* New Haven: Yale University Press, 1913.

Tindall, George, ed. *A Populist Reader.* New York: Harper Torchbooks, 1966.

Tucker, Carl. "Squeeze Play." *Saturday Review* 5 (August 1978): 68.

Turk, Herman. "Imageries of Social Control." *Urban Life* 8 (October 1979): 335–58.

Ubbelohde, Carl, et. al. *A Colorado History.* 3rd ed. Boulder: Pruett Publishing Company, 1972.

Vincent, Barbara. "Expanding the Process," *The Initiative Press & Seminars* (February 1996): 6.

Wiles, Peter. "A Syndrome, Not A Doctrine: Some Elementary Theses on Populism." Ghita Ionescu and Ernest Gellner, eds. *Populism.* London: Weidenfeld and Nicolson, 1969.

Wilkinson, Paul. *Social Movement.* New York: Praeger Publishers, 1971.

Woodward, C. Vann. *Tom Watson: Agrian Rebel.* New York: Macmillian Company, 1938.

Yin, Robert. *Case Study Research: Design and Methods.* Newbury Park, CA: Sage Publications, 1989.

Zimmerman, Joseph. *Participatory Democracy: Populism Revived.* New York: Praeger Publishers, 1986.

Zisk, Betty. *Money, Media, and the Grass Roots: State Ballot Issues and the Electoral Process.* Newbury Park, CA: Sage Publications, 1987.

## Newspapers and Magazines

Anderson, Eric. "Bruce Blast Rival Proposal." *The Denver Post.* May 21, 1992, B2.

Anderson, Eric. "Bruce Tax Initiative to Make Ballot." *The Denver Post.* January 28, 1992, A6.

Anderson, Eric. "Tax Crusader Vows to Get Initiative on Ballot." *The Denver Post.* January 7, 1992, B2.

Anderson, Eric. "Alternative Proposals in the Works." *The Denver Post.* December 24, 1991, B3.

Anderson, Eric. "Tax-Limitation Petitions Ruled Invalid." *The Denver Post.* December 7, 1991, A1.

Anderson, Eric. "Voters Favor Plan to Limit Taxes 2-To-1 Ratio." *The Denver Post.* December 4, 1991, B1.

Anderson, Jack. "Jarvis A Veteran of Political Stings." *Washington Post.* July 27, 1978.

"Anti-Democracy in California." *New York Times.* October 18, 1911.

Aucoin, Don. "Asking Your Signature, Leaving Theirs." *The Boston Globe.* October 2, 1993, B1.

Ayres, Drummond. "Politics: The Initiatives." *New York Times.* November 4, 1996, B6.

"Behr's Tax-Relief Bill Passes Assembly Test." *Long Beach Independent.* February 18, 1978.

"The Big Tax Revolt." *Newsweek.* June 19, 1978, 20–30.

Black, Chris. "How Proposition 2 1/2 Became Law." *The Boston Globe.* 1 July 1981, 41.

Blaustein, Arthur. "Proposition 13=Catch 22: California's Rush for Fool's Gold." *Harper's Magazine.* November 1978, 18–23.

Booth, Michael. "TV Blitz to Promote Amendment 2." *The Denver Post.* October 20, 1992, B1.

Broder, David. "Initiative Fever Still Grips California." *The Denver Post.* August 15, 1997, B7.

Brookes, Warren T. "Property Taxes Were the Key to Governor Dukakis' Loss to King." *The Boston Globe.* September 28, 1978.

Brookes, Warren. "How the Legislature Destroyed the Initiative Petition Process." *The Boston Globe.* July 11, 1980, A15.

Brown, Fred. "What's Wrong With the Public." *Denver Post.* November 2, 1994, B7.

Brown, Fred. "Voting on Taxes." *The Denver Post.* October 28, 1992, B7.

Brown, Fred. "Amendment 1 Remains Out in Front." *The Denver Post.* November 1, 1990, A18.

Brown, Fred. "Bruce Files New Tax-Limit Petition." *The Denver Post.* October 18, 1989, B1.

Brown, Fred. "Bruce Preaches the Gospel on Friendlier Turf." *The Denver Post.* December 12, 1990, B11.

Brown, Fred. "El Paso Led Failed Anti-Tax Charge." *The Denver Post.* November 11, 1990, A14.

Brown, Fred. "Hearing Turns Nasty a la Bruce." *The Denver Post.* April 21, 1990, B3.

Brown, Fred. "Tax-Limit Campaign Rekindled." *The Denver Post.* April 4, 1991, A1.

Brown, Fred. "The Grace of A Simple Idea." *The Denver Post.* October 3, 1990, B7.

Bruce, Douglas. "Should We Vote on Tax Hikes? Yes, Let's Vote." *The Denver Post.* October 18, 1992, G1.

Bruce, Douglas. "Tabor II offers Coloradans a Chance to Limit Taxes." *The Denver Post.* June 9, 1990, B7.

"Bruce Ready to Go to Court over Election Reform Plan." *The Denver Post.* May 26, 1992, B4.

"Bruce's Big Lies." *The Denver Post.* October 22, 1992, B6.

Bush, Ed. "Howard Jarvis." *Personality.* December 1978, 13–20.

"California Earthquake." *The Nation.* June 17, 1978, 714–15.

"Campaign '78: The Jarvis Amendment." *Political Animal.* January 27, 1978.

Carroll, Jerry. "The Return of Howard Jarvis." *New West.* May 5, 1980, 59–66.

Claiborne, William. "In Colorado, the Chips Are Down – and Out." *The Washington Post.* February 20, 1993, A4.

Cobb, Nathan. "Some People Put Drama in Their Lives By Going to Horror Movies. I Work in Massachusetts Politics." *The Boston Globe.* (Magazine) January 14, 1990, 16.

Collins, Lawrence. "GOP King Backs Governor on Zero Cap." *The Boston Globe.* April 25, 1979, 18.

Collins, Lawrence. "Petitions to Cut Bay State Taxes Filed for 1980 Ballot." *The Boston Globe.* August 2, 1979, 18.

Collins, Lawrence. "Tax Data and 2 1/2." *The Boston Globe.* November 2, 1980, 25.

"Colorado Lawmakers Pay School Bill; Governor Urges Sales Tax Rise for Future." *The Bond Buyer.* May 11, 1992, 2.

"Colorado's Amendment 1 is Just Common Sense." *The Denver Post.* October 27, 1990, B7.

Conniff, Michael. "Jarvis Brings His Message to Newton." *Boston Herald American.* October 16, 1978, A19.

Connolly, Peter. "The Voice of Raw Greed." *The Nation.* July 22, 1978, 77–78.

Cordtz, Dan. "Voter Initiatives Warn Politicians to Curb Spending." *Financial World.* October 30, 1990, 22.

Cortez, Angela. "No Fury Like Woman Raided: IRS Case Victor Expects Violence Against the Feds." *Denver Post.* June 7, 1997, A1.

Cowen, Peter. "In Boston, Official Opposition Is Low-Key." *The Boston Globe.* October 31, 1980, 21.

Crawford, Charles. "Proposition 13: 'The Sky. . . Has Not Fallen.'" *Enterprise* 2 (July 1978): 3–5.

De Lama, George. "Colorado Springs Showdown: Gays Facing Fundamentalists." *The Chicago Tribune.* April 27, 1993, A1.

"Denver Post/Center 4 Poll." *The Denver Post.* October 5, 1986, A14.

Dittemore, Betty Ann. "Should We Vote on Tax Hikes?" *The Denver Post.* October 18, 1992, G1.

Dubroff, Henry. "Businesses Unite Against Tax Limits." *The Denver Post.* October 31, 1988, A1.

Egelko, Bob. "Jarvis Skips Dues, Says Didn't Call Behr Senile." *Long Beach Independent.* February 28, 1978.

Eisenberg, Richard. "Tax Trends." *Money.* May 1983, 214.

"Election Roundup." *The Nation.* June 23, 1978, 758.

Finley, Bruce. "Tax-Limit Initiative Faces New Opposition." *The Denver Post.* July 22, 1988, B2.

"Four Who Also Shaped Events." *Time.* January 1, 1979, 40–1.

Fox, Jack. "Jarvis Reveals Shrewd Mind and Ambitions." *Newark Star Ledger.* October 15, 1978.

Fox, Joel. Letter to the Editor. *Los Angeles Times.* March 11, 1996, B4.

Freemantle, Tony. "The 'Hate State' Label Dividing Colorado." *The Houston Chronicle.* January 17, 1993, A1.

Fulcher, Michelle and Jeffrey Roberts. "Tax Limits Lose; English Issue Wins." *The Denver Post.* November 9, 1988, A1.

Fulcher, Michelle. "Business Raising $250,000 to Fight Tax-Limit Plan." *The Denver Post.* October 19, 1988, A11.

Fulcher, Michelle. "Ex-Governors Warn of 'Disaster' and 'Paralysis.'" *The Denver Post.* October 26, 1988, A9.

Fulcher, Michelle. "Gambling, Cap on Terms Get Nod From Voters." *The Denver Post.* November 7, 1990, A1.

Fulcher, Michelle. "High Property Taxes Spark Debate, Ignite Colorado Tax Revolt." *The Denver Post.* October 31, 1988, B7.

Fulcher, Michelle. "Specter of Tax Limit Frightens State Leaders." *The Denver Post.* September 30, 1988, B3.

Fulcher, Michelle. "Tax-Limit Author Says Foes Misleading Voters." *The Denver Post.* November 1, 1988, A1.

Fulcher, Michelle. "Tax-Limit Issue Disallowed." *The Denver Post.* September 22, 1988, B1.

Furlong, Tom. "Jarvis' Mr. Inside Has Outsize Job." *Long Beach Independent.* May 19, 1978.

Garnaas, Steve. "New Tax-Limit Petitions Filed." *The Denver Post.* October 7, 1988, B1.

Gavin, Jennifer. "Alternative Tax-Limit Plan Fails." *The Denver Post.* March 20, 1992, B1.

Gavin, Jennifer. "Amendment 1 Foes Unite." *The Denver Post.* September 1, 1990, B3.

Gavin, Jennifer. "Andrews Joins Bruce in Tax War." *The Denver Post.* October 17, 1990, B3.

Gavin, Jennifer. "Bruce Threatens to File New Tax-Lid Plan." *The Denver Post.* April 10, 1991, B1.

Gavin, Jennifer. "One Goal: to Head Off Tax Revolt." *The Denver Post.* January 6, 1991, C1.

Gavin, Jennifer. "Support Growing, Tax-Lid Author Says." *The Denver Post.* June 28, 1990, B2.

Gavin, Jennifer. "Tax-Limit Plan Gains Strength." *The Denver Post.* October 10, 1990, A1.

Gavin, Jennifer. "Tax-Limit Proposal Loses." *The Denver Post.* November 7, 1990, A1.

George, Mary. "New Tax-Control Ramrod Promises to Keep Trying." *The Denver Post.* July 27, 1988, B5.

Gibney, Jim. "Springs Caps Taxes, Limits Political Terms." *The Denver Post.* April 3, 1991, A8.

Gibney, Jim. "Tax Foe Bruce Is Back at It." *The Denver Post.* February 4, 1991, B2.

Glenchur, Paul. "Interview: Paul Gann, 'Downhome' Crusader for the Taxpayer." *The Guide.* August 31, 1978, 4–5.

Graf, Thomas and Michelle Fulcher., "Armstrong Opposes Amendment 6." *The Denver Post.* November 2, 1988, A1.

Grossman, Gary. "Prop 13 and Jarvis Won't Play in Boston." *Boston Herald American.* September 23, 1978.

"The Hidden Referenda." *The Wall Street Journal.* October 29, 1980.

Hillgren, Sonja. "General News." United Press International. November 5, 1980.

Hilliard, Carl. "Douglas Bruce: Reporter's Nightmare." *The Denver Post.* July 1, 1990, C2.

Hirth, Diane. "Proposal May Make State Even More Of A Tax Haven." *Orlando Sentinel Tribune.* October 30, 1996, A1.

Hornby, Bill. "Amendment 1 Is Fighting a Paper Tiger." *The Denver Post.* October 15, 1992, B7.

Johnson, Dirk. "Coloradans to Vote on Drastic Tax Curb." *New York Times.* November 5, 1988, A6.

Johnson, Dirk. "Taxpayer Revolt in Colorado Vote Raises Alarm About Lost Services." *New York Times.* November 15, 1992, A18.

Kazin, Michael. Letter to the Editor. "The Populist Tongue." *The Washington Post.* July 2, 1995, X14.

Kenney, Charles. "Proposition 2 1/2 Going Directly to the Voter." *The Boston Globe.* October 19, 1980, 82.

Kenney, Charles. "Who Gave Us 2 1/2." *The Boston Globe.* October 31, 1980, 22.

Kenney, Charles. "In Mass., Prop. 2 1/2 Going Directly to the Voter." *The Boston Globe.* November 4, 1980, 1.

Kershner, Vlae. "Anti-Tax Crusade Is Losing Steam." *San Francisco Chronicle.* June 3, 1978.

King, Nick. "Jarvis Takes to Bay State Television to Give King's Candidacy A Boost." *The Boston Globe.* November 3, 1978, 1.

Knight, Al. "Amendment 1 Changed the Landscape." *The Denver Post.* November 22, 1992, D1.

Kraft, Joseph. "And, Finally A Message of Populist Hedonism." *Los Angeles Times.* June 13, 1978.

Kristol, Irving. "The Meaning of Proposition 13." *The Wall Street Journal.* June 28, 1978.

"Lamm Lashes Out at Amendment Four." *The Denver Post.* September 14, 1986, B7.

"Last Hope for Tax Relief: Brown Willing to Back Republican Bill." *Long Beach Independent.* February 18, 1978.

Lawrence, Steven. "Peter Behr." *Long Beach Independent.* February 13, 1978.

Lipsher, Steve. "Ballot Drive A Job for Pros." *The Denver Post.* September 19, 1994, A1.

Lipsher, Steve. "Grassroots on the Airwaves to Push 13." *Los Angeles Times.* May 28, 1978.

Lynch, Mitchell. "Will Massachusetts Be the First State to Set Tax Limits?" *The Wall Street Journal.* December 19, 1977.

Lyons, James. "Tax-Cutting Frustration." *Forbes.* November 12, 1990, 164.

Marois, Michael B. "Trends in the Region: Initiatives: The People's Will Or Sound-Bite Government?" *The Bond Buyer.* February 14, 1997, 30.

Mathews, Tom. "Mr. Proposition 13." *Newsweek.* June 19, 1978, 25.

Mazanec, Jana. "Colorado 'Tax Revolt' Hard to Interpret." *USA Today.* November 19, 1992, A8.

McDougal, Dennis. "Jarvis at 75, Nurses A Rebellion." *Long Beach Independent.* March 12, 1978.

"Me First." *The New Republic.* June 17, 1978, 5–6.

Menzies, Ian. "Proposition 2 1/2: It's Time to Forget All Those Doomsday Cries." *The Boston Globe.* August 18, 1980.

Meyer, Eugene J. "California's Proposition 13 Spawned Brood of Anti-tax Laws." *Washington Post.* August 15, 1983, A23.

Milbank, Dana. "Ballot Warriors Challenge State, Local Governments." *The Wall Street Journal.* May 20, 1997, A20.

Miller, Carl. "Foes of Tax Measure Surge Ahead in Poll." *The Denver Post.* October 31, 1988, A7.

Miller, Carl. "Looking Closely at Amendment 4." *The Denver Post.* October 5, 1986, F6.

Miller, Carl. "Wirth, Kramer Even Amendment 4 Slips." *The Denver Post.* October 22, 1986, B4.

Moehringer, J.R. "Experts Fear Long Ballot Will Scare Away Voters." *Rocky Mountain News.* November 2, 1994, A4.

Morian, Dan. "Consultants Win in Fight Over State Initiatives." *Los Angeles Times.* November 3, 1996, A3.

O'Brien, Greg. "Mass. OKs Prop. 2 1/2 By 2–1." *Boston Herald American.* November 5, 1980, A1.

O'Brien, Greg. "Proposition 2 1/2 Has the Pulling Power at the Polls." *Boston Herald American.* November 3, 1980, A6.

"Opponents of Tax-Limit Measure Raise $161,000." *The Denver Post.* October 29, 1988, B2.

"Other Income?" *US News and World Report.* June 13, 1985, 87.

Pankratz, Howard. "Taxpayers Bill of Rights Reprieved." *The Denver Post.* October 5, 1988, A1.

Perry, James and Hyatt, James. "Stopping the Bucks." *The Wall Street Journal.* June 6, 1978, A1.

Pettier, Michael. "High Court Hearing Tax Limitation Arguments." *Port St. Lucie News* (Stuart, FL) December 2, 1996, B2.

Pope, Keith. "Groups Launch Tax-Limitation Drive." United Press International. June 10, 1986.

Powers, John. "The Stress of the Cities." *The Boston Globe.* (Special Edition, *The Squeeze on State and Local Spending*) May 11, 1981, 3.

"Property Taxes and the Revolt." *Los Angeles Times.* May 9, 1978.

"Property Taxes: A Painful Tradition Nobody Has Been Willing to Change." *The Boston Globe.* (Special Edition, *The Squeeze on State and Local Spending*) May 11, 1981, 25.

"Proposition 13 Paved Way for Tax Revolts Across Us" *Los Angeles Times.* February 14, 1988, A3.

"Proposition 2 1/2 Alluring, Confusing." *The Boston Globe.* October 13, 1986, 25.

"Proposition 2 1/2 at the Wire." *Boston Herald American.* November 3, 1980, A10.

"Proposition 2 1/2: Both Sides Step Up Their Crusades." *The Boston Globe.* October 22, 1980, 26.

"Proposition 2 1/2: Vote 'No.'" *The Boston Globe.* October 27, 1980, 14.

Rabey, Steve. "Court Strikes Down Homosexual Rights Ban." *Christianity Today.* June 17, 1996, 68.

Racine, John. "Colorado Lawmakers Consider Measure to Steal Thunder of Citizen's Tax Drive." *The Bond Buyer.* March 4, 1992, 2.

Racine, John. "Colorado." *The Bond Buyer.* February 4, 1992, 28.

Racine, John. "From Bears to Bonds, Colorado Voters' Ballot Likely to Have It All." *The Bond Buyer.* August 3, 1992, 1.

Racine, John. "One Way Or Another, Colorado May Get Tax, Spending Limits in 1992 Referendum." *The Bond Buyer.* November 15, 1991, 5.

Racine, John. "Sweeping Anti-Tax Proposal in Colorado Rattles Government and Bond Industry." *The Bond Buyer.* October 11, 1990, 1.

Racine, John. "Tax Rollback Drive Scores Voter Victory in Colorado Springs; Two Amendments Win." *The Bond Buyer.* April 4, 1991, 4.

Roberts, Jeffery. "Bruce: Taxpayers Must Seize Control." *The Denver Post.* October 14, 1992, A1.

Roberts, Jeffrey and Robert Kowalski. "Proposal to Limit Taxes Takes Jump Toward Ballot." *The Denver Post.* August 2, 1986, C3.

Roberts, Jeffrey. "Big Bucks Being Spent to Defeat Amendment 4." *The Denver Post.* October 25, 1986, A5.

Roberts, Jeffrey. "Campaign for Tax Limit Plan Kicks Off." *The Denver Post.* January 14, 1988, B4.

Roberts, Jeffrey. "Citizens Group Starts Drive to Limit Taxes." *The Denver Post.* March 8, 1988, B3.

Roberts, Jeffrey. "Colorado Tax-Curb Plan Wins '90 Ballot Spot." *The Denver Post.* December 9, 1989, B1.

Roberts, Jeffrey. "Foes of All Political Stripe Call Plan A Skunk." October 5, 1988, A10.

Roberts, Jeffrey. "Foes Vow Media Blitz to Defeat Tax Issue." *The Denver Post.* October 15, 1988, A1.

Roberts, Jeffrey. "Office-Holders, Bureaucrats Wringing Hands Over Impact of Amendment 1." *The Denver Post.* November 8, 1992, A8.

Roberts, Jeffrey. "Poll Shows Support Slipping for Tax-Limit Measure." *The Denver Post.* October 20, 1992, B4.

Roberts, Jeffrey. "Tax Limit Hailed and Decried." *The Denver Post.* November 5, 1992, A1.

Roberts, Jeffrey. "Tax-Limit Advocate Plows $50,000 Into Campaign." *The Denver Post.* November 2, 1988, A1.

Roberts, Jeffrey. "Tax-Limit Amendment Passes." *The Denver Post.* November 4, 1992, A1.

Roberts, Jeffrey. "Us West President Blasts Amendment 6." *The Denver Post.* October 28, 1988, B4.

Roberts, Jeffrey. "Voted Down Last Year, Tax-Limitation Initiative Likely to Be Resurrected for '88." *The Denver Post.* October 12, 1987, B3.

Robinson, Walter. "Proposition 2 1/2 Would Slash Auto Excise, Too." *The Boston Globe.* October 14, 1980, 17.

Robinson, Walter. "Proposition 2 1/2 Fight: Pros v. Enthusiasts." *The Boston Globe.* September 30, 1980, 13.

Robinson, Walter. "Proposition 2 1/2 Would Help Some Tenants. *The Boston Globe.* October 15, 1980, 19.

Robinson, Walter. "Q&A: Pressman on Proposition 2 1/2." *The Boston Globe.* October 26, 1980, 2.

Robinson, Walter. "Question 3—Its Tax 'Limit' is the Issue." *The Boston Globe.* October 29, 1980, 26.

Robinson, Walter. "Tax-Curb Backer Wants Services Cut." *The Boston Globe.* May 10, 1979, 20.

Robinson, Walter and Lawrence Collins. "Q&A on Proposition 2 1/2: MTF President Richard Manley Opposes 2 1/2." *The Boston Globe.* October 19, 1980, 2.

Romano, Michael. "Ballot Issues Limit Power of Politicians." *Rocky Mountain News.* September 25, 1994, A4.

Romano, Michael. "Bruce Proposal Going Down." *Rocky Mountain News.* November 9, 1994, A5.

Salisbury, Ann. "After 15 Years on the Sideline, Howard Jarvis Man of Hour." *San Francisco Herald Examiner.* July 7, 1978.

Sanko, John. "'De-Brucing' Measures Popular Throughout State, Voting Shows." *Rocky Mountain News.* November 17, 1995, A6.

Sanko, John. "Voters Loosen Amendment 1 Restrictions." *Rocky Mountain News.* November 9, 1995, A5.

"Scary Fiction and Scary Facts." *Boston Herald American.* October 26, 1980, B10.

Scharfenberg, Kirk. "Steering Clear of 2 1/2 Fire." *The Boston Globe.* October 11, 1980, 2.

Scheibman, Jack. "Jarvis, Behr in Heated Exchange." *Long Beach Independent.* May 13, 1978.

Schmidt, Bob. "Jarvis Opponents Map Plans to Beat Initiative." *Long Beach Independent.* January 20, 1978.

Schomp, Caroline. "Douglas Bruce Just Won't Give Up." *The Denver Post.* December 13, 1991, B5.

Schrader, Ann. "California Tax Activist Backs Amendment 4." *The Denver Post.* October 28, 1986, B3.

Schrader, Ann. "Coloradans Turn Down Amendment 4." *The Denver Post.* November 5, 1986, A1.

Schrader, Ann. "Harvesting Reform." *The Denver Post.* September 28, 1986, A10.

Segal, Michael. "Proposition 2 1/2: It's One Election That Money Could Not Buy." *Boston Herald American.* November 3, 1980, A19.

Sinisi, Sebastian. "Proposal's Author Not Picture of A Firebrand." *The Denver Post.* October 30, 1988, B7.

Smith, Brad. "Governor Romer Seeks Re-Election." United Press International. April 2, 1990.

Soble, Ronald. "California Elections." *Los Angeles Times.* October 2, 1986, A3.

Soble, Ronald. "Proposition 13 Backers Lead Foes in Fund Raising." *Los Angeles Times.* May 31, 1978.

"Sound and Fury Over Taxes." *Time.* June 19, 1978, 12–21.

Stata, Ray. "The Right Message." *The Boston Globe.* November 3, 1980, 15.

"Statewide Vote on Referendums." *The Boston Globe.* November 9, 1980, E20.

Stewart, Richard. "Many in Hub Say Tax Bills Steer Them to Proposition 2 1/2." *The Boston Globe.* October 23, 1980, 34.

"Tax Crusader Tries to Save Petitions." *The Denver Post.* December 24, 1991, B1.

"Tax Cut Plan Unveiled." *The South Middlesex News.* (United Press International) December 9, 1978, 2AY.

"Taxes Overboard." *Economist.* June 17, 1978, 11.

"Taxpayer Revolt: Where It's Spreading Now." *Us News and World Report.* June 19, 1978, 25.

"Taxpayers Rebel, Take the Initiative." *Los Angeles Times.* May 7, 1978.

"Tax-Limit Signatures Total 80,000." *The Denver Post.* August 1, 1986, B3.

Tracy, Phil. "The Jarvis Revolt: Rallying 'Round An Old Man's Obsession." *New West.* May 17, 1978, 17.

Turner, Robert. "Don't Put All the Blame for High Taxes on the Legislature." *The Boston Globe.* October 23, 1980, 19.

"Voter Trends." *The Denver Post.* October 28, 1998, B1.

Wash, Don. "Barbara Anderson's on the Money." *Cape Cod Times.* May 25, 1989.

Weber, Brian. "State Voters Jump Off the Anger Wagon." *Rocky Mountain News.* November 9, 1994, A11.

Weber, Tracy. "Making Politics Pay: Cashing in on Causes." *Los Angeles Times.* March 3, 1996, A1.

Weber, Tracy. "Mystery Surrounds Suit Against O.C. Consultants." *Los Angeles Times.* November 20, 1994, A1.

Weber, Tracy. "Suit Challenges Accounting on Political Funds." *Los Angeles Times.* November 22, 1994, A3.

Weber, Tracy. "Tax Group Guilty of Campaign Violation." *Los Angeles Times.* May 11, 1995, A3.

White, Keith. "Group Says Tax Revolt Alive, Well Out West." *Gannett News Service.* August 24, 1990.

Wicker, Tom. "A 'New Revolution.'" *New York Times.* June 9, 1978.

Wilson, Dave. "A Vote for 2 1/2." *The Boston Globe.* October 12, 1980, 31.

Yates, Albert. "Amendment 1 Could Devastate Higher Education in Colorado." *The Denver Post.* October 24, 1992, B7.

# INDEX

Adams, Charles, 22, 24
Adams, James Ring, xiii, 55–56, 79, 94
Alabama, 158
Alaska, 5
Amendment 1 (Colorado; 1990 tax limitation), 143–144, 146
Amendment 1 (Colorado; 1992 tax limitation), 10, 19, 34, 155; ballot title, **149**; and business opposition, 130–131; 149–150, 163; and business support, 150; campaign for, 147–154; conventional wisdom of, 130; and "de-Brucing" measures, 210n.179; effects of, 131, 167, 210n.179; grassroots support for, 155–156, 163; media coverage of, 130; 152, 155; opponents of, 130–131; 148–150, 152–153; and political consultants, 130, 151–152, 163; passage of, 128; 154; and Proposition 13, 149; provisions of, 128, 148–149, 207n.146; public opinion towards, 130–131; 135; 147–148, 152–153; signature collection for, 131; 147–148, 200n.9; and unresponsive government, 147; volunteers for, 131, 147, 155. *See also* Bruce, Douglas; Taxpayers Bill of Rights
Amendment 1 (Florida, 1996 tax limitation), xiii

Amendment 2 (Colorado, 1992 anti-gay rights), 129, 153
Amendment 4 (Colorado, 1986 tax limitation), 137–141, 203n.59
Amendment 6 (Colorado, 1988 tax limitation), 139–143
Amendment 6 (Colorado, 1992 sales tax for education), 163, 205n.108
Amendment 7 (Colorado, 1992 school vouchers), 163
Amendment 13 (Colorado, 1996 petition rights), 211n.19
America Group, The, 77–78; *See also* United Organizations of Taxpayers
American Conservative Union, 195n.129
American Federation of Labor-Congress of Industrial Organizations (AFL-CIO), 124, 141
American Federation of State, County and Municipal Employees, 152, 187n.161
American Tax Reduction Movement (ATRM), 32, 104, 107, 151, 176n.42
Americans for Tax Reform, 21
Anderson, Barbara, 8, 9, 50–51, **89**, 95, 108, 127, 130, 156; and *faux* populism, 48, 95; and the initiative process, 165; leader of Proposition 2 1/2, 35–36, 87, 89, 109–110, 113, 116–117, 162; media's portrayal of,

239